Encouraging and Supporting Student Inquiry

Researching Controversial Issues

Harriet S. Selverstone

Libraries Unlimited Professional Guides
in School Librarianship

A Member of the Greenwood Publishing Group

Westport, Connecticut • London

Library of Congress Cataloging-in-Publication Data

Selverstone, Harriet S.
    Encouraging and supporting student inquiry : researching controversial issues / Harriet S. Selverstone.
        p. cm. — (Libraries Unlimited professional guides in school librarianship ; ISSN 1074-150X)
    Includes bibliographical references and index.
    ISBN-13: 978-1-59158-496-4 (pbk. : alk. paper)
    1. Research—Methodology—Study and teaching (Secondary) 2. Library orientation for high school students. 3. High school libraries—Activity programs. 4. Inquiry-based learning. 5. Intellectual freedom. 6. School librarian participation in curriculum planning. I. Title.
ZA3075.S45   2007
001.4′20712—dc22   2007009266

British Library Cataloguing in Publication Data is available.

Copyright © 2007 by Libraries Unlimited

All rights reserved. No portion of this book may be reproduced, by any process or technique, without the express written consent of the publisher.

Library of Congress Catalog Card Number: 2007009266
ISBN-13: 978-1-59158-496-4
ISSN: 1074-150X

First published in 2007

Libraries Unlimited, 88 Post Road West, Westport, CT 06881
A Member of the Greenwood Publishing Group, Inc.
www.lu.com

Printed in the United States of America

The paper used in this book complies with the Permanent Paper Standard issued by the National Information Standards Organization (Z39.48–1984).

10 9 8 7 6 5 4 3 2 1

I dedicate this book to my beloved grandchildren: Joshua, Rebecca, Jacob, and Alison who I know grow up in an environment where inquiry, scholarship, and the joy of learning is encouraged. They are the future.

Contents

Acknowledgments xi
Introduction xiii
Controversial Issues: Definition xv
Student Assignments xvi
Administrative Support xxiii
Public Relations: Necessary for Support of Programs xxviii
Teaching, Learning, and Student Inquiry during the
    Research Process xxxv
Controversial Issues: What Are They? xliii
Researching Controversial Issues xlvii
Presentation of Controversial Issues xlix

Biology/Health 1
    Abortion 3
    AIDS Reappraised and AIDS, the Epidemic 6
    Alternative Medicine 10
    Birth Control 12
    Circumcision 15
    Cloning 18
    Cryonics 20
    Eugenics 22
    Euthanasia 24
    Evolution and Creationism 26
    In Vitro Fertilization 29
    Medical Marijuana 32
    Mind Control 35
    Overpopulation 37
    Performance-Enhancing Drugs in Sports 39
    Psychoactive Drugs 42
    Race and Intelligence 45
    Racial Profiling 48
    Stem Cells 51
    Tobacco Smoking 54
    Transracial Adoption 57

Entertainment 61
    Entertainment Software Rating Board 63
    Media Bias 65
    Media Restrictions 68
    MPAA Film Rating System 71

viii   Contents

Environment 75
    Acid Rain 77
    Global Warming 80
    Nuclear Power 83
    Ozone Depletion 86
    Pesticides 89

Geography 93
    Israeli-Occupied Territories 95
    Persian Gulf 98
    Puerto Rico Self-Determination 101
    United States–Mexican Border Dispute 104

History 109
    Apartheid in South Africa 111
    Cyprus Dispute 114
    Genocide 117
    Holocaust Revisionism 120
    Roswell UFO Incident 123
    Unidentified Flying Objects (UFOs) 126
    White Supremacy 129

People 131
    Salvador Allende 133
    Yasser Arafat 136
    Cesar Chavez 139
    Hugo Chavez 142
    David Duke 145
    Galileo Galilei 147
    Malcolm X 150
    Martin Luther King, Jr. 153

Politics 155
    Anarchism 157
    Black Separatism 160
    Communism 163
    Fascism 166
    Feminism 169
    Gays in the Military 172
    Gun Politics 175
    People for the Ethical Treatment of Animals (PETA) 178
    Public vs. Private School Education 181
    USA Patriot Act (H.R. 3162) 184

Religion 187
    Anti-Semitism 189
    Atheism 192
    Fundamentalism 195

New Age Spirituality 198
Opus Dei 201
Scientology 204
Sharia 207

Sexuality 211
Homosexuality 213
Polygamy 216
Pornography 219
Same-Sex Marriage 222

Index 225

Acknowledgments

I wish to thank Sharon Coatney for her invaluable assistance, cogent suggestions, and advice throughout the writing process. Her friendship, mentoring, and professional expertise were most important to me.

I also want to extend my appreciation to my husband, Bob, for his loving support, encouragement, and editing assistance during the writing of my manuscript. He has been a constant source of inspiration throughout my professional career. His reassurance has inspired me to continue to provide professional guidance to others in the school library media field.

Introduction

Controversy, in its implicit sense, is bound to cause a stir in any venue in which it appears, certainly in the media and in literature. Controversy implies argument, disagreement, dissent, dissatisfaction, and often leads to contentious debates.

Therefore, materials that are considered controversial because the subject matter might be considered offensive and inappropriate for some readers/viewers, are often challenged or removed from collections in public libraries and from school library media centers or from curriculum reading lists.

Students are eager for the opportunity to participate in the process of debating. They enjoy the chance to reflect and deliberate on topics which have been considered contestable. They want to justify their research and present cogent ideas which would substantiate their investigation of specific topics. They feel challenged; they accept the responsibility to thoroughly research their topics; they acquiesce when informed that if they believe in one side of a topic, they will readily switch gears and defend the opposing side of an idea or situation. Students also relish the opportunity to discover, to assess, to investigate, to explore, and to inquire about material to substantiate their theses without prior constraints placed upon their research capabilities. In essence, students achieve the important capability of accessing ANY material that would justify their point of view or the views of others and develop ownership in making discoveries. This ability reflects in the creativity of thought that culminates in the final product/presentation/debate and enhances the resourcefulness of their searching for knowledge.

Accessing controversial materials should be "a given" in our democratic society, where opportunity to discover, to realize, to contest, to dispute are all a part of the educational process.

The library media specialist and the classroom teacher have the opportunity and the responsibility to foster and encourage student inquiry. They have the pedagogical expertise to understand the importance of motivation and the resultant meaningful learning that can take place when students are fully engaged in the learning process. When students are encouraged to be creative, critical thinkers, their curiosity will be piqued and they will become active learners and researchers and be good candidates for life long learning. They will become active, knowledgeable citizens in our democratic society. This society should foster inquiring minds of our present students who will become productive and efficient seekers of information throughout their lives. A citizenry allowed to question, to raise issues, to object to issues, to propose opposing points of view should have had these seeds of inquiry planted in their formative years of schooling. I propose that it is the obligation of the library media specialist working in collaboration with the classroom teacher, with administrative support, to encourage this teaching/learning environment that enables the healthy responsive attitude of our students toward the excitement of learning and acquiring new knowledge and competencies.

Let us now explore student needs, student curiosity, student assignments, and opportunities afforded our students in our educational environment, the marketplace of ideas.

Let us understand the significance of enabling our students to be not only effective users of data and knowledge, but also the importance of the opportunity and freedom to research topics of their choosing with non-judgmental guidance. The positive attitudes of the library media specialist and the classroom teachers toward student involvement in their researching materials for academic or recreational needs is tantamount to our own credibility as "coaches" and supporters within the educational sphere.

Controversial Issues: Definition

Controversial issues are often referred to as "hot topics." "Hot" because for some people there is a discomfort in discussing, researching, or reading about them. This discomfort may stem from ignorance regarding the subject matter, religious or moral perspectives and dictates, or concern about "protecting" children and young adults from participating in or viewing or reading about what might be considered or construed as adult behaviors, activities, or thoughts.

There are parents, caregivers, and educators who are aware that when the children begin their school years, these children are no longer under the daily "protection" and governance that being at home provided. When children enter school they begin to socialize; they become more aware of and are exposed to the interests of others: the lives, thoughts and teachings of those from families other than their own. The values that have been inculcated at home may differ from their newly found peers, so they begin to question, to discover, to experiment, and to challenge what has been taught in the home.

For some families this is an exciting opportunity for their children, for others this becomes a frightening time because of a sense of loss of control over what their children are exposed to in their daily lives. As a result of the discrepancies between value systems taught at home and what may be learned at school, some parents opt for home schooling so they can be certain what material their children will cover in various subjects and the children will understand the parents' or guardians' point of view.

Controversial issues become controversial when the ideas inherent in the content are questioned or challenged by adults in a community, by religious groups, by community leaders or elected officials, by organized national groups, by political activists, by board of education members, or by school administrators. In a democratic society, and in a public school setting, students are entitled to be exposed to a myriad of topics, and to viewpoints of others that may differ from their own or those of their families. A public school environment provides a safe place where ideas may be explored, where discussions are open, viewpoints of others respected and tolerated, and where new discoveries are made. A public school environment provides for enrichment of knowledge and the engagement of students in the pursuit of this knowledge.

Controversy is natural; controversy should be encouraged, not stifled in a school community. This adds to the intellectual growth of the child and should nurture the curiosities inherent in growing up to be a responsible citizen.

Student Assignments

School systems are increasingly becoming aware that many students are deficient in writing skills. Teaching these skills in isolation instead of as part of a prescribed assignment may not encourage student interest in a topic nor motivate them to fully articulate and communicate their thoughts in writing. Increasingly, teachers are being encouraged to teach "writing across the curriculum," even in higher education. No longer are students given writing assignments only in English and Social Studies classes. Curriculum coordinators and administrators have been encouraging various other subject teachers to assign research papers on topics related to science subjects, world languages on cultural topics, music and art themes, and areas in physical education classes.

In conjunction with "writing across the curriculum," "reading across the curriculum" has also been instituted. The federal initiative, No Child Left Behind Act, requires school systems to concentrate on reading and mathematics, since those are the areas where competencies are tested. School systems, therefore, must decide on priorities. Should these systems want recognition for having attained high scoring in areas of reading, comprehension, editing, and mathematics, then other subjects need to be placed on the "back burner," unless they teach in an integrated manner. Teachers often feel stressed about lack of time to cover the curriculum because of so much clerical/paper work. If teachers are mandated to stress reading and math, and to spend time in remediation, how would they be able to offer instruction in other subject areas and have students engage in research and reference activities, particularly in the school library media center?

This creates an opportunity for library media specialists to seek out faculty members and provide them with their consulting services and truly to be an instructional partner. This may be done by identifying curriculum links to information needs; integrating resources into instructional units and helping the teacher design authentic learning tasks and accompanying assignments. (Authentic learning is discussed in the section: "Teaching, Learning and Student Inquiry During the Research Process.") These activities form the basis for an important collaborative teaching/learning situation. Teachers, students, and library media specialists all benefit from such interrelated activities.

The National Assessment of Educational Progress (NAEP) and other similar groups are also very concerned about writing and reading in the nation's classrooms. The groups' research has shown: "Most students are poor writers. In July 2003, surveys revealed that fewer than one in three of the nation's 4th, 8th, and 12th graders were proficient in writing, capable of composing organized, coherent prose in clear language with correct spelling and grammar. Only 24 percent of high school seniors, referenced above, achieved that goal."[1] It was also reported that teachers themselves are not proficient in writing. Another fact is that students are often not required to work on high level writing assignments, even in their English classes. NAEP reported that "nearly all elementary school students (97 percent) spent only three hours a week or less on writing, yet, they spent about twenty hours watching television. Only one-half of high school seniors (49 percent) receive writing assignments of three pages or more for English class, and then only once or twice a month."[2] Clearly, teachers need professional development opportunities to strengthen their skills in order to assist students in this very important area.

Teachers should avail themselves of the opportunity to study theories and best instructional practices. Library media specialists ought to join with teachers in various professional development activities, and collaboratively engage in action research projects that can then be implemented with the instruction and assignments in which the students will be participating. By attending reading/writing (literacy) professional development courses, teachers and library media specialists can jointly share reflections on current practices. They will be provided with new skill exercises that will embellish the instructional assignments offered to the students. Everyone—students, teachers, and library media specialists—all benefit from the new learning opportunities which provide intellectual growth and empowerment.

The Educational Testing Service (ETS) which administers the SAT exam has also entered the fray of encouraging more writing opportunities for students, and the 2005 SAT exam had an essay added to the multiple choice questions which have in the past made up the bulk of the exam.

Schools not only need to strengthen the writing skills for students who plan to continue their education beyond high school, this remediation is important for those students who are seeking employment directly from high school. During my years working as a department chair in a high school library media center, I designed challenging faculty meetings that sought to engage the faculty in meaningful activities. During a few such sessions, several employers in the surrounding community addressed the faculty regarding skills they wished the students to have mastered in order to succeed in the workplace. Among these skills were reading and correctly interpreting information (reading comprehension), ability to write in a precise, meaningful manner, and the ability to participate in group problem solving behavior. Students need to understand group dynamics in order to function well and efficiently as part of a team. The employers also highlighted the importance of computer skills (computer literacy, different from information literacy) in order to produce data which would help the workplace compete in the economic marketplace. Of course, information literacy (data formulation, interpretation, analysis, and retrieval) encompasses skills learned in the library media center in collaboration with the classroom teacher.

Access to the School Library Media Center for Student Assignments and Class Discussion of Topics

Along with writing and reading across the curriculum, and collaboration in these skill-oriented and cognitive growth experiences, the library media center must be open and available for students and teachers to access materials and to take advantage of the collaborative relationship between library media center professionals and subject teachers. School library media specialists must encourage the use of the media center's materials as further enrichment beyond what is found in textbooks. The process of resource-based instruction, rather than reliance on textbook information, not only enables students to experience in-depth study of subject matter, it also solidifies the importance of the library media program as an integral part of the curriculum. Of course, in conjunction with the library media center's policy of open access to materials, a flexible schedule must be in place so that students and teachers will have the opportunity to visit the library media center when the need arises. Prior scheduling of classroom visits to the library media center is also most helpful both for the teachers and the library media specialists, especially when they have collaborated on lessons, on topic assignments, and on teacher and student expectations for their work. As students increase their library media center usage, their information literacy skills are also enhanced. In addition to programs of writing and reading across the curriculum, student mastery of information literacy skills contributes to student competence and confidence in their pursuit of knowledge and their delivery of that information.

When faculty are given the opportunity to work with their students on curricula topics and are given the time and support by their administrators to help students develop their research and reference skills potential—rather than teaching to a specific test or program such as No Child Left Behind—students benefit from an exciting approach to learning.

There are specific steps to follow when teachers request library media center time with their classes. Classes do work at their maximum academic level when students have the ability to locate the information they need to complete their research tasks and when they are able to process the information according to the objectives put forth by the teacher.

Therefore, before the teacher schedules a class for time in the library media center, the library media specialist should:

1. Consult with the teacher about the assignment, what the teacher's objectives are for the students,
2. Assist the teacher in framing the questions so there is a coherent theme, and

3. Spend time with the teacher on focusing exactly what is expected of the students: the topics assigned, the information problem-solving process of research, the mechanics of the assignment (length of work to hand in, the manner of the final product (written, oral, artistic endeavor, media oriented, etc.)—the entire presentation.

It is very important for the library media specialist and the teacher to troubleshoot possible misinterpretation of the assignment. Too often, the teacher is not really sure what he/she expects the student to produce. Of course, once the assignment/project is understood by both the teacher and the library media specialist, it then behooves the library media specialist to investigate which materials are available for the students' research needs, including print, databases, and Internet sites.

The next major step before the students visit the library media center is for the library media staff to provide some skills overviews in class and help students to focus, narrow, and define their topics. This may be done through a webbing process.

The webbing process assists the students in organizing ideas and thoughts based upon their main topic or thesis statement. In webbing, ask students to draw a large circle with their main general research topic in the center. From this center circle lines are drawn to other circles or triangles or whatever shape is desired. Within these smaller shapes other aspects of the topic are to be developed. These additional shapes can be categorized into comments of persuasion or processes needed to be expanded upon.

The process of webbing may lead the student to a deeper understanding of the topic and provide greater conviction and inducement to research in a more focused direction. The student may well generate more excitement in researching a particular topic and be persuaded to expand his/her range of research opportunities. This excitement of discovery of possible new learning will influence the outcome of the student's research endeavors. Therefore, many of these "informational" shapes mentioned above, might support the main theme, or might even provide the student researcher with a more challenging and interesting topic to research, rather than the originally planned area of research/thesis. This whole process is one of reflection, where the student develops new understandings of the topic and creates new knowledge for him/herself. All of these processes take time and this time frame should be built into the assignment parameters. This will serve to prevent the student from approaching a wider topic, for example, global warming, and to be more thoughtful in the process of narrowing the topic. An example of this process is shown in Figure 1.

The library media staff also assists students in the process of interpreting and explaining the information. At this point any number of problem-solving processes may be taught, whether it be the BIG6 Skills, Kulthau model, the Washington Library Media Association model (Essential Skills for Information Literacy), the Pappas/Tepe Pathways to Knowledge model, and others. (These will be discussed later.)

xx Student Assignments

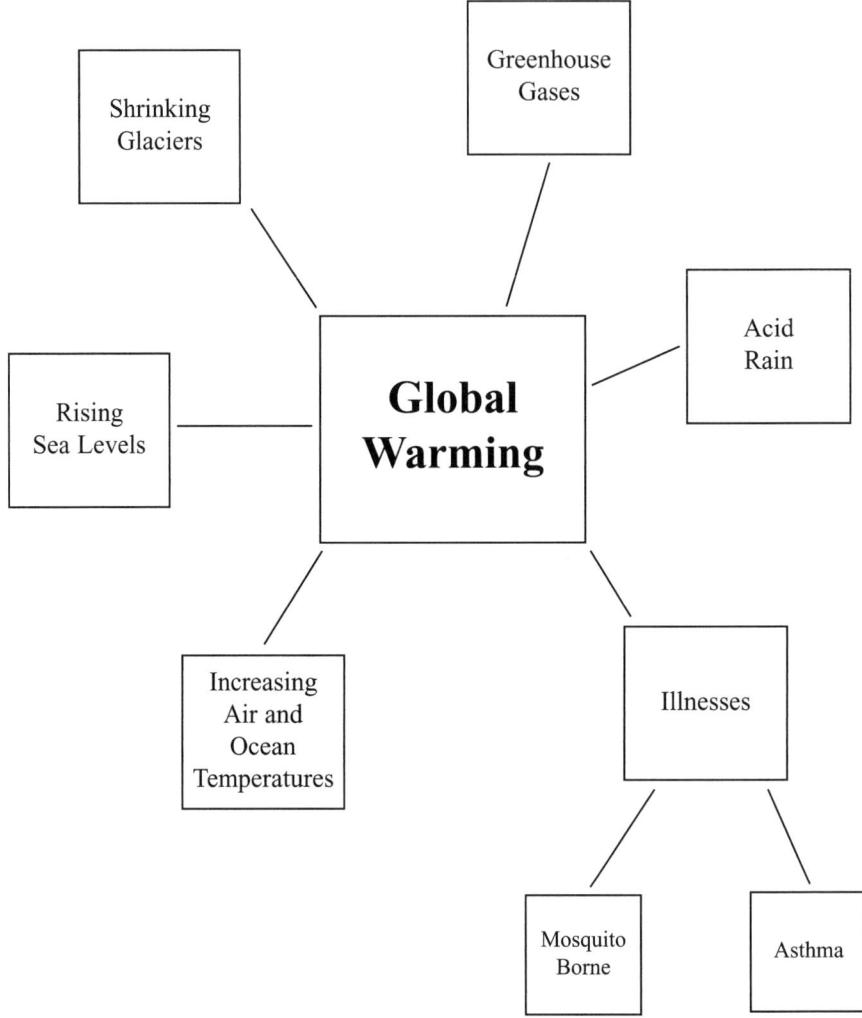

Figure 1. The webbing process.

At this time it is also appropriate to discuss with the class and teacher the various methods the students use when they are engaged in note taking. Some school systems have system-wide procedures required for note taking. This is also an excellent opportunity to discuss plagiarism, to define it, and illustrate the difference between paraphrasing and copying word for word from sources.

Plagiarism has become an all too often used method to write a research paper. If research were inquiry-driven there is less likelihood of a student copying information. If a student is assigned to investigate a specific topic, in all likelihood the research done will be nothing more than copying and reproducing the information that was found either online or in print. However, if the student can be challenged by his/her presenting a series of questions, based upon previous readings or observations, or asking for solutions to several issues, then the student will define his own thesis and present data in his/her own writing. The teacher can also request the student to submit reflective comments about the whole research process and what parts were successful and how improvement could have been achieved in other sections. Built into the process of researching for a topic should be the submission of periodic drafts and/or outlines to show the teacher the progression not only of the research but of the thinking process of the student. It is important to request an annotated bibliography/webliography from each student indicating also how useful the resource was in fulfilling the necessary information to complete the research process. When the student is able to narrow the topic, he/she is engaged in more critical thinking which encourages a more meaningful educational experience. Researching for information is a learned process. It is important for both the library media specialist and the classroom teacher to instruct students in the ethical use of information. Students are not innately aware of copyright infringement or being respectful of intellectual property rights. Students are not really cognizant of intellectual freedom issues. All of these concepts must be brought to the students' consciousness before they embark on the research process. This should also act as a deterrent to plagiarism. It also fosters the application of the student's individual interest and inquiry, which is so very important in creating an educational environment that is meaningful, creative, and fun.

When the students do finally come to the library media center, give them an opportunity to look up their topics on the OPACs and locate materials themselves. While it is easier for the students if the library media specialist removes print materials from the shelves and places them on carts for the students to start the reading and research process, that does not help the students to understand the mechanics of using a library media center or to learn to locate materials on their own. It is at this time that the teacher and the library media specialist must be available to assist in this process and for the teacher, in particular, to be available for direction to the students.

Upon completion of the assignment/projects, suggest to the teacher that if the project presentation is a visual one, it might be a wonderful idea to display the final product in the library media center for maximum exposure to other students, staff, and administrators. It is important to the students for others to see their exemplary work. It also encourages them to continue to learn and excel, and for the administration to understand the collaborative effort that took place in order for the students to successfully complete their assignments.

Administrators do want to understand the nature of the library media program and it behooves the library media specialist to provide the administrators with every opportunity to view and hear about the involvement of their media specialist(s) within the curriculum. It is also a good public relations effort on the part of the library media staff to support and maintain the administrators' commitment to the library media program (especially in times of severe budgetary constraints).

The exhibition of student work is also an encouragement for teachers who have not previously utilized the services and programs of the library media center to do so in the future. Students are most respectful of work that is exhibited by their fellow students. Students tend not to deface or destroy artistic, creative, and literary presentations. These opportunities for student expression are enjoyed for what they are intended to be—the sharing of work accomplished.

Notes

1. *American School Board Journal*, March 2004, Vol. 191, No. 3; http://www.asbj.com/2004/03/0304coverstory.html

2. Ibid.

Administrative Support

It is essential that school library media specialists develop positive, collegial alliances with administrators, with their school community, and with the community surrounding their school system. The real challenge is: "How do library media specialists succeed in creating an environment of confidence, good will, and respect within this sphere of constituencies?" What characteristics and strategies does a library media specialist need to possess in order to build a sense of belief and conviction among his/her colleagues and community so that decisions made are considered sound, commendable, and accepted?

The following characteristics also reflect the nature of the job that a library media specialist can provide. These distinguishing features are essential in order to conduct a successful library media program. This is not a totally inclusive list, but possession of any number of these is vital. A library media specialist should:

1. Be self-sufficient and self-confident,
2. Value communication with others,
3. Not work in opposition to or in isolation from other colleagues,
4. Assume a leadership role within the school community and in curriculum planning,
5. Be willing to be a risk-taker to achieve leadership,
6. Be a caring, attentive person,
7. Be a good listener,
8. Be a good communicator of ideas,
9. Enjoy people, and
10. Be willing to accept change and paradigm shifts in order to promote new learning.

School media specialists must be active advocates for their media centers and their programs. As part of the American Library Association's "Campaign for America's Libraries," the American Association of School Librarians (AASL) developed their own @ Your Library Campaign and the key/core messages that were imparted as part of this campaign for advocacy are:

1. "School library media programs are critical to the learning experience"— where there is collaboration between library media specialists and classroom teachers to help to make an impact on student achievement;
2. "School library media specialists are crucial to the teaching and learning

process"—where they are involved in developing and implementing curriculum, working with students to hone their research and reference skills and the use of resources in all formats;

3. "School library media centers are places of opportunity"[1]—where students can become successful in the learning process, where collections are managed to support the curriculum, where students can work in an environment conducive to learning and exploring various fields of knowledge.

Advocacy is an essential proactive activity in achieving a well-conceived, respected library media program and in turn a respect for the producers and implementers of that program(s). Although there are many constituencies who need to be reached and convinced of the worth of the program, the administrator is a key person in this effort. However, since students are the prime recipients of a successful program, they must be involved in the process of advocating for the library media program. A student advisory group is a good way to begin to get them involved in thinking and acting positively about the library media center and its staff. Of course, the school staff, and that includes professional, paraprofessional, and support people, should all be considered part of the school community who would also benefit from the library media program and its services. Parents and guardians are an essential constituency that must be nurtured, listened to, and communicated with to develop acceptance of decisions made by the library media staff regarding materials and services. Members of the wider school community should be informed of library media activities through newspaper articles in local publications, and in interviews on local cable channels so that a "relationship" can develop and recognition be established for future communication.

Relationships, respect, and acceptance are effective if all parties/constituencies are in agreement regarding expectations and outcomes. Dr. Gary Hartzell, of the University of Nebraska indicated in his presentation material at a Connecticut Educational Media Association Conference, January 23, 1999, that a partnership between the administrator and the library media coordinator or library media specialist is critical to achieve success in academic achievement. "The media coordinator is the only person outside the administration who has consistent opportunity to observe and evaluate what is going on in every area of school operation. The media coordinator has information, and access to information and materials, that can make a positive difference in your ability to improve instruction, bring about change, prevent damaging surprises, and foster the most positive image of the school. The media coordinator can also help to bring additional resources to your school—and resources are the very foundation of influence and change control."[2] Dr. Hartzell expressed the importance of the relationship between the school library media specialist and the administrator, initially, in a *School Library Journal* article, November 1997, "The Invisible School Librarian." The subtitle of the article, "Why Other Educators are Blind to Your Value," was an important call to action for library media specialists

Administrative Support xxv

to become more involved within the school community, to show their value, and prove their worth in the academic program. His concern was that all too often the library media specialist did not create an awareness of the worth of the library media program within the context of teaching and learning. Dr. Hartzell postulated a few reasons for teacher and administrative lack of awareness of the important roles the library media specialist could play in a collaborative relationship.

1. Teacher training programs do not offer information on the effectiveness of library media specialists in curriculum planning or staff development. Personally, I have often thought that pre-service teachers should spend at least one third of their student teaching experience working with the library media specialist within the library media center to understand how a collaborative relationship would provide meaningful teaching and helpful learning on the part of the students. Both the faculty and the students would be enriched by this effort.

2. The type of work the school library media specialist performs. Many perceive the school library media specialist as a helper, an assistant, one who does not work toward the success of the student's academic performance. If the library media specialist is a passive member of the staff, just working as a person in charge of a warehouse of material and not at all involved in any pedagogical interaction with the student and teacher, then this attitude reflects the importance or lack of importance of the library media specialist in a teaching/learning situation.

3. Dr. Hartzell's third reason for the invisibility of the library media specialist as a true partner on the teaching staff stems from the conventional or historic concept of the culture of a school library media center. Also, many administrators were themselves participants in the culture and customary/ordinary experiences of the peripheral help they received, or did not receive, from the library media specialist, then known as the school librarian. Traditionally the school library was a place to go to get material, maybe to read, or to work on homework assignments, but certainly not a significant contributor to the academic environment.

Therefore, it behooves the school library media specialist to be assertive, develop a collegial relationship with the administrator, and build a support system of teachers and students. Effective library media specialists should offer to conduct staff development programs, write articles for professional journals, and have these acknowledged among the staff. Library media specialists should also offer to present at conferences and be certain that your school community and the community at large is aware of your involvement in the educational environment. These presentations should also be offered at conferences other than educational media conferences, at meetings of administrators, and/or boards of education. It is important to get the word out about the essential contribution the library media program can make to the academic achievement of students. In addition, the library media specialist should get involved in the state, regional, or national association where he/she can network, learn about conditions in other school settings, be encouraged by others who have been successful in being recognized, and share library media programs that have made a difference in the lives and teaching of their staffs and the knowledge obtained by students and the instruction offered to them.

It is very important for the library media specialist to periodically have one-on-one meetings with the administrator/principal. The library media specialist should take the initiative in scheduling these sessions. This will be a time to inquire what expectations the administrator has for the library media program vis-à-vis the academic curriculum. I also took this opportunity to present the administrator with a copy of *Information Power; Building Partnerships for Learning* (ALA/AECT, 1998) so the administrator would more fully understand the importance of collaboration in the teaching and learning process. These scheduled meetings enable you, the library media specialist, to inform the administrator how teacher/library media specialist collaboration can enhance and enrich the lessons taught by the classroom teachers and the resultant achievements and learning by the students. These sessions also provide an opportunity to request library media specialist participation on important school-wide committees, that is, curriculum, accreditation, staff development. In my own school situation, I served on the Curriculum Committee, the Human Relations Committee, the Professional Development Committee, and the Faculty Council, an advisory team consisting of faculty, administrators, students, and community members. With all of this participation and exposure to staff and community, I was also appointed co-chair of our accreditation process, probably the ultimate in recognition of leadership within the school environment. This appointment also reflected the respect that the administration had for not only the library media specialist as an individual, but filtered down to the importance of the library media program within the school.

Another way in which the relationship between the library media specialist and the administrator might be strengthened is for the media specialist to offer to write a column within the newsletter that is mailed home to the parents that included information on classes utilizing the library media center for that month and the other activities in which the library media center and staff was involved.

Since many school administrators and teachers actively pursue advanced degrees and take advanced course work, the library media specialist can demonstrate his/her reference capabilities by assisting their research. A "Professional Library" collection as part of the library media collection is a wonderful public relations tool for any staff members needing material on curricular areas for lesson planning or for those taking advanced courses in their fields.

As an extension of meetings with the school administrator, it is also important to participate in, or even just attend, district school board meetings. This acknowledges the interest the library media specialist has in school curriculum, academic improvement, and school administration which furthers the support for the library media program.

Notes

1. *Toolkit for School Library Media Programs*, American Association of School Librarians, 2003, "Key Messages," p. 8.

2. "The Principal Partnership; Developing Opportunities For and With School Library Media Specialists," paper presented at the Connecticut Educational Media Association Conference, Hartford, CT, January 23, 1999.

Public Relations: Necessary for Support of Programs

The library media department must continue to "sell itself" and its self worth in order to gain the respect, admiration, and consideration in the eyes of the administration and teaching staff. All of these qualities will result in full support of the library media program and an understanding of the important role the library media program and the professional staff play in the academic achievement of the students.

In order for the library media specialist to advocate for the implementation of various programs, it is imperative that a collegial relationship be developed with faculty and administrative staff. This positive, respectful relationship can be created through the efforts of library media program advocacy. This entails a concerted effort on the part of the library media specialist in the context of curricula assistance, achievement of academic excellence by students, the availability of resources, and accessibility of the collection.

Peripheral to and complementary with developing support for programs, a viable public relations campaign can also be used to gain financial support for the library media program and, therefore, for the resources needed to implement the program. A public relations/public awareness effort also reveals all the services that a library media specialist and library media program can provide to enhance the teaching and learning within the curriculum. The public relations effort may also help build confidence in the effectiveness of the library media program, so when new concepts or suggestions for research topics are offered the teachers and administration would not be too quick to negate the recommendations of the library media specialist about students researching controversial issues.

Another important aspect of gaining support for the library media program is to present to the faculty and administration at the beginning of the school year a well articulated narrative of the goals and objectives of the library media program and the various services the library media staff is willing to render, with a possible increase in services as a dialogue ensues with staff and administration. The latter must realize that to ensure an effective library media program, the faculty, and library media specialist must develop a collaborative, cooperative relationship. The library media program does not exist in isolation from the curriculum; the program is integral to a well honed curriculum.

The library media advocacy effort is a continuous process. The library media staff must continually think of ways to attract users, to meet the needs of present and potential users, and to decide on which constituencies are to be reached. Aside from teachers, students, and administrators, the library media center staff must also consider parents, community leaders, community members, and even particular groups of students. The following represent some ways in which the library media staff can reach out to its constituencies:

Teachers and Administrators

1. Invite them at the beginning of the school year, early in the morning, before the school day, to a breakfast and introduce them to new acquisitions that have already been displayed by you and your staff. Also present the different departments with subject area lists of new acquisitions.
2. If a brochure of your library media center programs and rules has been printed (and it is wise to construct this brochure), disseminate these.
3. Turn the computers on to new websites and/or databases that you know would interest the staff and help in their lesson planning.
4. If you have developed a professional collection, this is a good opportunity to share this section with the staff. Inform the staff that you would be more than willing to help them with their research if they are pursuing advanced degrees. Let them know that you subscribe to professional journals just for this reason.
5. Consult with the department chairs and encourage them to conduct their meetings in the library media center. Take a moment of their time to indicate newly acquired materials that would be of help to them.
6. Also print up special memo pads with the library media center logo that you can use to inform the staff when material they would be interested in or material they requested arrives at the media center.
7. Be a good communicator of the library media center's activities and send this data to the administrator on a periodic basis and if there is a school newsletter be certain to include some library media activity with each issue.
8. Suggest to your administrator that you are very willing to work on school committees—this increases your visibility among the staff and adds to your credibility as a specialized teacher.

Students

1. Be certain that all students new to the school have an opportunity to participate in an orientation.
2. Solicit print suggestions from the students and when these materials arrive, send notes to the students that the material is ready for their use.

xxx   Public Relations: Necessary for Support of Programs

3. Set up a bulletin board and post articles about the students' academic accomplishments, or sports activities in which they are involved, especially if these have been written up in local papers. (This also means you are to read the local papers on a regular basis.)

4. Encourage students (through their teachers) that you would be delighted to display any projects that they have produced.

5. Form an advisory group in which students and faculty may participate. They can suggest materials or activities in which they feel the media center should be involved.

6. Display colorful posters and frequently change exhibits that would attract student interest and that would make the library media center an inviting place in which to work.

7. Participate in student debates or other forensics activities as a judge; become involved in a Quiz Bowl and initiate an information "scavenger" hunt; students really enjoy your involvement.

8. Have career material available for students to borrow.

9. Become involved in extracurricular activities in which students are involved. It indicates your interest in all aspects of the students' academic and co-curricular experience. Take tickets at a sporting event; attend theatrical productions, or other activities in which the students are involved.

Parents

1. A newsletter article about media center activities (mentioned above) is an informative tool for getting out the message about what is happening in the media center, what new material was acquired, and activities in which the professional staff is involved. It is essential that you publicize your activities since this acknowledges your engagement in students' lives and earns you more appreciation among staff and community.

2. Offer to give a computer update "course" in the evening so they can feel as savvy as their students. Suggest particular research websites for them to help their students with their homework.

3. Sponsor a reading night or book club for parents and students when they can discuss a book that all have read. Grants can help to provide funding for ordering paperbacks. It is helpful to have an initial meeting with students and parents interested in this activity and elicit book choices from them. That personal involvement will enhance their level of interest.

Community

1. It is important to make periodic presentations at board of education meetings about library media activities.
2. Contact a local educational access channel and speak about the media center and programs.
3. Inform newspaper reporters, through the school system's public relations person, when you will be celebrating different events: Banned Books Week, Read-Ins, National School Library Media Month activities. Reporters are eager for material for their columns. For years I had been interviewed by local newspaper reporters, especially during Banned Books Week. These interviews are further enhanced by having students (with parental permission) be interviewed, as well. It is critical to hear from the students' perspective on issues of intellectual freedom and the celebration of the freedom to read. This, too, makes it easier when students are researching their own projects which might be deemed controversial by different constituencies. Let the community know that you visit classrooms, especially during Banned Books Week, to discuss intellectual freedom issues. This encourages students and staff to deal with issues that might be discouraged if the policy/policies of the library media center/program were in question.
4. Invite people to mentor students and meet them in the library media center.
5. Of course, send a note in the newsletter requesting volunteer library media center help.

In addition, do not forget about students with special needs. They must also be accommodated. Consultations with the special needs faculty will help to clarify what resources/devices are needed to assist these students in their research and recreational requests. In addition, students who are studying world languages will need material in these other languages, possibly some materials that follow a bi-lingual format for ease of translation and understanding specific nuances within those languages. Meeting with the world languages staff will assist the library media center staff in their acquisitions requests.

Surveying both the staff and students is an important activity which provides both feedback and input to the library media program. How well is this program meeting the needs of the faculty? This might well be a terrific opportunity to enhance the library media program and services you might offer. This does not only involve resource acquisitions but also assistance in lesson planning and units of instruction. Involving the school staff is an acknowledgment that both the library media specialist and classroom teacher can together facilitate greater learning on the part of the students and offer helpful learning/teaching activities that would ease the burden of solo planning by the classroom teacher. A survey distributed to the students also indicates the desire of the library media staff to acquire recreational and resource related material that students would need or those which they may have requested. This line of open communication is essential for developing a user friendly library media environment. After the surveys have been submitted it is critical to divulge the summaries to the school community when the results are collated. When consideration is given to requests for materials, and the subsequent ordering of material is completed, it is important to keep track of what materials were requested and by whom so that notes can then be sent to the subject teachers and/or students when the material arrives. This is not only a considerate activity, but one that adds to your credibility as a partner in the educational endeavors of the students.

Another public relations activity is to promote new materials each week to the staff and students. My school disseminated a weekly calendar of schedules, school activities, and sporting events. To this weekly schedule I added an annotated description of newly acquired materials that could be taken out at the conclusion of the school week, although during that first week, these materials were on display. It was amazing the interest that this generated for library media visits. This same approach was used whenever there was a special holiday, or sports season, or an event taking place in school for which the library media center had material. During holiday times, information about the particular holiday was featured as well as holiday cookery. For the various sporting seasons, books on a particular sport were displayed. Whenever school functions were occurring, that is, an art show, art books were also featured. There was a time when for years the art show was set up in the library media center to which classes were invited and one evening was ear-marked when a musical quartet played during the exhibit time, coffee and pastries were served, and the town and school system dignitaries were invited. Students and parents also attended during the evening hours. Eventually the art show grew too large for the library media center to accommodate all the art, musicians, etc., so the art show had to be moved to a larger location in school. This might also serve as a good opportunity to advocate for a larger space. The art show provided an opportunity for the library media staff to present the library media center as a center of cultural activity, not just a place to study, work on homework, be involved in class research projects, or just read and relax. This art show production brought a sense of vitality, student/staff enthusiasm, and school community involvement in the educational process.

Another exciting, but time-consuming project involved a collaborative effort with the English department. An honors class produced original work by each student. I offered to catalog these materials and add them to the library media collection, which enhanced the credibility of these students as viable authors, and by extension, the library media center as a special repository of these materials for future readers. This successful project idea came to fruition during a meeting I requested with the English department chair. Of course, the administration was informed of this collaborative effort and when the new "books" (actually lengthy essays) were all catalogued and placed on the shelves and the data inputted into the catalog, the administrators were invited to actually view the materials as part of the library media collection.

Sophomore students in my state at the end of May were all required to take specific exams administered by the State Department of Education. These Connecticut Academic Performance Tests were offered over a period of days. When the results were received early in the next school year, a congratulatory event was held in the library media center to which those students who received excellent scores were acknowledged. This event was attended by school board members, the school administration, students, their parents, and teachers. The press was alerted, they reported on the event, and the school community knew that this took place in the high school library media center. Student pictures were mounted on posters and these were on display for several months during the school year. What a wonderful opportunity to highlight the library media center as a special part of school functions. This event was supported financially by the administration and parent-teacher organization.

To further gain administrative support, it is suggested that the library media specialist send a monthly report of library media center activities to the principal and all supervisors. The information embedded within the report should indicate classes that utilized the library media center's services—topics students were involved in researching, professional activities in which the media center staff was participating, extracurricula school events the library media staff attended or was part of, and circulation and attendance statistics. By implication, if after a number of months a supervisor saw the same classes coming to the library media center, he/she could take appropriate action—either commending those teachers who utilize the library media center's services, and/or encouraging other teachers to do the same.

At the conclusion of the school year, the monthly reports should be compiled and re-submitted with an accompanying narrative that indicates the goals and objectives of the media center program that were met. In addition, it is important to convey concerns about program facilitation and future plans. The latter would be helpful when the principal needs to consider his/her budget for the following year. I found that this detailed analysis proved helpful when school accreditation visits took place because all of the statistical and anecdotal information was in place.

Both the monthly and annual reports express to your administrator the significant contributions the library media center makes toward the academic achievement of the students. These reports also highlight the interest the library media staff takes in the entire well-being of the student body through interest in the students' academic and extra-curricular activities.

It is also extremely important to cultivate classroom teacher interest in the library media program and services that may be offered to them and their students. Aside from classroom visits which draw attention to the fact that the library media specialist is a specialized teacher, the students and staff will see that the library media specialist wishes to extend him/herself within the school, not to just have people come to the media center. The media specialist must extend his/her services physically outside the library media center environment. This activity may be difficult when the library media specialist is the only library media professional on the staff, but if the clerical assistant(s) will fill in and assist students in the media center in the absence of the professional, it would work to the advantage of the media specialist.

Another way to increase interest in the library media program is to suggest to the department chairs that they hold their department meetings in the media center. The library media specialist can suggest that he/she will spend a few moments prior to the department meeting to highlight some new materials that would interest the staff members' both professional and personal reading. It is at this time that suggestions might be made regarding consultations with staff to enhance their lesson planning with new materials and assistance with lesson planning. The library media specialist could also attend these meetings and be an integral part of all the planning. This library media visit by departments will bring into the media center teachers who, in the past, would not consider the media center as a viable help to them in their lesson planning or for their curriculum needs. This may well lead to more collaborative work sessions than were held in the past. Attendance at these meetings by the library media specialist would necessitate staying a bit later after school hours than originally intended or expected, but it is worth the effort to extend oneself to gain the extra support you might need in the future. It will also endorse and affirm the library media program as an integral part of curriculum planning and implementation. Sometimes department/grade level meetings are held during common planning time during the day—elementary schools and middle schools—and this points out the need for a flexibly scheduled library.

Much of this advocacy activity will also help to create an environment that becomes a showplace for visitors to experience when they come to the building. When the principal or another administrator accompanies visitors on tours of the building, the library media center becomes number one on an academic expedition. This further enhances the importance of the library media program through pride in achievements of the students. The library media center is seen as a hub of activity with visual acknowledgment of student studies and exhibits of student work. The media center becomes an attractive place to work and spend time, other than when accompanied by a teacher.

Teaching, Learning, and Student Inquiry during the Research Process

In order for the library media program to become integrated within the school curriculum, it is important for the library media specialist to "create and sustain an environment that encourages information literacy, independent and collaborative inquiry, and life long learning, to orchestrate access to information resources within and beyond the school ... promote curriculum and instructional development based on the information literacy standards for student learning to equip students with the knowledge and skills they need to participate actively and effectively in the learning community."[1]

As indicated previously, it is very important for the library media specialist to work on various committees within the school whose responsibilities are related to curriculum. Both subject area and grade level teams offer the possibility to effect enriching change within curriculum development. A significant change that ought to be proposed by the library media specialist would be to incorporate information literacy skills in the teaching learning environment while recommending appropriate information resources that support information literacy and critical thinking throughout and across curriculum areas. Most content area standards have some standard that suggests information literacy.

The concept of learning is enhanced and made more meaningful when eight specific constructs are considered. This list was generated by the ideas gleaned from the "Information Literacy Standards for Student Learning" highlighted in *Information Power; Building Partnerships for Learning*, Chapter 2.

1. Learning must be challenging.
2. It should often be hands on so the student is engaged in the process.
3. There should be some value to the process that could lead to awareness.
4. New learning should take place, and, therefore, development of new meaning.
5. Learning should involve a defined order of events, processes, or concepts.
6. Learning must definitely be relevant and meaningful to the student.
7. The process of learning ought to be creative as well as the presentation.
8. The last, but not least, aspect of learning, is that the student develops pride in the final product of the research process.

In order to be assured that learning for the student is meaningful and relevant, the concept of *authentic learning* becomes evident (Eisenberg, Lowe, Spitzer). "Through authentic learning, students address and investigate real world problems or personal situations . . . Through authentic learning, all students would be able to:

1. articulate the purpose of activity
2. analyze and practice what they do know
3. acknowledge what they do not know
4. formulate questions that lead to further knowledge
5. synthesize connections between knowledge and life experience now and in the future, and
6. evaluate what was learned, how it was learned, and how it could be more effectively learned as a formal part of the assignment."[2]

Meaningful learning is also quality-based learning. There should be every attempt to apply academic discipline, to be certain that the information sought within the topic could be applied to the real world (authentic learning), that the student should be engaged in active exploration of the topic, and most importantly, assessment should be conducted not just to evaluate the research which produces a final product, but also an assessment of the entire research process. The latter concept is what the student can use throughout his/her academic career and life experiences. There are a number of indications of whether authentic learning is taking place.

1. To begin with, this type of learning is student-centered wherein many of the questions raised become owned by the students working collaboratively.
2. The student should also be encouraged to be skeptical of the information located. Many students assume that all information they obtain from the Internet, or in printed text, is factual. Students must learn to corroborate facts and in addition, gain various perspectives from their researching to determine the credibility of the concepts and issues they are investigating. Students should be encouraged to find several resources that would substantiate the data they have located, to be certain that what they are reporting is accurate.
3. Authentic learning is also equated with reality research where the student might find information through surveys, interviews, or experiments which would enhance and support the data they are searching.
4. The students could access primary source material, go on virtual field trips to museums or other subject-area related locations. When the teacher and library media specialist coach the students in this process of inquiry and collaboration, the students more fully value the process since they have

the adult coaches as role models. Probably the most significant advantage to the student of processing information through authentic learning is that students are thoroughly engaged in the information problem-solving process. They assume a most active role as the researcher or explorer throughout the course of the inquiry method.

During the teaching/learning process there are questions that the teacher and library media specialist and students must consider:

1. Why they are requiring this research,
2. What specific concepts do they want the students to learn,
3. How will the students, record, process, and organize the information,
4. How will the students produce their findings and
5. How will the product and the process be assessed?

For the student, the issues to dwell upon are:

1. What am I interested in learning more about,
2. Why does this particular topic interest me,
3. Will the teacher accept this topic of my choosing,
4. If I pursue this topic will there be enough relevant information to locate.

Sometimes the classroom teacher will suggest topics. In this case the teacher may have to consider whether enough topics have been suggested and whether or not these topics are appropriate. At this point in the teacher's thinking, it would be important to work collaboratively with the media specialist to make sure that there would be enough resources in all formats for the students to research these topics and in elementary school to be certain there are materials for all reading levels plus age appropriate Internet resources. In the higher grades there is access to inter-library loan, the Internet, and databases which can enhance the availability of additional resources. The teacher may even consider whether or not to allow the students to suggest their own topics within the larger topic. All of these thoughts reflect what elements are important in order to have a successful library media and teaching program. Cooperative/collaborative planning must take place; scheduling library media center use or time with the library media specialist should be flexible. Of course, the latter also depends upon the needs and demands of the curriculum. The library media specialist should be as responsive as possible to the teachers' and students' needs to nurture positive attitudes toward use of the library media center. The media facility ought to be attractive, functional and well-organized. What is vastly important is there must be library media program support from the administration in order to have sufficient funding for staffing, equipment, and collection development.

In order for the information literacy standards to be integrated into content learning, classroom teachers and the library media specialist must have joint responsibility for teaching information literacy skills in every unit of study and across the curricula spectrum. The information literacy standards as outlined in *Information Power; Building Partnerships for Learning*, are grouped into three significant areas: information literacy, independent learning, and social responsibility. Essentially these standards indicate the various academic acuities the students obtain through being information literate and the resulting capabilities that can be effectuated as a result of this literacy. They can access and use information effectively, appreciate the learning process, understand why it is so important to be knowledgeable and ethical in pursuit of knowledge, and how satisfying it is to generate new information.

The teaching/learning process becomes ever more challenging when resource materials and the various teaching approaches need to accommodate diverse learning styles, abilities and needs. Joy H. McGregor, in *Learning and Libraries in an Information Age; Principles and Practice*, relates how we learn and groups the learning processes by: multiple intelligences, learning styles, and motivation. The concept of multiple intelligences was developed by Howard Gardner. In his research he discovered that each person has stronger and weaker intelligences in different areas. The eight intelligences Gardner related are: "linguistic, logical-mathematical, spatial, bodily kinesthetic, musical, interpersonal, intrapersonal, and naturalist."[3] It is Gardner's contention that teachers should use this data to understand the uniqueness of each student and to enhance his/her strengths. This would encourage student success in learning and ultimately enable students to become more competent as success is achieved. As students build up their self-confidence and self-esteem, it is possible that other intelligences may be enhanced. In learning styles, the student should work in his/her area of preference and/or strength. Students may prefer to search and present material through an auditory mode, others, through a visual or kinesthetic process. This approach will also have ramifications as the student approaches presenting the final outcome/product of his/her research. Presentation formats, therefore, could differ considerably. Depending upon the topic, the written format may produce a written report, a brochure, a bibliography, a game, a crossword puzzle, a magazine, a survey, a dramatic production, a newspaper article, an interview. A visual presentation may result in a slide show, a collage, a banner, cartoon and/or a political cartoon, diorama, model, painting, photographs. An oral presentation might be a dialog, an oral report, a play, puppet show, a dramatization, or an audio tape. Any of these combinations will enable the student to produce a project that would enhance the individual student's specific intellectual ability in relation to his/her learning style and add to the student's self esteem.

During the teaching/learning process, it has been noted that the library media specialist and the classroom teacher should collaboratively foster student inquiry. In an article by Barbara Stripling, she discusses the inquiry process and indicates that there are six steps in which the student ought to become involved. These are "*connecting*—to self, to previous knowledge; gain background knowledge to set context for new learning; *wonder*—develop questions, make predictions; hypotheses; *investigate*—find and evaluate information to answer questions, test hypotheses; *construct*—construct new understandings connected to previous knowledge; draw conclusions about questions and hypotheses; *express*—express new ideas to share learning with others, apply understandings to a new context; *reflect*—reflect on own process of learning and on new understandings gained from inquiry, ask new questions."[4]

In *connecting*, the student will use his/her senses of listening and communicating to concepts presented by others to develop a new awareness. Regarding *wonder*, the student will try to find divergence in views to help in interpretation of data. When the student *investigates*, he/she uses many types of resources to test hypotheses, and as a result may ask additional questions. When the student *constructs*, he/she will come to an understanding of varying points of view and realize there are other perspectives than what was originally conceived. When the student is ready to *express* his/her thoughts, these can be presented in a variety of formats, depending on the comfort level of the student, and will reveal the justification for all the research previously conducted. Finally, when the student is able to *reflect* on his/her research process, either through peer review, teacher and/or library media specialist critiques, new comprehension and insight will have taken place and possibly additional questions may be pursued.

All of these steps will ensure that the student is actively engaged in the inquiry/research process. Active engagement also results in more meaningful, creative learning.

The student inquiry process is also part of the various information literacy skills models. There are a number of them and they incorporate the steps indicated above. The information literacy skills models are discussed in many texts related to information searching techniques, so I will not delve into a lengthy discussion of them here other than to mention some of them along with their accompanying constructs (*Learning and Libraries in an Information Age; Principles and Practices,* edited by Barbara K. Stripling, pages 60–67).

The BIG6 Skills model (Eisenberg & Berkowitz)

1. Task definition
2. Information seeking skills
3. Location and access
4. Use of information
5. Synthesis
6. Evaluation

xl   Teaching, Learning, and Student Inquiry

Pathways to Knowledge Model (Pappas and Tepe)

1. Appreciation
2. Preresearch
3. Search
4. Interpretation
5. Communication
6. Evaluation

Essential Skills for Information Literacy (Washington Library Media Association)

1. Recognizing a need for information
2. Constructing strategies for locating information
3. Locating and assessing information
4. Evaluating and extracting information
5. Organizing and applying information
6. Evaluating the process and product

INFOhio DIALOGUE Model (Ohio statewide library automation and information network)

1. Define
2. Initiate
3. Assess
4. Locate
5. Organize
6. Guide
7. Use
8. Evaluate

These foregoing models are all process models. The Colorado Information Literacy Guidelines and the AASL/AECT Information Literacy Standards for Student Learning are not process models.

Model Information Literacy Guidelines (Colorado)

1. Students as knowledge seekers
2. Students as quality producers
3. Students as self-directed learners

Teaching, Learning, and Student Inquiry   xli

4. Students as group contributors
5. Students as responsible information users

AASL/AECT Information Literacy Standards for Student Learning

1. Information literacy
2. Independent learning
3. Social responsibility

Since students will be researching materials in many formats, their information literacy skills and inquiry methods will also involve being able to fully understand the development of new competencies. These competencies involve media literacy. The latter might be considered a new form of communication that provides information in our electronic age. The reason to discuss this here is that consumers of this type of information are often passive and not given to determining accuracy, authenticity, and relevancy of the data they are hearing or viewing. Media is widely used by students, but generally for entertainment, not often considered as a resource for their research. The information they receive is rarely questioned. The media referred to encompasses television, the Internet, billboards, newspapers, magazines, maybe even the radio. In order for the students to become effective users of this type of information emanating from these sources, they must develop critical viewing skills. These skills should enable the student to understand such things as stereotyping, camera angles, body language, lighting, sound, and voice. Lessons in media viewing and listening should be offered by the library media specialist and/or classroom teacher.

One approach might be to have the class watch news segments with the sound turned off for a while, and then comment on what they observe. Then, have students listen to the information imparted without looking at the picture. Give them an opportunity to produce their own news story.

An additional approach would be to have students obtain information from an Internet source. Then have them research that information elsewhere to corroborate that information. Help develop their inquiring minds, not to be skeptical, but to search for authenticity and accuracy. When the students are using an Internet site, they should also be taught how to evaluate those sites. There are various criteria for judging whether an Internet site is valuable and credible. There are four main areas to consider: authority, content, design, and access. Regarding authority, it is important to note who developed the site and to seek to discern if the individual or group is knowledgeable and credible. The site should offer an indication about whether it is affiliated with an institution or a commercial company. It is important to check for stereotyping or bias and whether the bias is personal, political, or religious. For content, the student needs to understand whether the information on the site is unique and/or is the data accessible from another source. The information should be checked for accuracy through another resource. It is important to note if the data given is updated on a regular basis. When design of the site is considered, it is necessary to see if the information is organized logically and whether one can progress easily from one section to the next. If graphics are offered, determine whether they really serve a purpose. Access to the site is important, therefore, the student should consider whether the site can be reached consistently, and in a timely manner, or whether it takes too long to load. A major question regarding access is whether there is a charge or fees for using all or parts of the site.

Many school systems require student and/or parental or guardian permission to use the Internet. There are many examples of policies in print. One may be located in: *The School Library Media Manager*, Blanche Woolls, published by Libraries Unlimited in 2004, pp. 91, 92. There are also a number of policies accessible on the Internet. These policies work as contracts between the students and the school, with parental guidance, as well. In my library media center, we kept the signed hard copy policies on file and used a field on our Follett management software to indicate that a policy was on file. Of course, if the contract was not adhered to by the student, that student lost his/her Internet use privileges for a specified period of time. These consequences were written into the contract so all signers were fully aware of the effects of a broken agreement.

To reiterate, teaching/learning methods described in this section which incorporate the process of student inquiry, is a collaborative process, one that will generate new knowledge, new skills and new perspectives on the process of learning that the student will rely upon for his/her lifetime.

Notes

1. *Information Power; Building Partnerships for Learning* (Chicago: American Library Association, 1998), pp. 72, 73.

2. Michael B. Eisenberg, Carrie A. Lowe, Kathleen L. Spitzer, *Information Literacy; Essential Skills for the Information Age,* 2nd ed. (Westport, CT: Libraries Unlimited, 2004), p. 97.

3. Barbara K. Stripling, ed. *Learning and Libraries in an Information Age; Principles and Practice* (Colorado: Libraries Unlimited, 1999), p. 38.

4. Barbara K. Stripling, "Fostering Literacy and Inquiry" (*School Library Journal's Learning Quarterly*, September 2003) p. 5; Barbara K. Stripling and Sandra Hughes-Hassell, eds. *Curriculum Connections Through the Library* (Westport, CT: Libraries Unlimited, 2003), pp. 10–17.

Controversial Issues: What Are They?

Controversial issues are those that reflect differences of opinion. They may be inherently political, philosophical, and/or religious. Students and faculty come to school with value systems that have been inculcated into their lives from parents/guardians, their clergy, their friends, the media, or from the opportunity to be reflective citizens. Since controversy implies disagreement or dissent to either an established value system, or to a new area or issue not considered previously, this area of study becomes a unique challenge for the library media specialist and classroom teacher. Everyone has a set of opinions on most subjects, but it is imperative that educators who work with children do not influence or unduly propagandize opinions of their students. Faculty and staff have the responsibility to present neutral points of view. Their goal should be to get students to *think critically* without being persuaded in one direction or another. When students research issues, analyze and synthesize their data, they become better able to make more informed decisions. When students research topics that are more challenging, provocative, and creative, they are conducting a paradigm shift from the standard, "safe" topics that have been assigned in days past.

Classroom teachers and library media specialists must anticipate that students will wish to research some issues which will instigate debate. This is healthy and ought to be encouraged. Debate, disagreement, consternation, and anxiety are what encourage students to think critically. Students enjoy this challenge, especially because they become engaged in the process of argument, judgment, the legitimate opportunity to become opinionated. The library media specialist and/or the classroom teacher must be skilled in handling these discussions so that students are respectful and not antagonistic. The following are some ground rules for classroom discussion:

1. "Always listen carefully, with an open mind, to the contributions of others
2. Ask for clarification when you don't understand a point someone has made
3. If you challenge others' ideas, do so with factual evidence and appropriate logic
4. Always critique ideas or position, not people
5. If others challenge your ideas, be willing to change your mind if they demonstrate errors in your logic or use of the facts
6. Point out the relevance of issues that you raise when their relevance might not be obvious to others in the class
7. If others have made a point with which you agree, only repeat it when you have something important to add

8. Be efficient in your discourse; make your points and then yield to others—take turns speaking
9. Above all, avoid ridicule and try to respect the beliefs of others, even if they differ from yours."[1]

It is also important for the faculty member to be aware of the students with whom he/she is working. It is critical to be cognizant of students' backgrounds, perspectives, and experiences. Students enter school with a set of values, beliefs, and judgments from their families which must be respected. Classroom discussions, therefore, present a wonderful opportunity for students to gain respect for other viewpoints.

In my experience of working with classroom teachers during preparation for debates and also as a "judge" of these debates (I was asked by the classroom teacher to perform this responsibility, along with my school principal and another administrator), I had found it most exciting when the students who had been working in groups on a particular issue, are then told to reverse their previous position on the issue and take the other side. Students are then sometimes asked to develop a compromise situation/statement that both sides can agree on. It is most important for students to understand that the classroom or library media center is a safe, protected, harmless environment, where the students and adults will not be judgmental of strong opinions. The students might need periodic reminders of the ground rules stated above, and perhaps even a break in time might be necessary to cool tongues, and the possibility of some volatility. Yet, how exciting an opportunity this is for students and staff. The atmosphere becomes electric; students are thinking and learning.

Who Is Dealing with Controversial Issues?

I sent an e-mail message to each state board of education and territory inquiring whether they had adopted a statement/policy regarding "Teaching About Controversial Issues." The following state/territories responded: Arizona, Connecticut, Delaware, Florida, Guam, Hawaii, Illinois, Indiana, Kentucky, Maine, Maryland, Missouri, New Hampshire, New York, North Carolina, Pennsylvania, South Dakota, Texas, Washington, and West Virginia. The only respondent who had a specific policy was Hawaii. This reads:

CONTROVERSIAL ISSUES POLICY
Student discussion of issues which generate opposing points of view shall be considered a normal part of the learning process in every area of the school program. The depth of the discussion shall be determined by the maturity of the students.
Teachers shall refer students to resources reflecting all points of view. Discus-

sions, including contributions made by the teacher or resource person, shall be maintained on an objective, factual basis. Stress shall be placed on learning how to make judgments based on facts.[2]

There was a time when the Connecticut State Board of Education had a lengthy, and I believe a model, policy on this topic. It was adopted on October 4, 1978. However, they no longer have such a policy. The closest they now come to any policy, even though remotely related to this subject, is a statement titled: "Position Statement On Creating a Healthy School Environment." Basically it calls for school personnel to "consistently enforce rules and provide opportunities to develop and foster ethical reasoning, self-control and a generalized respect for others. Academic subjects should be used as vehicles for examining and reflecting upon ethical issues." And students must appreciate differences and respect all other persons.[3]

The October 4, 1978 policy is worthy of note here, since I do believe it should be a policy adopted by state boards of education, or at least by individual school districts:

CONTROVERSIAL ISSUES

Learning to deal with controversial issues is one of the basic competencies all students should acquire. Controversial issues are those problems, subjects or questions about which there are significant differences of opinion based for the most part on the differences in the values people bring to the appraisal of the facts of the issue.

Controversy is inherent in the democratic way of life. The study and discussion of controversial issues is essential to the education for citizenship in a free society. Students can become informed individuals only through the process of examining evidence, facts and differing viewpoints, by exercising freedom of thought and moral choice, and by making responsible decisions. The perpetuation of the fundamental principles of our society requires the guarantee that there be opportunity for students to read, to gather information, to speak and to hear alternative viewpoints, and to reach honest judgments according to their individual ability.

In order for students to learn these competencies, teachers must be free to help students to identify and evaluate relevant information to learn the techniques of critical analysis, and to make independent judgments. They must reinforce the students' rights to present and support their conclusions before persons who have opposing points of view. Teachers should also endeavor to develop a flexibility of viewpoint in students so that they are able to recognize the need for continuous and objective re-examination of issues in the light of changing conditions in society and as new and significant evidence becomes available to support a change in point of view. Further, teachers should direct the attention of learners, at the appropriate levels of maturity, to significant issues and to promote a lively exchange of ideas about them. Although teachers have the right to express their own viewpoints and opinions, they do not have the right to indoctrinate students with their personal views.

It is recommended that all Connecticut boards of education develop and disseminate a written policy which supports the concept of Teaching About Controversial Issues.[4]

In the responses I did receive from the various states and one territory indicated above, the comments were either that the state does not have such a policy, or that each community is responsible for the development of curriculum and policies.

The next sections will delineate the many categories of controversial issues and some but not all of the issues in each category. The issues are numerous and to some might not even be considered controversial.

Notes

1. "Teaching Controversial Issues," Staff of the Center for Teaching and Learning (CTL Publications: For Your Consideration #21); http://ctl.unc.edu/fyc21.html.

2. Robert McClelland, "Hawaii's "Controversial Issues Policy," Robert_McClelland/PEG/HIDOE@notes.k12.hi.us

3. "Position Statement On Creating a Healthy School Environment," Adopted February 7, 2001.

4. *Learning Resources & Technology; A Guide To Program Development* (State of Connecticut Board of Education, 1991), Appendix E, "Controversial Issues," p. 73.

Researching Controversial Issues

Researching controversial issues necessitates investigating, locating, and securing information that might well be challenged or rendered inaccessible. Print and electronic materials might be considered inappropriate for students for a number of reasons: interest level, intellectual capacity, emotional/maturity level, or reading level, or because some people disapprove of anyone (or students) knowing about certain topics. Websites may be blocked because of the installation of filters on computers. It would be impossible to have materials that would offend no one; this would be the "dumbing down" of subject matter and learning.

Students enjoy the process of debate and should be given every opportunity to engage in researching materials that would substantiate the ideas upon which they have reflected and deliberated. The school library media specialist, in collaboration with the classroom/subject teacher, must provide an environment where students have every opportunity to inquire and perform their research. Students should be able to access materials that justify their viewpoints. They must learn to make responsible decisions based upon researching an array of material. This will provide the students with a chance to be the critical, creative thinkers they ought to become to be responsible, participating citizens in our democratic society.

Students need to be challenged. They need to have the freedom to select material which will support their inquiring minds. In order for this scenario to be viable, school library media collections need to reflect all points of view. Material selection policies, board of education approved, must reflect this philosophy. Material selection policies should also pertain to the accessibility of electronic resources. Since computers with filtering software will not permit total freedom for accessing data, investigating the controversial issues presented in this text necessitates using computers without filters. The biology, health, sexuality, and political issues presented in this text require freedom from restrictions to access those issues.

As was previously noted, controversial issues are often called "hot topics." This is because many people feel uncomfortable in discussing, reading, and hearing about these issues. This is often the case when people are ignorant of or frightened by the subject matter. This results in adults wanting to protect and shield their children from topics they themselves cannot discuss.

School library media specialists have a responsibility to provide material that will not only support the curriculum, but enrich it, as well. Of course, they must consider the different reading levels, interests, and emotional readiness of the students. Should restrictions be placed upon a school library media's collection, the school library media specialist would not be able to deliver a diverse, varied selection. As indicated in the American Library Association's *Access to Resources and Services in the School Library Media Program, An Interpretation of the Library Bill of Rights*, "School library media professionals assume a leadership role in promoting the principles of intellectual freedom within the school by providing resources and services that create and sustain an atmosphere of free inquiry."[1]

To rectify a situation of restrictions, computers should not be filtered. Internet filtering is not a new phenomenon, but it is a policy that must be seriously debated before installation is implemented. Many producers who provide filters do not always reveal what information is being blocked. While some of the material may be clearly objectionable other material may be protected by the First Amendment. Also, school library media specialists cannot guarantee to parents that blocked material will remain that way. Students are technically savvy and can often override the blocking software. The important issue is to enable students to access information in all formats. It is critical that school library media specialists provide the most effective learning environment for the students and staff.

Students should also be made aware of both safety and "netiquette" issues when they are online. The benefits far outweigh the risks when using online services. There is some inappropriate material available. Students should not provide personal information to anyone online. Students should agree not to meet anyone in person with whom they have communicated online. School library media specialists should educate students about these dangers and letters of reassurance and risk ought to be mailed to parents and guardians prior to the school year. It is important for families to be involved and interested in their students' work. Adults should teach students how to make effective and wise choices when researching and reading any material.

School library media specialists, teachers, and their school systems in a democratic, pluralistic society, need to fulfill their obligations to serve a diverse community by teaching students to tolerate, respect, and honor differences. This can be done by offering material that expresses conflicting perspectives so students can develop an understanding and respect for different viewpoints. This can be accomplished by having unfettered access to material in all formats.

Note

1. American Association of School Librarians, division of the American Library Association, 2001. 0838970532.

Presentation of Controversial Issues

When students research controversial issues, it is beneficial to approach the subject from a neutral point of view, unless, of course, the intent and the ultimate reason for conducting the research is to debate the issue in a forum. Then a particular viewpoint needs to be addressed from a distinct perspective. However, it is also imperative that information used to project an opinion be documented in order to be deemed credible.

A short bibliography and/or webliography will be provided for each issue highlighted, so that students, library media specialists, and classroom teachers will have a point of reference to begin their own research on each topic.

Wikipedia, the free online encyclopedia, enables one to obtain not only an extensive listing of controversial issues, but also the fact that these issues are arranged under specific categories. These broad categories enable the researcher to narrow his/her focus on a particular area of interest. As was mentioned previously, the student doing research will become much more engaged in the research process when he/she is interested in the topic and has personally selected the subject of study.

The specific broad categories of controversial issues listed in the *Wikipedia* should not be considered the only definitive ones available, and each category might be further delineated into a narrower search sub-section. These categories are presented here only as a guide, and since they vary in scope, breadth, and depth, students can make their own determination about the direction in which the study will proceed.

The nine broad categories are:

1. Biology/Health
2. Entertainment
3. Environment
4. Geography
5. History
6. People
7. Politics
8. Religion
9. Sexuality

It is significant that a number of these topics might straddle several categories, so that "Stem Cell Research" could be placed under Biology, Politics, or Religion depending on the approach used to discuss this topic; similarly "Anarchism" may be listed under Politics, History, or People.

Biology/Health

Abortion

AIDS Reappraised and AIDS, the Epidemic

Alternative Medicine

Birth Control

Circumcision

Cloning

Cryonics

Eugenics

Euthanasia

Evolution and Creationism

In Vitro Fertilization

Medical Marijuana

Mind Control

Overpopulation

Performance-Enhancing Drugs in Sports

Psychoactive Drugs

Race and Intelligence

Racial Profiling

Stem Cells

Tobacco Smoking

Transracial Adoption

Abortion

Many students have debated and written about abortion. It is a highly charged issue that has inflamed religious groups, political organizations, and ethicists. There are a number of aspects to the abortion issue, and this is certainly one that can be "webbed" to narrow the focus. This topic might be approached from the standpoint of medical ethics, from weeks of gestation, mother's health or the health of the fetus, the various procedures employed, the type of intervention, marital status, cultural norm, family values, religious perspective, and/or age of pregnant person.

There are several good websites. The Internet websites typically are coming from two perspectives: pro-life and pro-choice. If the website represents a specific religious or any other advocacy group, one must be cautious about the possibility of inaccuracies and distortions.

http://www.religioustolerance.org/abortion.htm

ReligiousTolerance.org. This website offers an interfaith perspective and, therefore, different viewpoints are given. The site presents a critical and non-biased overview of what the process of abortion is, options available, demographic statistics, the differing views about when the fetus assumes personhood, and the various perspectives of pro-choice and pro-life.

http://en.wikipedia.org/wiki/Abortion

The *Wikipedia* site offers definitions, statistics, types and forms of abortion, health issues, including mental health, the history of the process of abortion, social issues, laws concerning abortion, and public opinion in different countries. This site is rather inclusive and offers not only the specifics mentioned above, but also ethical aspects, information on fertilization, and incidents of anti-abortion violence.

http://members.aol.com/abtrbng/

Abortion Law Homepage. This site features constitutional law (i.e., *Roe v. Wade*), state abortion laws, issues of privacy, canon-law, oral argument transcripts, and an index of primary source materials from legal texts.

Journal Articles through the Web

http://www.nytimes.com/library/national/abortion-index.html

The New York Times. There are several links to articles on abortion. One concerns a bipartisan group of law-makers who mounted a drive in the US House and Senate to overturn the George W. Bush Administration policy on international family planning assistance, which they feel is counterproductive and cruel. This drive was the result of the Bush Administration moving to deny federal aid to overseas groups that provide abortion counseling or abortions. Another article mentioned that thousands of opponents

4 Encouraging and Supporting Student Inquiry

of legalized abortion cheered because they felt they had a supporter in the White House who would change abortion policy. In another article, First Lady Laura Bush indicated that she did not think the *Roe v. Wade* 1973 Supreme Court decision, declaring a woman's constitutional right to abortion, should be overturned.

http://websearch.cnn.com/search/search?source=cnn&invocationtype=search%2Ftop&sites=web&query=abortion

CNN.com. This site contains articles on the challenges of abortion—depression and physical complications such as infection and infertility. The site also provides links to articles providing all sides of the issue and listings for pregnancy help centers. In addition, there is data on political updates regarding this controversial procedure.

Books

Bearing Right: How the Conservatives Won the Abortion War, With a New Preface by William Saletan (University of California, 2004). 0520243366.

Thirty years after *Roe v. Wade* the author contests that conservatives won the abortion war—on legality, parental notification, reproductive autonomy inaccessible to the young and the poor.

When Abortion Was a Crime: Women, Medicine, and Law in the United States, 1867–1973 by Leslie J. Reagan (University of California Press, 1997). 0520216571.

This text deals with the criminalization of abortion, death, and suffering. It concerns a college freshman who had an abortion before *Roe v. Wade*. The information is reflective of the author's doctoral dissertation.

Wrath of Angels: The American Abortion War by James Risen and Judy Thomas (Basic Books, 1999). 046509273X.

This book offers the history of the anti-abortion movement since *Roe v. Wade*, as social protest that turned violent.

Back Rooms: Voices From the Illegal Abortion Era by Ellen Messer and Kathryn E. May (Prometheus Books, 1994). 0879758767.

In this text, women share experiences with back room abortions, forced abortions and marriages. The narrative is concerned with the need for legalization of abortion.

Targets of Hatred: Anti-Abortion Terrorism by Patricia Baird-Windle and Eleanor Bader (Palgrave Macmillan, 2001). 0312239254.

The book offers the perspectives of two pro-choice advocates. The targets referred to in the text are clinics, workers, clients, people behind the attacks, leaders, and the strategies they use.

Ethics of Abortion by Jennifer A. Hurley (Greenhaven, 2000). 0737704691.

The articles offer a wide range of viewpoints on abortion—moral, religious, legal, constitutional issues, and *Roe v. Wade*.

The Abortion Rights Controversy in American History by N.E.H. Hull and Peter Charles Hoffer (University of Kansas Press, 2001). 0700611436.

This text presents an historical analysis of the abortion debate—key events, legal issues, and social consequences of this issue since the 1973 case.

Democrats for Life: Pro-Life Politics and the Silenced Majority by Kristen Day (New Leaf Press, 2006). 0892216379.

The author is National Director of Democrats for Life—a grassroots pro-life organization in Washington, DC. She indicates how the Democratic Party has been hijacked by the extremely liberal members of the party and special interest groups like NARAL Pro-Choice America (National Abortion Rights Action League). She illustrates that only 25 percent of people in the United States support the Democratic Party's agenda of abortion on demand.

Pro-Life Activists in America: Meaning, Motivation, and Direct Action by Carol J.C. Maxwell (Cambridge University Press, 2002). 0521669421.

This text presents an oral history of pro-life direct activism in the United States from the late 1970s through the 1990s. The author offers stories of leaders, followers, Catholics, and evangelicals and explores the complex beliefs and desires that gave rise to this activism.

AIDS Reappraised and AIDS, the Epidemic

In the 1980s, after the discovery of AIDS and the HIV virus, much attention was given to the cause and subsequent treatment of the virus and the full-blown disease. As in the case of a number of issues, there has been a debate about the accuracy of the subject matter, the true existence of the issue, and the validity of the occurrence. There are those who would deny the scientific data, so the debate and controversies continue.

AIDS Reappraised

http://www.virusmyth.net/aids/data/epmedhypo.htm
"Reappraisal of AIDS—Is the Oxidation Induced by the Risk Factors the Primary Cause?" The thesis proposed here indicates that there are causes of AIDS other than the HIV virus and conditions which suppress the immune system different from those previously offered.

http://www.virusmyth.net/aids/data/ppisolation.htm
"The Isolation Question" by Paul Philpott, 1997. This article challenges and disputes the AIDS model. This is a technical article, but some high school students who excel in science might well find it provocative.

http://www.suppressedscience.net/aids.html
"The Suppression of Dissent in AIDS Science." This is an interesting redefinition of the disease factors, and questions the purity of symptoms.

Journal Articles through the Web

http://www.virusmyth.net/aids/data/nheuropean.htm
The European. "AIDS: Is Anyone Positive?" by Neville Hodgkinson, June 22, 1998. The author feels HIV is a "myth." He claims that the photos of the virus that have appeared worldwide are artists' impressions and computer simulations, based on indirect observations by molecular biologists. Some scientists believe that HIV is not a new virus but the result of cell stress. They have indicated that HIV researchers have failed to demonstrate the existence of HIV in AIDS patients. The author felt that the enormous investment of money and energy allocated to study this illness has made it difficult for ideas about the nature of AIDS to change. Those in the public health field and AIDS advisory groups became defensive about their re-

search and claimed that the application of new drugs is decreasing the devastating illnesses associated with HIV/AIDS.

http://www.thenhf.com/articles_30.htm

Journal of Scientific Exploration. "AIDS: Scientific or Viral Catastrophe?" by Neville Hodgkinson; Vol. 17, No. 1, pp. 87–120, 2003. Despite more than $100 billion spent on AIDS, this author indicated that scientists have not been able to explain how HIV causes AIDS. He mentioned that AIDS deaths have fallen in Europe and the United States. He felt the drug "cocktails" taken by AIDS patients may have contributed to the decline in cases, but this has not been supported by evidence. He also thinks there is a vast overdiagnosis of AIDS and HIV disease reported in Africa.

Books

As They See It: The Development of the African AIDS Discourse by Raymond Downing (Adonis & Abbey Publishers, Ltd., 2005). 1905068077.

The author and his wife, both doctors, have lived in various African countries. They trace the development of the AIDS story. The authors suggest that the reader should understand how Africans view health and diseases.

AIDS: Virus Or Drug Induced? edited by Peter H. Duesberg (Springer, 1996). 0792339614.

Two dozen scientists, scholars, and journalists investigated AIDS research. They discuss the AIDS hypothesis. This book urges that ideas on the disease be freely discussed, without being judgmental, so a consensus can be achieved.

Unraveling AIDS: The Independent Science and Promising Alternative Therapies by Ho Mae-Won (Vital Health Publishing, 2005). 1890612472.

This book addresses whether AIDS is a real disease and whether it is a single disease. The author further discusses the HIV virus and whether it is the cause of AIDS. Also addressed are the issues of conventional anti-HIV drugs and whether they help in the containment of the disease. This book is evidently very readable for the general public.

AIDS, the Epidemic

The AIDS/HIV epidemic continues to grow and increase rapidly among women. It is no longer just the disease affecting homosexual men, as it was in the 1980s. Since this disease is striking heavily in the female gender population, it is also being passed to the unborn fetus during pregnancy. The disease is also passed on by IV drug users, since needles are often shared.

The most recent world statistics on this disease reflect the 40+ million people living with the illness of whom "17.5 million are women and 2.3 million are children under age 15 . . . In 2005, 3.1 million people died of HIV/AIDS related causes."[1]

Many of these new HIV/AIDS cases are developing in sub-Saharan Africa. However, there are a number of antiretroviral drugs that are helping to sustain lives. Yet countries that are still suspect of the disease and/or enmeshed in poverty, illiteracy, or considering the disease in prejudicial terms are not supplying these life-sustaining medications. Scientists worldwide, the Global Fund to Fight AIDS, Tuberculosis and Malaria, the Gates Foundation, and others, are still committed to fighting this pandemic and searching for a cure.

Some excellent websites to search for information:

www.aidsvaccineclearinghouse.org

This is the AIDS Vaccine Clearinghouse which is a link to people and organizations interested in AIDS vaccine advocacy, research, and reaching people worldwide.

http://www.iavireport.org/BackissuesVAX.asp

VAX is a bulletin, released monthly and published by the International AIDS Vaccine Initiative (IAVI). The articles are written in nontechnical versions on AIDS research. Vaccine trial information can be used by journalists, policymakers, and health workers.

http://www.unaids.org/en/HIV_data/2006GlobalReport/

2006 Report on the Global AIDS Epidemic. One hundred twenty-six countries submitted reports, a most comprehensive set of data. These reports deal with the political commitment of each country, quality, and service offered in an equitable manner and how the countries are approaching issues of discrimination.

Journal Articles through the Web

http://www.thebody.com/aac/aacix.html

The Body; The Complete HIV/AIDS Resource. This site contains articles from 1995 to 2006; material is also available in Spanish. The areas of concentration are: HIV/AIDS Basics & Prevention, Just Diagnosed, HIV Treatment, Living with HIV, AIDS Policy & Activism, HIV Around the World, and Conference held in Glasgow, November 12–16, 2006.

http://www.newstarget.com/AIDS.html

NewsTarget.com. This site has feature articles on AIDS with related concepts: HIV, Infections, Hospital, Bad Medicine, AIDS Drugs, Pharmaceutical Companies, Advertising, Nutrition, Africa, and South Africa.

Books on AIDS

AIDS: Science and Society, 4th edition by Hung Fan, Ross F. Conner, and Luis P. Villarreal (Jones & Bartlett Pubs., 2004). 076370086X.

This text is written for lay people with clarity and good illustrations. The information enables non-professionals to understand the biological, social, and psychological aspects of this disease.

And the Band Played On: Politics, People, and the AIDS Epidemic by Randy Shilts and William Greider (Stonewall Inn Editions, originally published in 1987, but new edition in 2000). 0312241356.

This was the first major book on AIDS and considered a landmark work. It criticizes the medical and scientific communities' first response to the disease.

AIDS in the Twenty-First Century: Disease and Globalization Fully Revised and Updated Edition by Tony Barnett, Alan Whiteside (Palgrave Macmillan, 2nd ed., 2006). 1403997683.

This text examines the social and economic effects of the HIV/AIDS epidemic and the failures to respond appropriately and what needs to be done to combat this disease. The authors do emphasize much of what is happening in Africa and the factors that gave rise to such a horrific epidemic.

Note

1. http://globalhealth.org/view_top.php3?id=227

Alternative Medicine

This method of medical care is also referred to as complementary and alternative medicine (CAM). Approximately 36 percent of adults in the United States use some form of CAM (2004 study by NCCAM and the National Center for Health Statistics). This percentage increases to 62 percent when the definition of CAM includes megavitamin therapy, and prayer, especially for health reasons. There are a number of hospitals, doctors, and managed care plans and facilities that have incorporated some use of CAM. In addition, medical institutions—medical and nursing schools—are offering instruction in aspects of CAM. The National Institutes of Health (NIH) and the National Center for Complementary and Alternative Medicine (NCCAM) plus the Agency for Healthcare Research and Quality are convening meetings to discuss use of such medical care in private and academic medicine. All of this collaboration is lending credibility to this form of medical treatments.

http://www.pitt.edu/~cbw/altm.html
This is the Alternative Medicine Homepage. The website offers sources of information on unconventional, unorthodox, unproven, or alternative, complementary, innovative, interpretive therapies.

http://nccam.nih.gov/
This site is the National Center for Complementary and Alternative Medicine. The website offers information on research, clinical trials, training, and health information on a variety of treatments for various illnesses.

http://www.altmedicine.com
This website, the Alternative Health News Online, reflects information offered by various journalists who have surfed the Internet to find credible sites, even adding a conventional health site to present an integrative approach to health care. Some sites are updated daily and/or weekly. It is important to look at all websites with a healthy skepticism since some sites are maintained by those who adhere to certain procedures and want to put a positive outlook on their approaches to medical care.

Journal Articles through the Web

http://www.jsu.edu/depart/library/graphic/handouts/althandout.pdf
"Finding Journal Articles in Alternative/Complementary Medicine." This website provides access to EBSCO health databases, to Oxford Journals database, and to the specific database of the *Journal of Alternative and Complementary Medicine*.

http://www.biomedcentral.com/bmccomplement.alternmed/
BMC Complementary and Alternative Medicine. This is an open access journal which provides articles dealing with: studies of homeopathic reme-

dies, use of herbal medicines, use of treatments with cancer and chronic pain, skin and stomach problems, and uses of alternative and complementary medicines and procedures worldwide.

http://nccam.nih.gov/camonpubmed/

National Center for Complementary and Alternative Medicine/National Institutes of Health. This site provides links to full text articles at journal websites. This is also a database of the National Library of Medicine and provides access to the Medline database. This website does not provide specific medical advice, but enables the user to access sources of information on complementary and alternative medicine and care.

Books

Complementary and Alternative Medicine: Challenge and Change by Merrijoy Kelner and Beverly Wellman (Routledge, 2003). 9058230996.

This book brings together many leading North American and European social scientists who identify who uses CAM, why they use it, and how they find out about it.

Blackwell Complementary and Alternative Medicine: Fast Facts for Medical Practice edited by Mary A. Herring (Blackwell Pub., 2002). 0632045833.

This text helps physicians in educating themselves and their patients about alternative therapies and how these treatments impact conventional therapies.

Complementary and Alternative Medicine in the United States, by Institute of Medicine (The National Academies Press, 2005). 0309092701.

This book outlines areas of research in CAM therapies and ways of integrating these therapies with conventional medicine. It also offers models to guide decision-making and various curricula that provide education for health professionals.

Birth Control

Birth control involves taking certain courses of action to prevent pregnancy. The various methods help to reduce the likelihood of fertilization of an ovum with spermatozoa. Contraceptive devices help to reduce the chances of pregnancy, which differs from abortion. The latter ends a pregnancy. Birth control is a controversial political and ethical issue. There are cultures and religions that oppose its use.

People's attitudes and beliefs are often developed as they are growing up. These reflect their parents' value system as well as their experiences with religion.

American social conservatives have had a major campaign against abortion. This campaign became more aggressive with *Griswold v. Connecticut*, a U.S. Supreme Court case in 1965 which, in effect, legalized contraception. Then the issue became more problematic with *Roe v. Wade*, 1973 U.S. Supreme Court decision. This decision was a landmark one. The essence of this decision indicated that laws against abortion violate a constitutional right to privacy under a liberty clause of the 14th Amendment. This case overturned all state and federal laws outlawing or restricting abortion that were inconsistent with this decision.

The American Life League, a lay Catholic organization, contends there is a connection between the practice of contraception and that of abortion. They consider contraceptive use to be anti-child. The organization wants to stress the importance of building a culture of life and they feel life begins at conception.

The anti-birth control campaign is not necessarily centralized but evolved within the conservative movement. The topic is discussed in evangelical churches and on the agendas of Bible-based conservative organizations like Focus on the Family and the Christian Coalition.

http://www.4woman.gov/faq/birthcont.htm

United States Department of Health and Human Services; Women's Health.Gov. This site lists birth control methods, and the methods best for different situations. Also discussed are methods with estimates of their effectiveness: continuous abstinence, periodic abstinence, the male condom, oral contraceptives, the mini-pill, the intrauterine device (Copper T IUD), the female condom, Depo-Provera, diaphragm, cervical cap or shield, contraceptive sponge, the patch (Ortho Evra), hormonal vaginal contraceptive ring, surgical sterilization (tubal ligation or vasectomy), non-surgical sterilization (Essure permanent birth control system), emergency contraception, withdrawal—how effective is it, and protection from HIV.

http://en.wikipedia.org/wiki/Birth_control

The *Wikipedia* offers an extensive discussion of the history of birth control, various birth control methods, a section of modern folklore about this topic, the effectiveness of the many methods, and religious and cultural attitudes.

http://www.fda.gov/fdac/features/1997/babytabl.html
United States Food and Drug Administration (FDA); "Birth Control Guide," updated 2003. This site discusses a number of birth control methods that have been approved by the FDA. It also lists failure rates noted in clinical trials submitted to the FDA.

http://www.medem.com/MEDLB/article_detailb.cfm?article_ID= ZZZ480I527C&sub_cat=5
Medical Library—American College of Obstetricians and Gynecologists; "Birth Control." This article discusses the various methods of birth control: barrier, hormonal, intra-uterine devices, pills, injections, vaginal ring, skin patch, natural family planning, withdrawal, and sterilization.

Journal Articles through the Web

http://ils.unc.edu/dpr/path/birth_control/pathfinderjournalarticles.html
FDA Consumer Magazine. "Protecting Against Unintended Pregnancy: A Guide to Contraceptive Choices" by Tama Nordenberg, 1997. This article attributes the excessive number of unintended pregnancies in the United States on the lack of knowledge of contraceptive options. Therefore, the author provides lists of such options and describes them. Included, too, is a chart showing the effectiveness, risks, and convenience of each option.

http://www.agi-usa.org/pubs/journals/3209500html
Family Planning Perspectives. "In Clinical Trial, Women Using Once-A-Month Injectable Contraceptive Avoid Pregnancy and Approve of Method" from the Alan Guttmacher Institute, March/April 2000. This article discusses the safety of injectable contraceptives to prevent pregnancy.

http://www.opinionjournal.com/taste/?id=110008814
Opinion Journal from the *Wall Street Journal.* "God's Protection—Evangelicals Embrace the Contraceptive Culture" by Christine J. Gardner, August 18, 2006. This article was written after the FDA approval of over-the-counter Plan B, the "morning after" pill. The author indicates that American evangelicals are pro-contraception by 88 percent. However, the author contends that acceptance of contraception by Protestants has a rather short history. The 1930 Lambeth Conference of Anglican bishops first authorized contraceptive use in marriage.

Books

Contraception: Your Questions Answered by John Guillebaud (Churchill Livingstone, 2003). 0443073430.
This book offers a detailed explanation of the various methods of contraception. There are also full explanations of how each method works.

It's Perfectly Normal: Changing Bodies, Growing Up, Sex, and Sexual Health by Robie H. Harris (Candlewick Press, 2004). 0763624330.

This text provides unbiased answers to every question a child or young adult might ask about sexuality, from conception to birth control, and AIDS. This book also has age-appropriate illustrations.

Natural Birth Control Made Simple by Barbara Kass-Annese (Hunter House Publishers, 2003). 0897934032.

This book provides information on reproduction, fertility, and natural conception, and offers instructions on natural family planning.

The Birth Control Book by Jennifer Cadoff and Samuel Pasquale (Ballantine Books, 1996). 0345400372.

This text offers information on the female condom, natural methods of birth control, the mini-pill, the IUD (intrauterine device), cervical cap, and the "morning after" pill. The book is a contraceptive encyclopedia to help the reader make informed decisions.

Circumcision

This topic concerns a procedure about which decisions have been made based on cultural values and religious and health practices. When considering the ramifications of this procedure, which is often thought of as applied to the male gender, attention must also be given to female circumcision, which is practiced in a number of African countries and elsewhere in the developing world. Male circumcision involves surgery that removes the foreskin covering the glans of the penis. Female circumcision is a surgical procedure in which all or part of the clitoris and sometimes the labia are removed. It is also called clitorectomy or clitoridectomy. The latter rite is oftentimes referred to as mutilation by those in the developed world.

The International Coalition for Genital Integrity considers circumcision as genital mutilation, whether it is performed on males or females. Those in favor of not having the surgery performed consider three functions of keeping the foreskin intact: protective, sensory, and sexual. Those in favor of the surgical procedure usually consider their cultural and religious reasons. They also regard the circumcised penis as being cleaner, or easier to keep clean. Medically, considerations are reduced risk of urinary tract infections, reduced risk of penile cancer, reduced risk of cervical cancer in female sexual partners, and reduced risk of sexually transmitted infections.

The male circumcision procedure is most often performed by either a doctor while the baby is still in the hospital or by a trained religious person several days after the baby is born, often at home. It is sometimes performed on adolescents as a rite of passage.

http://www.cirp.org/

Circumcision Information and Resource Pages (CIRP). This site provides information on all aspects of this genital surgery. CIRP is divided into two parts: "The Circumcision Reference Library" contains technical material, medical and historical articles, statistics, and "The Circumcision Information Pages" which offers a more readable/understandable collection of data which is much more suitable for parents and educators and, therefore, less technical. There are links to both male and female circumcision. Offered, as well, are rationales for routine circumcision in males. The link to female circumcision is entitled: Female Genital Mutilation.

http://www.cirp.org/pages/whycirc.html

This site discusses original motivations behind this procedure; it is historical in nature. This site offers very similar information as the previous site, information on both male and female circumcision.

http://www.cirp.org/pages/cultural/

This site offers many links to Jewish, Christian, Latter Day Saints, and Muslim issues regarding this procedure. This site is mostly about male

16   Encouraging and Supporting Student Inquiry

circumcision. The section on "Muslim Issues" frowns upon female circumcision, and refers to this procedure as mutilation. It further states that female circumcision is mentioned nowhere in the Koran.

http://www.cirp.org/pages/female/
   This website offers information on culture, medical society statements, links to organizations, scholarly journal articles on the Internet, law resources on the Internet, and Human Rights Charters and Declarations. This site only deals with "female genital mutilation."

http://www.cirp.org/news/mercurynews07–12-03/
   This is an anti-circumcision site. "Saying No to Circumcision." This site discusses the fact that an increasing number of Jews are choosing not to circumcise their sons, but perform alternative birth ceremonies. The site only deals with male circumcision.

Journal Articles through the Web

http://www.mothering.com/articles/new_baby/circumcision/against-circumcision.html
   Mothering; Natural Family Living. "The Case Against Circumcision" by Paul M. Fleiss; Issue 85, Winter 1997. This article is about male circumcision and reflects views on the harm it causes: desensitizes, disfigures, and disrupts circulation.

http://www.cirp.org/library/history/gollaher/
   Journal of Social History. "From Ritual to Science: The Medical Transformation of Circumcision in America" by David L. Gollaher; Vol. 28, No. 1, pp. 5–36. This article is about male circumcision. The author indicates that America differs from Western Europe and the rest of the world where circumcision was either a religious ritual or infrequent medical intervention to treat a specific disease.

http://www.questia.com/Index.jsp?CRID=female_genital_mutilation &OFFID=se1&key=female_circumcision
   Daedalus. "What About 'Female Mutilation'? And Why; Understanding Culture Matters in the First Place" by Richard A. Shweder. This author could find no evidence that this procedure leads to death, or to medical complications. The latter were rare. However, the author indicated that there are not too many studies done on female responses. The custom appears to persist on men's insistence.
   Australian Journal of Social Issues. "Responding to Female Genital Mutilation: The Australian Experience in Context" by Ian Patrick. This issue has become controversial in Australia because of the arrival of refugees from Northern African countries, parts of the Middle East, and Asia. The procedure transgresses human rights standards in Australia.

Books

Circumcision: A History of the World's Most Controversial Surgery by David L. Gollaher (Basic Books, 2000). 0465043976.

The author discusses circumcision practices throughout the ages within their social and anthropological context. This account shows how the procedure was viewed by ancient Greeks, who disliked the procedure, and the medieval church. The book also highlights how this procedure was performed in the United States in the late nineteenth century and at that time considered a necessary medical procedure.

Circumcision: What It Does by Billy Ray Boyd (Taterhill Press, 1990). 0961679239.

In this short book, fewer than 100 pages, the author deals openly with the denial, fear, pain, anger, myths, and ignorance about this procedure.

Female Genital Mutilation: Legal, Cultural and Medical Issues by Rosemarie Skaine (McFarland & Co., 2005). 0786421673.

This book discusses the definition and types of FGM (Female Genital Mutilation) and explores common justifications for the procedure, along with data about this procedure in Africa and elsewhere. Global laws, legal issues, rights, and religion are also cited. Personal interviews are also offered.

Cloning

Biologically, a clone could be both single-celled or a multi-cellular organism which is genetically identical to another living organism. There are "natural" clones and those that are produced scientifically and intentionally. Natural clones are made "when an organism reproduces asexually or when two genetically identical individuals are produced by accident, as with identical twins."[1]

Cloning has received much derisive and divisive media attention. There are ethical, moral, medical, health, and technical concerns. Some religious groups are against this process. "The main moral objection to attempts at human cloning right now is that a child might be damaged by such an origination . . . Libertarian views on the subject suggest that it is a person's constitutional right to conduct this process, similar to abortion."[2] Regarding health aspects, there is hope for therapeutic cloning, that when creating stem cells, research that follows might find cures for various diseases.

http://www.euthanasia.com/clone.html

Cloning Information Website. This site has links to specific cloning facts, to medical articles, statements by those in the medical professions, articles that raise legal and ethical issues, and a list of organizations against cloning.

http://www.cloninginformation.org/info.htm

Cloning Information. This site has links to other sites regarding Americans wishing to ban cloning; with fact sheets, state laws, a United Nations report, and reports developed by the United States Government.

http://www.ornl.gov/sci/techresources/Human_Genome/elsi/cloning.shtml

Human Genome Project Information. This is a cloning fact sheet indicating what exactly cloning is; what types of cloning exist (DNA cloning, reproductive, and/or therapeutic); how cloning technologies can be used; what animals have thus far been cloned; the question of organs to be cloned for use in transplant procedures; what the risks are; and whether humans be cloned.

Journal Articles through the Web

http://www.lib.msu.edu/skendall/cloning/news.htm

"Latest News and Science of Cloning." This site contains current and older news articles and interviews.

http://bioethicsweb.ac.uk/browse/mesh/D016428.html

Wellcome Library; Bioethics Web. This site provides information on stem cell research and different perspectives on cloning from various religions.

Books

Who's Afraid of Human Cloning by Gregory E. Pence (Rowman & Littlefield Publishers, Inc, 1998). 0847687821.

The author is a medical ethicist and professor of philosophy. He argues for human cloning as a reproductive option.

The Second Creation by Ian Wilmut, Keith Campbell and Colin Tudge (Farrar Straus Giroux, 2000). 0374141231.

This book confronts genetic engineering and cloning. These authors cloned Dolly the sheep. They discuss how they cloned Dolly, the implications for the future, from attacking diseases to human cloning. The authors are against human cloning.

The Naked Clone by Professor John Charles Kunich (Praeger Publishers, 2003).
0275979644.

This author advocates reproductive cloning. He feels that restricting cloning affects constitutional rights. The author feels it is necessary to preserve personal autonomy, privacy, reproduction, and the freedom of expression. Professor Kunich also discusses the need for rational, scientific evaluations of both reproductive and therapeutic cloning.

Notes

1. http://en.wikipedia.org/wiki/cloning
2. Ibid.

Cryonics

According to the website http://www.cryonics.org/prod.html, "cryonics is a technique designed to save lives and greatly extend life span. It involves cooling legally-dead people to liquid nitrogen temperature where physical decay essentially stops, in the hope that future technologically advanced scientific procedures will someday be able to revive them and restore them to youth and good health. A person held in such a state is said to be a 'cryopreserved patient', because we do not regard the cryopreserved person as being really 'dead.' The cryopreservation state is sometimes described as 'cryonic suspension,' although it is not really 'suspended animation.' The person is more buoyant, but not really 'suspended' in liquid nitrogen."[1]

The term often associated with this procedure has been cryogenics, but cryonics is the more widely accepted term. This process was first suggested by Benjamin Franklin in 1773. He thought that it would be possible to preserve human life in a suspended state for eons. The date given for the modern era of this process is 1962. The most famous person to undergo this process was the former baseball star, Ted Williams. His procedure occurred in 2002.

http://en.wikipedia.org/wiki/Cryonics

The *Wikipedia* site offers several sections: obstacles to success, neuropreservation, financial issues, philosophy, ethics, history, culture, and links to institutes and societies.

http://www.cryonet.org/other.html

More Cryonics-Related Web Sites. This site cites people who are knowledgeable about cryonics. The site also links to organizations and institutes worldwide, plus highlights discussion lists.

http://www.randomhouse.com/features/firstimmortal/links.html

Online Resources: Cryonics, Nanotechnology, Cloning. This website provides a free electronic forum on cryonics, frequently asked questions, a cryonics newsgroup on Usenet, a quarterly magazine about future and advanced technologies, information on Alcor Life Extension Foundation (which is the largest cryonics facility in the world), and links to other organizations.

Journal Articles through the Web

http://www.alcor.org/sciencerefs.html

Alcor Life Extension Foundation. This site presents selected journal articles supporting the scientific basis of cryonics.

http://www.quantium.plus.com/lr/funerals.htm

Funeral Service Journal. "Cryonics and Autopsy." The greatest fear of the cryonicist is autopsy because the procedure involves a violation of the body and the brain. Much information on the brain is lost during autopsy. The brain is of great interest to the cryonicist because it contains the program and data that make humans individuals. This article also offers information on alternatives to cryonics and on the procedure, itself. This site has many articles published from 1987–1995 that offer worthwhile background information on aspects of cryonics.

Books

Forever for All: Moral Philosophy, Cryonics, and the Scientific Prospects for Immortality by R. Michael Perry (Universal Publishers, 2000). 1581127243.

This book refers to death and the hereafter, but death is not seen as inevitable. The text reveals hopes in future advances in technology.

Modern Mummies: The Preservation of the Human Body in the Twentieth Century by Christine Quigley (McFarland & Company, 1998). 0786404922.

This text includes a comprehensive study of the successful prolonged preservation of the human body and considers the law and science of modern mummification.

The Scientific Conquest of Death by Immortality Institute (Libros en Red, 2004). 9875611352.

Nineteen scientists, doctors, and philosophers share their views on this scientific development which could eradicate aging and mortality. This anthology also explores the ethics, politics, and philosophy behind the scientific conquest of aging.

Note

1. http://www.cryonics.org/prod.html. "Cryonics: A Basic Introduction." This website has FAQs that would help a student grasp the essence of the process of cryonics, and who or what (animal) has undergone this technique.

Eugenics

This topic is very controversial since it deals with medical ethics, and moral and religious issues. The movement, or philosophy, advocates improving human heredity traits through some type of intervention.

The goals of this movement are to create healthier and more intelligent humans. Originally, selective breeding was the suggested mode of effectively promoting this philosophy. Presently, the goals of eugenics may be achieved through pre-natal testing and screening, genetic counseling, birth control, in vitro fertilization, and genetic engineering.

http://www.splcenter.org/intel/intelreport/article.jsp?sid=240

Southern Poverty Law Center: Intelligence Report. A number of the links found in this website promote the Eugenics Movement, and many are racist. However, in an effort to present all points of view, this information is important.

http://www.pbs.org/teachersource/thismonth/june03/index3.shtm

PBS Teacher Source, "Concepts Across the Curriculum." This site has a number of links to genetic testing, the cloning debate, high school bioethics, and embryonic stem cell research, plus a Eugenics Archive.

http://www.albany.edu/jmmh/vol3/wwwlinks-v3.html

The Journal for MultiMedia History, Volume 2000. This is a noteworthy website on the "Archive On the American Eugenics Movement." There are more than 1200 web pages divided into ten sections: social origins, scientific origins, research methods, traits studied, research flaws, eugenics popularization, marriage laws, sterilization laws, immigration restriction, and author information and references.

Journal Articles through the Web

http://www.dnafiles.org/resources/res07.html

"Genes and Society." This site lists several journal articles, plus a link to the *American Journal of Bioethics Online*, updated February 2005. There are also radio programs cited on the topic of eugenics.

http://jme.bmjjournals.com/cgi/content/abstract/25/2/176

Journal of Medical Ethics, 1999, Vol.25, No. 2, pp. 176–182; "Ethics Briefing; Preimplantation Genetic Diagnosis and the 'new' eugenics."

Books

Preaching Eugenics: Religious Leaders and the American Eugenics Movement by Christine Rosen (Oxford University Press, 2004). 019515679X.

This text discusses how Protestant, Catholic, and Jewish leaders confronted and, often times, were enthusiastic about the eugenics movement.

Eugenics and Other Evils: An Argument Against the Scientifically Organized State by G.K. Chesterton (Inkling Books, 2000). 1587420023.

Chesterton vehemently opposed eugenics and considered the process one of the great evils of modern society. He also prophesied that the movement might take root in another society—and it did during the period of Nazi Germany. The first edition was published in 1922. This new edition includes writings of Chesterton's opponents.

In the Name of Eugenics: Genetics and the Uses of Human Heredity by Daniel Kevles (Harvard University Press, 1998). 0674445570.

The author discusses the relationship between the genuine science of genetics and the political program and prejudices of the eugenicists. He traces the study and practice of eugenics from its beginnings in the late nineteenth century to the present field of genetic engineering.

Euthanasia

The dictionary definition of this procedure is to bring about a gentle death in the case of incurable and painful disease. Generally, the term implies that the act is initiated by the person who wishes to die. Yet, some define euthanasia as both a voluntary and involuntary termination of life.

There is passive euthanasia, altering support or just letting the person die naturally by: removing life-support equipment, stopping medicating, terminating food and water intake, and/or not delivering CPR (cardio-pulmonary resuscitation). The most common passive type is to prescribe large doses of morphine to dull pain and cause death by suppressing respiration.

Active euthanasia involves the injection of controlled substances. There is also physician-assisted suicide (PAS), when the patient receives a lethal dose of sleeping pills or carbon monoxide gas.

Involuntary euthanasia is the killing of the person who has not requested dying. Often, these people are in a persistent vegetative state.

http://www.religioustolerance.org/euthanas.htm

Religious Tolerance.Org; Euthanasia and Physician Assisted Suicide (PAS). This site discusses the status of euthanasia/PAS around the world, the medical management of pain, ethical and religious aspects and issues, and public opinion.

http://en.wikipedia.org/wiki/Euthanasia

This site offers a wealth of information: terminology, eugenics, ethics, religious perceptions, legal aspects, types of suicides, crisis hotlines by country, plus sections offering "for and against" links.

http://www.nrlc.org/euthanasia/

National Right To Life. This site provides various definitions, some Frequently Asked Questions, and legal cases. This site is solely about assisted suicide and defines the procedure as "Euthanasia is the intentional killing by act or omission of a dependent human being for his or her alleged benefit."

http://plato.stanford.edu/entries/euthanasia-voluntary/

Stanford Encyclopedia of Philosophy. This site lists necessary conditions for someone to be a candidate for voluntary euthanasia, plus objections to the moral possibility of voluntary euthanasia, and provides additional Internet resources.

Journal Articles through the Web

http://sprojects.mmi.mcgill.ca/ethics/x/topics/eutha/eutha_main.htm

Euthanasia and Physician-Assisted Suicide. This site has a lengthy list of journal articles and web resources.

http://www.jco.org/cgi/content/abstract/15/2/418

Journal of Clinical Oncology. "Euthanasia and Physician-Assisted Suicide; A Comparative Survey of Physicians, Terminally Ill Cancer Patients, and the General Population," 1997. This site lists several other journal articles, from many different journals.

http://www.deathwithdignity.org/resources/articles.asp

Death With Dignity National Center. This site provides various articles from the *New England Journal of Medicine.*

Books

Negotiating a Good Death: Euthanasia in the Netherlands by Robert Pool (Haworth Press, 2000). 0789010801.

This text offers a discussion on two years of observation about decisions on this procedure in a Dutch hospital. The topics include: why patients request euthanasia, social and non medical factors that influence doctor's decisions about whether or not to grant requests for this procedure.

Angels of Death: Exploring the Euthanasia Underground by Roger S. Magnusson (Yale University Press, 2002). 0300094366.

This book explores all dynamics of helping victims of AIDS to die. The research occurred in Australia and San Francisco. This text brings the process of aid-in-dying into the open.

A Merciful End: The Euthanasia Movement in Modern America by Ian Dowbiggin (Oxford University Press, 2003). 0195154436.

This is a full scale historical account of this movement. The author also documents the movement's place with other social causes: women's suffrage, birth control, and abortion rights.

Evolution and Creationism

"Evolution involves the development of species from earlier forms. It is a process that results in heritable changes in population over many generations. Within the scientific community, biological evolution concerns the change in the properties of populations of organisms that transcend the lifetime of a single individual. It is the genetic material that is passed on from one generation to the next."[1] Another definition from WordReference.com states that "Evolution is a process in which something passes by degrees to a different stage (especially a more advanced or mature stage)."[2]

Creationism may be defined this way: "In the Abrahamic religions, creationism is the belief that humans, life, the Earth, and the universe have a miraculous origin in a deity or supreme beings with supernatural intervention . . . In modern usage, the term creationism has come to be specifically associated with the brand of conservative Christian fundamentalism which conflicts with various aspects of evolution, cosmology, and other natural sciences that address the origins of the natural world."[3]

There is another concept regarding the origin of species from its early forms and this is referred to as intelligent design. Natural selection is not considered part of this concept. The proponents of this theory feel that intelligent design is a scientific theory superior to current scientific theories on evolution and origin of life. However, there are a number of groups that disagree with the proponents of intelligent design. For example, the U.S. National Academy of Science has stated that the supernatural intervention theory has not been tested through experiments. There was also a U.S. federal court case, *Kitzmiller v. Dover Area School District* which ruled that teaching intelligent design as an alternative to evolution violated the Establishment Clause of the First Amendment to the U.S. Constitution because intelligent design was not considered to be a science and was found to be a religious concept.

http://www.talkorigins.org/origins/other-links.html
   The Talk.Origins Archive. "Exploring the Creation/Evolution Controversy." This site has a number of links—one approaches the creation/evolution controversy from an evolutionary or anti-creationist perspective. There is a link to critical thought that takes a skeptical approach to both sides of this topic. Another large section has links to general science and evolution links. In addition, there are online forums to discuss and debate creationism and evolution.

http://physics.syr.edu/courses/modules/ORIGINS/origins.html
   Evolution vs. Creationism. This site features news groups, Frequently Asked Questions, creationist sites and evolution links.

Journal Articles through the Web

http://www.actionbioscience.org/evolution/nhmag.html
 "Evolution: Science and Belief; Intelligent Design?" This is a special report reprinted from *Natural History* magazine, April 2002.

http://content.nejm.org/cgi/content/full/354/21/2277
 The *New England Journal of Medicine*, May 25, 2006. "Intelligent Judging-Evolution in the Classroom and the Courtroom" by George J. Annas.

http://www.ncseweb.org
 National Center for Science Education. This site has articles that defend the teaching of evolution in public schools. There are articles in newspapers and journals around the country.

Books

Evolution vs. Creationism: An Introduction by Eugenie Scott (University of California Press, 2005). 0520246500.
 This book provides a balanced survey, but it is written by a leading advocate for the teaching of evolution in the United States. Many facets of the debate are offered: scientific evidence for evolution, legal and educational basis for its teaching, and various religious points of view, plus a concise history of the evolution-creationism debate.

From Genesis to Genetics: The Case of Evolution and Creationism by John Moore (University of California Press, 2003). 0520240669.
 This author shows how faith can exist alongside science; however, he indicates one must support the teaching of science and the scientific method in the public schools. He describes both schools of thought. He begins by analyzing the Genesis story, looks at other creation myths and then discusses the history of evolutionary thought.

Refuting Evolution 2 by Jonathan Sarfati, Mike Matthews (New Leaf Publishing Group, 2002). 0890513872.
 This author exposes the false premise behind many evolutionary theories in this study, which is an update of a previous text on *Refuting Evolution: A Handbook for Students, Parents, and Teachers Countering the Latest Arguments for Evolution* (Master Books, 1999). 0890512582.

Evolution, Creationism and Other Modern Myths: Critical Inquiry by Vine Deloria, Jr. (Fulcrum Publishing, 2004). 1555914586.
 The author discusses Western science and religion and presents the current state of evolutionary theory, science and religion. He incorporates non-Western and Native American ideas and offers a new way of looking at the world.

Notes

1. http://www.talkorigins.org/faqs/evolution-definition.html
2. http://www.wordreference.com/definition/evolution
3. http://en.wikipedia.org/wiki/creationism

In Vitro Fertilization

The full name for this procedure is In Vitro Fertilization Pre-Embryo Transfer (IVF-ET). This procedure had its first successful results in 1978 in England. The process has been further developed since then, with approximately 20,000 babies born as a result of this method of fertilization. Essentially, egg cells are fertilized outside the woman's body. The success of this procedure cannot always be predicted. The age of the wife and husband and their reproductive health are factors in determining success of this process.

The success or failure rate of IVF-ET can be confirmed thirteen days after egg aspiration, and the pregnancy can be confirmed by ultrasound 30–40 days after aspiration. The aspiration procedure is as follows:

In an outpatient procedure with local anesthesia, the female's egg can be visualized by ultrasound and then retrieved from the ovary by placing a needle through the vaginal wall (aspiration). Then the embryologist will place sperm with the eggs when they are ready for fertilization. The sperm with the eggs are kept in a nutrient mixture. A special catheter, containing the pre-embryos, will be passed through the vagina and into the uterus two days after retrieval from the woman.

http://en.wikipedia.org/wiki/In_vitro_fertilization

The *Wikipedia* provides the history of the in vitro fertilization procedure, the methods used to aid pregnancy, ethics involving this procedure, separation of the traditional mother-father model, religious objections, and regulations. In the United States IVF programs are under voluntary guidelines; some other countries have specific regulations.

http://www.emedicinehealth.com/in_vitro_fertilization/article_em.htm

This site is eMedicine Health and discusses various aspects of in vitro fertilization: factors to consider (age, possibility of multiple births, cost, and safety), techniques, success rate, and many Web links.

http://www.asrm.org/Patients/faqs.html

American Society for Reproductive Medicine. "Frequently Asked Questions About Infertility." Aside from offering information on infertility, this site describes in vitro fertilization, the costs, whether it is a successful procedure, and whether insurance plans cover the process. The site is very helpful for those seeking quick answers to questions about infertility, with many links to sites specifically for patients, some sites for the media, and others for professionals.

Journal Articles through the Web

http://www.findarticles.com/p/articles/mi_mOFSL/is_5_71/ai_64424127

AORN Journal. "Social and Ethical Aspects of In Vitro Fertilization" by Edwina A. McConnell, May 2000. The author raises the issues of legality and ethical questions involving IVF. The questions are related to parenthood, children, and the beginning of life. An important social question concerns the effectiveness of IVF. Legally, in vitro fertilization is not regulated in the United States and elsewhere.

http://jfi.sagepub.com/cgi/content/abstract/13/1/99
Journal of Family Issues. "Adoption Actions and Attitudes of Couples Seeking In Vitro Fertilization" by Linda S. Williams, Vol. 13, No. 1, pp. 99–113, 1992. This study explores adoption actions and attitudes of sixteen childless women and husbands of fourteen of them. Wives were more in favor of adoption than husbands. However, since there is a lack of "adoptable" babies, there is a demand for in vitro fertilization. Yet, unless the success rate of IVF increases, more couples will tend to adopt.

http://www.questia.com/PM.qst?a=o&d=5001913466&er=deny
Columbia Journal of Gender and Law. "Disputes Over Frozen Pre Embryos and The 'Right Not To Be a Parent'" by Tracey S. Pachman, vol. 12, 2003. This article discusses the United States legal system, trying to create legal standards with respect to individual rights and reproductive rights. The "right not to be a parent" has been a standard by which several courts have decided disputes over frozen pre embryos. The author also describes the IVF process and how courts have responded to various disputes related to this procedure.

http://www.questia.com/PM.qst?a=o&d=5001018487&er=deny
Yale Law Journal. "Baby Contracts" by Chi T. Steve Kwok, vol.110, 2001. This article considers that many problematic legal issues have arisen as a result of IVF procedures. What happens to the pre embryos if the couple divorces after the IVF procedure, and both husband and wife cannot agree in the disposition of the pre embryos? What if a third party donated the eggs?

Books

In Vitro Fertilization: The A.R.T. of Making Babies by Geoffrey Sher et al. (Facts on File, 1998). 0816038279.

This book guides couples who are considering in vitro fertilization. It describes the process of conception. The authors also offer help by addressing emotional, financial, physical, and moral-religious issues about conceiving with medical assistance.

In Vitro Fertilization by Kay Elder and Brian Dale (Cambridge University Press, 2000). 0521778638.

This text discusses the range of assisted reproductive technology clinical treatments.

When Nature's Not Enough: Personal Journeys Through In Vitro Fertilization by Diane M. Olick (Lyons Press, 2005). 1592285422.

This is a personal story by journalist Olick about her own experiences with in vitro fertilization and interviews she conducted with other couples. Issues raised were: emotions during the process, financial issues, choosing the right doctor, Is the drug regimen difficult? Should failure with the procedure mean not to try again?

Medical Marijuana

Since marijuana (cannabis) has been used as a recreational drug, the use of this drug as medication is now controversial in most countries. Yet, cannabis has been used for medicinal purposes for over 4800 years. Ancient doctors used it for a variety of ailments: gastrointestinal disorders, insomnia, headaches, as a pain reliever, and even in childbirth.

The term, medical cannabis, refers to the use of this drug as herbal therapy. The chemical compound, THC, has both psychoactive and medicinal effects when used by smoking or ingestion.

http://medmjscience.org/

This site concerns a study commissioned by the White House. The report indicated that marijuana does have a medical benefit and should be prescribed to patients who could use this protocol. However, political opponents of the use of marijuana as a medicine do not believe in the scientific basis of the report. This site offers major reports/findings, scientific studies, history, overviews, and opinions.

http://www.drugwarfacts.org/medicalm.htm

Drug War Facts. Since 1996, eleven states have legalized medical marijuana use. These are Alaska, Arizona, California, Colorado, Hawaii, Maine, Nevada, Oregon, Rhode Island, Vermont, and Washington. The Institute of Medicine's report in 1999 on the use of marijuana for medicinal purposes stated, "The accumulated data indicate a potential therapeutic value for cannabinoid drugs, particularly for symptoms such as pain relief, control of nausea and vomiting, and appetite stimulation."[1] The site also lists the many organizations that have endorsed medical access to marijuana. In addition, some editorial boards of newspapers also endorsed the use of the drug, including the *New York Times*, *Boston Globe*, *Chicago Tribune*, *Miami Herald*, *Orange County Register*, and *USA Today*.

http://www.medicalmarijuanaprocon.org/

Medical Marijuana Pro Con.Org. This site offers a nonpartisan pro-con format to the question: Should marijuana be a medical option now? The medical marijuana issues presented are: medical value, risks, diseases/conditions for its use, United States government and medical marijuana, access to medical marijuana, non-smoked marijuana, legal issues, and public policy.

Journal Articles through the Web

http://www.commondreams.org/views03/0817–02.htm

Boston Globe. "The Shifting Medical View on Marijuana" by Lester Grinspoon, August 17, 2003. Common Dreams News Center. A recent poll

(2003) indicated that 76 percent of physicians and 89 percent of nurses felt marijuana should be made available as medicine. A decade ago this was not the case. This change is the result of research and clinical experience. Medical personnel have seen positive results with marijuana use for syndromes, multiple sclerosis, Crohn's disease, migraine headaches, nausea and vomiting, convulsive disorders, and chronic pain.

http://www.findarticles.com/p/articles/mi_qa4020/is_200201/ai_n9036522

Journal of Public Health Policy; "State Medical Marijuana Laws: Understanding the Laws and Their Limitations" by Rosalie Liccard Pacula et al., 2002. Even though the Federal government opposes use of medical marijuana, twenty-six states and the District of Columbia have laws for use of this drug under specific circumstances. There seems to be much confusion about these laws because of the different types of legislation by different medical, professional, and policy advocate groups.

http://cannabisnews.com/news/22/thread22130.shtml

Central Kentucky News Journal. "Medical Field Against Legalized Marijuana" by Ted Beam, September 3, 2006. The author doubts that most people have the knowledge and skill to use marijuana responsibly so that mental capacity will not be diminished. The author, a pastor, presents a religious perspective on this issue. He does recognize that the medical field uses a synthetic cannabis in some treatments, but those are supervised. His concern is the unsupervised use of the drug.

Books

Marijuana Medical Handbook: A Guide to Therapeutic Use by Ed Rosenthal et al. (Quick American Publishing Company, 1997). 0932551165.

This text is written for people with little or no experience with marijuana but wish an informative account of the medicinal value related to treatment of cancer, AIDS/HIV, glaucoma, and other ailments or diseases.

Understanding Marijuana: A New Look at the Scientific Evidence by Mitch Earleywine (Oxford University Press, 2005). 0195182952.

The author traces the medical and political debates surrounding marijuana in a balanced, objective manner. The author examines the biological, psychological, and societal impact of marijuana use.

Marijuana: The Forbidden Medicine by Lester Grinspoon and James B. Bakalar (Yale University Press, 1997). 0300070861.

The authors discuss the medical benefits of marijuana, why its use has been forbidden and advocate for full legalization for patients who need it.

Waiting to Inhale: The Politics of Medical Marijuana by Alan W. Bock (Seven Locks Press, 2001). 0929765826.

The author discusses the different initiatives that came before voters, the activists who got the issue on the ballot, and the methods used by opposition forces to discount the use of the drug. The author also provides the history of the plant as a drug, and the fact that marijuana was once an ordinary, acceptable prescription drug.

Note

1. *Marijuana and Medicine: Assessing the Science Base*, National Academy Press, 1999 by Janey E. Joy, Stanley J. Watson, and John A. Benson.

Mind Control

This is an all-inclusive term for several controversial theories indicating that a person's thinking process, behavior, emotions, or decisions can possibly be manipulated by outside sources. Psychologists, neuroscientists, and sociologists debate the possibility of such control and the methods by which it can be attained. The various views on mind control have legal implications. This topic has been discussed in conjunction with religion, politics, prisoners of war, totalitarianism, cults, terrorism, torture, parental alienation, neural cell manipulation, and with battered person syndrome.

The foregoing *Wikipedia* information is also enhanced by a discussion of theoretical models and methods, cults and mind control controversies, legal issues, mind control in fiction and popular culture. All this data may be found at: http://en.wikipedia.org/wiki/mind_control.

http://en.wikipedia.org/wiki/Mind_control#cults_and_mind_control_controversies

This is a section of the *Wikipedia* which comments on those who refute mind control as a factor in cult membership. There are also links to legal issues of some famous cases where the courts rejected mind control as a defense.

http://www.csicop.org/si/9609/conspiracy.html

"Conspiracy Theories and Paranoia: Notes From a Mind Control Conference" by Evan Harrington. Committee for the Scientific Investigation of Claims of the Paranormal. This article concerns a debate over recovered and false memories and whether mind control was actually practiced in certain situations.

http://skepdic.com/mindcont.html

The Skeptics Dictionary. This site provides the conceptions and misconceptions of mind control, clarifies the term, its appearance in fiction, in film, in government through the military using this process, and by subliminal advertising.

http://www.rotten.com/library/conspiracy/mind_control/

This site offers evidence of cults and secret societies, hypnotism, television and subliminal messages, behavioral conditioning (as in George Orwell's *1984*), and provides information on drug-induced and sci-fi techniques.

http://news.bbc.co.uk/2/hi/health/5167938.stm

This site is from the BBC News, July 12, 2006. "Brain Sensor Allows Mind Control." The article is about a sensor implanted in a paralyzed man's brain which has enabled him to control objects by using only his thoughts.

Journal Articles through the Web

http://www.newdawnmagazine.com/Articles/
Mind%20Control%20Experiments%20on%20Children.html

New Dawn Magazine. "Mind Control Experiments On Children" by Jon Rappoport. This article involves a CIA program, how extensive it was and the purpose of the experiments. The experiments were conducted on American, Mexican, and South American children over a forty year period. This article is derived from a book written by the author.

http://www.wanttoknow.info/mindcontrol

"The Secrets of Mind Control," based on excerpts from three landmark books: *Bluebird* by Colin A. Ross, M.D., *Mind Controllers* by Dr. Armen Victorian, and *A Nation Betrayed* by Carol Rutz. Much of the information is based on 18,000 pages of declassified CIA mind control documents.

Books

Bluebird; Deliberate Creation of Multiple Personality By Psychiatrists by Colin A. Ross, M.D. (Manitou Communications, 2000). 0970452519.

The author viewed 15,000 pages of documents obtained from the CIA under the Freedom of Information Act that the "Manchurian Candidate" (movie and book) is fact, not fiction. The text of this book exposes political abuse of psychiatry in North America in the second half of the twentieth century.

Mind Controllers by Dr. Armen Victorian (Lewis International Inc., 2000). 0966677196.

This text also discusses covert psychological manipulation. These techniques included prescribing psychoactive drugs, allowing sensory deprivation, hypnotic suggestion, disorientation from radiation, and complete restructuring of cognitive processes through cranial implants.

A Nation Betrayed by Carol Rutz (Fidelity Publishing, 2001). 097101020X.

This is the true story of secret cold war experiments performed on children and innocent people. The author was a child victim of government 'behavior modification' programs. The website review provides excellent insight into this program: http://www.raven1.net/nabetray.htm#BIBLIO.

Overpopulation

This situation refers to the relationship between the human population and its environment. The concern has been the number of people and the resources available to sustain them.

Overpopulation occurs when there are increases in birth, a decline in mortality rates, which deals with increases in life expectancy or from an unsustainable use and depletion of resources. The resources to be considered are clean water and air, food, shelter, warmth, arable land, medical/health care, employment, education, fuel, electricity, waste management and transportation.

http://www.overpopulation.com/faq/

This website has over 1000 pages which focus on a) basic information: current population, fertility rates, urbanization, birth rates, etc., and b) environmental issues: acid rain, air pollution, and endangered species. There is also information on health and welfare, economics/poverty, education/literacy, hunger/famine, infectious diseases/AIDS, cholera, malaria, mortality/infant mortality and life expectancy, natural resources/energy, food, crop yield, soil erosion, and population control.

http://www.overpopulation.org/impact.html

Impacts—July 27, 2006. This site features global warming, methane, air pollution, water, oceans, species extinction, desertification, food and water shortages, overcrowding, genetically modified food, diseases, and health hazards.

http://www.overpopulation.net/

"Lovearth Network." This site connects to 1000 ecohumane political and spiritual websites. This is a rather broad, but inclusive site for information on overpopulation.

http://www.henrygeorge.org/popsup.htm

"Overpopulation: Is There Such a Thing?" The author feels the Earth can sustain our population growth. The author further comments on the fact that vast capacities of the Earth's resources lie unused. Also, with more education birth rates will decline. In addition, the article states that present day miserable conditions are misnamed "overpopulation." What is happening is really a result of poverty.

Journal Articles through the Web

http://www.ecofuture.org/pop/reports.html

This site features publications and reports on overpopulation and sustainability. The reports are from: *Population Action International, Rockefel-*

ler Commission Reports, *U.S. News & World Report* articles, *New York Times Magazine* articles and those from various *Population Bulletins, World Watch Institute, Alan Guttmacher Institute* reports, and many others.

http://jcgi.pathfinder.com/time/archive/preview/0,10987,956645,00.html

Time Archive, 1923 to the Present. "Overpopulation: Too Many Mouths The Problem: Swarms of People Are Running Out of Food and Space" by Anastasia Toufexis. This is a site that features articles on the Earth and the consequences of overpopulation.

http://www.overpopulation.com/

Lancet. "Overpopulation Doesn't Kill People, War Kills People," January 7, 2006. This article claims that the ongoing civil war in the Democratic Republic of Congo is killing up to 38,000 people each month. As the title implies, this author is not concerned about overpopulation but what wars are doing to reduce the number of inhabitants.

Books

The Population Explosion by Paul R. Ehrlich and Anne H Ehrlich (Touchstone Books, 1991). 0671732943.

These authors are respected advocates of population control. They discuss connections between overpopulation, global warming, pollution, depletion of resources, widening gap between rich and poor nations.

Ecology and the Crisis of Overpopulation: Future Prospects for Global Sustainability by Anup Shah (Edgar Elgar Publishing, 1998). 1858984637.

This book discusses ancient and modern theories of population change.

Overpopulation by John Zeaman (Franklin Watts, 2002). 0531118932.

The author discusses better health care and improved grain crops. This text is an update of the Ehrlich's *Population Explosion*, 1991.

Performance-Enhancing Drugs in Sports

There have been many reports in the media about track-and-field athletes, and participants in other sports, using steroids. This is also called "doping." The latter may come from the Afrikaans word "dop"—a concoction of grape leaves that Zulu warriors drank before going into battle. In sports, the term was first used to describe illegal drugging of race horses at the beginning of the twentieth century. Doping in sports now includes a wide range of practices: "blood doping"—transfusions and use of a synthetic substance to increase the number of red blood cells; anabolic steroids and human growth hormone to grow skeletal muscle; stimulants to improve cognitive function and reduce fatigue; and nitrogen tents to stimulate effects of sleeping at high altitudes.

http://www.steroidabuse.org/

Anabolic Steroid Abuse site has a number of links to articles, resources and publications, initiatives by NIDA, the National Institute on Drug Abuse. The message from NIDA's Director, Dr. Nora D. Volkow, on the "Consequences of the Abuse of Anabolic Steroids" is that there is great risk that adolescents will be vulnerable to messages about these steroids yet not be concerned about long term health risks to their bodies and minds. The anabolic steroids—synthetic versions of a male sex hormone testosterone, can be injected, taken orally, or used transdermally. These drugs can stunt the height of growing adolescents, masculinize women, and alter sex characteristics of men. They can lead to premature heart attacks, strokes, liver tumors, kidney failure, and serious psychiatric problems. This site and NIDA try to create an awareness about the dangers of steroid abuse.

http://www.whitehousedrugpolicy.gov/prevent/sports/index.html

Drugs and Sports; Office of the National Drug Control Policy. This site offers links to: NIDA's (National Institute on Drug Abuse) steroid public service announcements; to a section on steroids and young people; publications on steroid abuse from the DEA (Drug Enforcement Agency); the FDA (Federal Drug Administration) statement on the designer steroid, THG, and another section of links to "What Can You Do?" for coaches, athletes, and parents. The section on steroids and young people describes the scope of the problem—a survey of middle and high school students showed an increased use of steroids since 1996. Another section titled "Steroids Threaten Young People's Health and Development" discusses side effects—liver and kidney tumors, cancer, severe acne, and stunted growth. Regarding the importance of professional athletes as role models, recent trends indicate a link between athletes' decisions on steroids and use of steroids among youth.

http://www.mayoclinic.com/health/performance-enhancing-drugs/HQ01105
MayoClinic.com. "Taking Performance-Enhancing Drugs: Are You Risking Your Health?" Young athletes take these drugs for a number of reasons: for a medal for their country, a college scholarship, or place on a professional team. There is a tremendous competitive drive to win, sometimes at all costs. The site reveals the effects of these drugs on the body. *Anabolic steroids*—the latest being THG (tetrahydrogestrinone)—can stunt growth, cause strokes and heart attacks. THG is often undetectable during testing for drug use. *Androstenedione*—produced by the adrenal glands, ovaries, and testes—risk of heart attack and stroke. *Creatine*—for quick bursts of activity—stomach and muscle cramps, damage to liver, kidneys, and heart. *Stimulants*—reduce fatigue—weight loss, convulsions, heart attack. *Diuretics*—change body's balance of fluids, exhaustion, heart arrhythmias.

Journal Articles through the Web

http://jpp.sagepub.com/cgi/content/abstract/16/1/37
Journal of Pharmacy Practice. "Health Risks of Selected Performance-Enhancing Drugs" by Peter A. Chyka, 2003, Vol.16, No. 1. This article reviews adverse effects of and the difficulty of attributing toxic effects to selected drugs and dietary supplements that are supposed to enhance athletic performance. Many adverse effects are exaggerations of excessive testosterone produced on liver, heart, or behavioral functions. The author indicates that some abnormalities do occur with the use of these drugs, but the extent and frequency are not known.

http://www.healthinschools.org/ejournal/2004/sept4.htm
Health and Health Care in Schools. "Athletes and Performance-Enhancing Drugs," September 2004. This article was written following the 2004 Summer Olympics in Athens. The article gives an overview of the drugs being used as early as 1948. Anabolic steroid use began after the 1948 Olympic Games. The drugs used initially were cocaine and heroin, then anabolic steroids, followed by erithropoyetin—regulates red-cell mass. Twenty-six young cyclists died after using this drug.

http://www.findarticles.com/p/articles/mi_qn4196/is_20060331/
  ai_n16202625
Milwaukee Journal Sentinel. "Selig Launches Steroids Probe; MLB Investigation to Revolve Around This Drug Use" by Tom Haudricourt, March 31, 2006. Baseball Commissioner Bud Selig promised an investigation in use of performance-enhancing drugs by major league players who were associated with the Bay Area Laboratory Co-Operative, like San Francisco's Barry Bonds. The investigation would be limited to events since September 2002 when Major League Baseball (MLB) and the players' union put a drug-testing program in place. Former Senator George Mitchell was to head up the probe. Results from the investigation are pending.

Books

At Issue Series-Performance-Enhancing Drugs edited by James Haley (Greenhaven Press, 2002). 0737711698.

The authors in this series debate whether use of performance-enhancing drugs is a serious problem and discuss ways of addressing the use of such substances, including Olympic oversight and drug testing.

The Juice: The Real Story of Baseball's Drug Problems by Will Carroll et al., (Ivan R. Dee, Publisher, 2005). 1566636681.

The authors consider these performance-enhancing drugs as not just a baseball or sports problem, but a social issue on par with the use of recreational drugs. This text is recommended for the high school athlete who might well confront the truth about the illegal substances. Carroll is an expert on medical matters related to baseball and for his analysis of steroid use.

Drugs in Sport by D.R. Mottram (Routledge, 2005). 0415375649.

Leading figures in the field explore the science behind every major class of drug, as well as the social, ethical, and organizational dimensions to the issue. Key topics discussed are: analysis of anabolic steroids, EPO (ErithroPOyetin) and human growth hormone, alcohol and social drug use in sport, creatine, and nutritional supplements.

Psychoactive Drugs

Drugs, which are chemical substances, often alter behavior and perception. Some drugs are also used for recreational purposes and/or performance enhancement. There are some drugs that are abused and misused and others that immediately help a patient feel better, even though they might be considered hard drugs.

There is concern that there may be long term effects with use of these drugs. They may affect a person's physical and mental well-being. Often, drug dependence (addiction) results from continued drug use. The dependence affects the normal processes in the brain related to perception, emotion and motivation. There is a sense of compulsion to take these drugs. Many times the body tolerates the level of drug use so that the person needs to increase dosage to achieve the same effects as the lower dosage. Therefore, using these drugs has negative long term effects.

Some psychoactive drugs are stimulants—caffeine, cocaine, amphetamines, and Ritalin; others are sedative/depressants—barbiturates, opium, codeine, morphine, heroin. There are hallucinogens or deliriants, or antipsychotics, which treat disorders such as schizophrenia, paranoia, and bipolar disorder.

Psychoactive drugs have been considered controversial for many years. During the nineteenth century Opium Wars between Britain and China and later between France and Britain, opium was considered good for trade with China for economic reasons. Today the issue of drugs being grown and harvested to bolster the economies of a number of places like Afghanistan, Latin America, and other regions of the world is of major concern to various groups. The issue over psychoactive drugs reflects the concern of religious and philosophical beliefs. Are the drugs sinful, therapeutic, ethical, or risky? Should governments remain neutral on the use of these drugs? Should prescriptions be required?

Many people do not consider alcohol or cigarettes as falling in the category of drugs. There is also an increased use of Ritalin. Much information on the use and abuse of this drug may be found at http://www.breggin.com/ritalin.html. Steroid use is also very controversial. The National Institute on Drug Abuse has a Research Report on anabolic steroid abuse at http://www.nida.nih.gov/ResearchReports/Steroids/AnabolicSteroids.html. Substance abuse refers to drug abuse, drug addiction, and chemical dependency. All of these issues make for lively debate, and research.

Those who are concerned about the use of certain drugs are concerned about a person's health, and often make decisions based on religious and moral influences. However, if drugs are forbidden, some say it increases criminalization because the drugs are not readily available by legitimate means; hence, the formation of drug cartels. Some are of the inclination that if there is little prohibition, the use of hard drugs is reduced, as in the Netherlands. The Dutch have liberal drug policies, especially related to marijuana and cocaine use. In the Netherlands the attitude about drug use is that it is a public health issue rather than one that needs to be litigated in the court system, and, therefore, not a criminal offense. Statistics show that the use of drugs has decreased among teens and adults.

There is a growing opposition to punitive drug policies worldwide. Physicians, lawyers, scientists, journalists, and public health officials are not in favor of punitive, criminalized forms of drug prohibition. They feel these policies are expensive and not effective in reducing drug use and are often racially and ethnically discriminatory. Since the 1980s, the Netherlands has successfully administered a system of regulated, decriminalized cannabis (marijuana) sales. Additional information on this topic may be found at:

http://www.cedro-uva.org/lib/levine.alcohol.htm

CEDRO: Amsterdam; "Alcohol Prohibition and Drug Prohibition" by Harry G. Levine and Craig Reinarman. This topic is very provocative, with many ramifications, but would certainly stimulate energetic discussion.

http://www.safeyouth.org/scripts/teens/drugs.asp

This website represents the National Youth Violence Prevention Resource Center. This site offers facts about teen use of drugs and subsequent violence, how to turn down offers of drugs, and links to sites that answer questions about teen safety, anti-drug campaigns, the research site from the National Institute on Drug Abuse, about effects of drugs on the brain, and general tips for teens.

http://www.well.com/~woa/

This site, Web of Addictions, was set up to deal with misinformation about drug abuse. It also serves as a resource for teachers and students, who need factual data.

http://www.nida.nih.gov/drugpages.html

This website, the National Institute on Drug Abuse, discusses the drugs that are abused and provides links to medical consequences of drug abuse, prevention research, stress and drug abuse, trends, statistics, and drug testing.

http://en.wikipedia.org/wiki/NORML

National Organization for the Reform of Marijuana Laws or NORML. This is a United States-based nonprofit corporation whose aim is to "move public opinion sufficiently to achieve the repeal of marijuana prohibition so that responsible use of cannabis by adults is no longer subject to penalty."

Journal Articles through the Web

http://www.harmreductionjournal.com/info/about/

The Harm Reduction Journal focuses on research, book reviews, case reports, and commentaries—all dealing with drug use and drug policies.

http://www.emedicine.com/news.asp?name=20060712elin001
  .xml&page=eMedicine%20Today
Medical and Science News. "Genetic Tendency to Drug Abuse Seen In Study" by Megan Rauscher, July 18, 2006.

http://www.findarticles.com/p/articles/mi_m0816/is_1_20/ai_89973149
  Pediatrics for Parents. "More Children On Psychoactive Drugs," January, 2002.

Books

A Primer of Drug Action: A Concise Non Technical Guide to the Actions, Uses and Side Effects of Psychoactive Drugs by Robert M. Julien (Owl Books, 2001). 080507158X.

This text has been updated since the 1975 edition. This new edition is considered to be the definitive guide to the effects of psychoactive drugs on the brain and on behavior.

Drugs 101: An Overview for Teens by Margaret O. Hyde (Twenty-First Century Books, 2003). 0761326081.

This book is very readable. It offers the review of health effects of illicit drugs to the debate over legalization.

The Legalization of Drugs by Doug Husak and Peter de Marneff (Cambridge University Press, 2005). 0521837863.

Both authors are philosophers of law. One author, Husak, favors drug decriminalization by discussing the meaning of legalization and decriminalization. Peter de Marneff is against drug legalization and discusses how drug prohibition can protect youth from being self-destructive when using drugs.

Race and Intelligence

This issue concerns intelligence research which "studies the nature, origins, and practical consequences of racial and ethnic group differences in intelligence test scores and other measures of cognitive ability."[1]

Evidence of research is based on IQ testing in the United States. The racial/ethnic groups may overlap, but the range is comparable. The difference occurs in the placement of groups in a cluster along the intelligence scale. This depiction is evident on the *Wikipedia* site noted above. There have been various hypotheses as to why IQs vary among racial/ethnic groups: environment-nutrition, education level, and though not limited to, home environment. There is also a debate about genetic make-up, brain size, and generally, the ancestry of the group. This issue has caused much controversy because research and test data conflict with social philosophies.

The *Wikipedia* provides a great deal of information in the areas listed above, plus data on media portrayal and biases.

http://www.dushkin.com/connectext/psy/ch08/raceintel.mhtml

"Exploring Psychology: Race and Intelligence." This website offers information from various researchers on their studies of race and intelligence. Some issues reflect the fact that intelligence tests could be biased, so testing instruments may not be that accurate.

http://skepdic.com/iqrace.html

"IQ and Race." This site is from *The Skeptic's Dictionary* by Robert Todd Carroll. The thesis in this piece discusses the facts of several kinds of intelligences and, therefore, an IQ test would reflect only some types of intelligence, but not all. The author cites genetic data and genetic differences which might have resulted through the years and could have been attributed to natural selection.

http://www.aaanet.org/stmts/race.htm

This site is from the American Anthropological Association, "Statement on 'Race' and Intelligence," adopted 1994. The concern of this association is that it is unwise to differentiate intelligence of species into biologically defined races. The members feel that this is not a scientifically accepted way of explaining differences in intelligence or other traits. The members stress respecting diversity.

Journal Articles through the Web

http://www.commentarymagazine.com/production/files/murray0905.html

This is from *Commentary Magazine*, "The Inequality Taboo" by Charles Murray, September 2005. The author describes reasons for establishing that some group differences in intelligence are "intractable." He focuses on two types of differences: between men and women and between blacks and whites. He did discover that the variation *within* groups is greater than *between* groups.

http://www.findarticles.com/p/articles/mi_m1282/is_n23_v46/ai_15988897
   National Review. "Going Public—Race and Intelligence—'The Bell Curve': A Symposium—Cover Story" by Richard Neuhaus, December 5, 1994. The author is pointing up the difficulties of assuming differences in intelligence in races. Sometimes the results found, as in the book, *The Bell Curve*, can be destructive. The author ponders why it was so urgent in the book to relate racial differences in cognitive functioning. This article raises more questions than answers.

http://lrainc.com/swtaboo/taboos/wsj_main.html
   The Wall Street Journal. "Stalking the Wild Taboo; Mainstream Science on Intelligence," December 13, 1994. The aim of this article is to promote more reasoned discussion of the vexing phenomenon that the research (on intelligence) has revealed in recent decades. The article is divided into specific sections: The Meaning and Measurement of Intelligence, Group Differences, Practical Importance, Source and Stability Within-Group Differences and Between-Group Differences and, Implications for Social Policy.

Books

Race and Intelligence: Separating Science from Myth edited by Jefferson M. Fish (LEA, Inc., 2001). 0805837574.
   The authors of this book represent a range of disciplines: psychology, anthropology, biology, economics, history, philosophy, sociology, and statistics. The authors offer the following information: the human species has no races in the biological sense, no single form of intelligence, and formal education helps people develop many cognitive abilities.

Race Differences in Intelligence: An Evolutionary Analysis by Richard Lynn. (Washington Summit Publishers, 2006). 159368021X.
   The author, a Ph.D. in psychology, has done much research on racial differences in IQ. He analyzes the results of over 500 published studies of ten population groups—races and sub races worldwide. He discusses the formation of races, meaning of intelligence, validity of race differences in IQ, environmental and genetic relationship to intelligence, brain size and relationship to intelligence, evolution of race differences in intelligence, and racial hybrids.

The Bell Curve by Richard J. Herrnstein and Charles Murray (Free Press, 1994). 0029146739.
   This was a best selling book, but its contents were also widely debated because of the authors' discussion in two chapters on race and intelligence.

The authors believed there was a large difference in intelligence among the races. There were many supporters and detractors of the theories posited in this text.

Note

1. http://en.wikipedia.org/wiki/Race_and_intelligence

Racial Profiling

This process/activity may be described as "any police or private security practice in which a person is treated as a suspect because of his or her race, ethnicity, nationality, or religion. This occurs when police investigate, stop, frisk, search, or use force against a person based on such characteristics instead of evidence of a person's criminal behavior."[1]

Racial profiling has resulted in the incarceration of people of color in a disproportionate amount. Since the "war on terrorism" in the United States has become a major governmental concern, the practice of racial profiling has been on the increase, specifically targeting Arabs, Muslims, and South Asians.

http://en.wikipedia.org/wiki/Racial_profiling
The *Wikipedia* site offers a number of links from the discussion of advocacy in one section, whereby advocacy groups deny that the disproportionate number of people representing certain racial groups who are arrested and prosecuted for crimes is really not necessarily due to racial profiling. There is also a section on criticism in which it is indicated that race should never be considered in a police action. In addition, there is a presentation of statistics on cases whereby racial profiling was a considered factor. There are links to "media and ethnicity" and to affirmative action, offering certain preferences to usually under-represented groups.

http://www.amnestyusa.org/racial_profiling/index.do
This is the Amnesty International USA site which is legislating for passage of the "End Racial Profiling Act" that is described in detail. The site also offers a summary of reports on racial profiling related to domestic security and human rights in the United States. The site also provides an opportunity for people to share their own experience with racial profiling.

http://www.racialprofilinganalysis.neu.edu/
Racial Profiling Data Collection Resource Center at Northeastern University. This resource center provides current data collection efforts dealing with racial profiling, community and civil rights initiatives, legislation and litigation, reporting and analysis, and a library and archives. This resource center is part of the Institute on Race and Justice at Northeastern University. It deals with strategic social science research methodologies to assist government agencies, educational institutions, and community members to develop policy changes to advance social justice.

Journal Articles through the Web

http://www.city-journal.org/html/11_2_the_myth.html
City Journal. "The Myth of Racial Profiling" by Heather MacDonald, Spring, 2001. The thesis in this journal article is that no credible evidence

exists to prove that racial profiling occurs and the efforts to abolish it would threaten crime-fighting success. Evidence is presented to substantiate this viewpoint.

http://findarticles.com/p/articles/mi_mOHSP/is_1_6/ai_106647777

Civil Rights Journal. "Flying While Arab: Lessons from the Racial Profiling Controversy" by David Harris, Winter 2002. This site dwells on the changes in security procedures as a result of September 11, 2001, and that profiling should no longer become a discredited law enforcement tactic. This article provides an interesting perspective on the procedure of racial profiling in an era of terrorism.

http://findarticles.com/p/articles/mi_qa3720/is_200509/ai_n15352196

The IRE Journal by Stephen Holly, September/October 2005. This is an interesting article that describes an investigation which uncovered a police database in San Antonio, Texas that was filled with errors and duplications in which drivers were listed as more than one race. The article discusses the action, DWB (driving while black or brown) and studied cases involving DWB. There were many inconsistencies in the reporting and the manner of recording the statistical data. In addition, this site (http://www.questia.com/library/sociology-and-anthropology/racial-profiling.jsp) lists many more journal articles on racial profiling.

Books

Profiles in Injustice: Why Racial Profiling Cannot Work by David A. Harris (W.W. Norton & Co., 2003). 1565848187.

The author is a law professor who has written extensively on racial profiling. In this book, he describes what this program is, what tactics are generally used, the cost of profiling in dollars, casualties, relations with police, and wasted police time. He recommends many alternatives to this procedure (i.e., departmental policies, incentives, training, and collecting data).

The Color of Guilt & Innocence: Racial Profiling and Police Practices in America by Steve Holbert and Lisa Rose (Page Marque Press, 2004). 0974664006.

Steve Holbert is a law enforcement veteran and Lisa Rose an attorney. They provide a readable discussion of racial profiling in the United States. They discuss data collection and analysis programs to determine whether racial profiling actually took place, issues of civil liberty, and police reactions to accusations.

Driving While Black: What To Do If You Are a Victim of Racial Profiling by Kenneth Meeks (Broadway, 2000). 0767905490.

The author uses stories to discuss this topic. This appears to be an excellent handbook for young adults on what to do if they find themselves in such a situation—whom to write to, what to say, what to notice when profiling is taking place, what one's rights are, what profilers look for aside from race (class, dress, age), and how one can reduce one's risk of being a victim.

Notes

1. http://www.aclu.org/racialjustice/racialprofiling/index.html; this site offers many press releases of instances of racial profiling, plus many links to reports and ongoing litigation.

Stem Cells

These cells are thought to develop into various different cell types in the body. They work to "repair" cells within the body and divide without limit to replenish other cells so long as the person or animal is alive. As a stem cell divides, each newly formed cell has the potential to remain a stem cell or become another type of cell that would have a specialized function (i.e., a muscle cell, a red blood cell, or a brain cell).

Scientists are investigating the possibility of using cell-based therapies to treat many different diseases. This process has been referred to as regenerative or reparative medicine.

There has been much debate within and outside the scientific community on the ethics of this developing science. The controversy concerns the techniques used in both the creation and use of stem cells.

http://stemcells.nih.gov/info/basics/

Stem Cell Information. This site is the official National Institutes of Health resource for stem cell research. The site covers the unique properties of stem cells: what are embryonic stem cells; what are adult stem cells; similarities and differences between these two types; the potential uses of human stem cells; and obstacles that need to be overcome so the implied uses will be realized.

http://en.wikipedia.org/wiki/stem_cell

From the *Wikipedia*. This site contains a vast amount of information on: stem cell types, treatments, and the controversy surrounding stem cell research. There is also a chronological listing of key events in stem cell research.

http://www.cnn.com/SPECIALS/2001/stemcell/

The Stem Cell Debate; "Scientists Clone Embryos." This site features four specific sections:

1. The issues and ethics of stem cell research.
2. The science of stem cells and the possibility of treating neurological diseases.
3. The politics and Bush Administration decisions, and congressional issues raised.
4. The analysis of stem cell research—looking for middle ground so as not to fall behind in research, and embryonic ethics.

Journal Articles through the Web

http://www.sciam.com/
   article.cfm?chanID=sa006&collD=1&articleID=000B1BED-0C0A-
   1498-8C0A83414B7F0000

Scientific American. "Stem Cells: The Real Culprits in Cancer?" by Michael F. Clarks and Michael W. Becker, July 2006. This article offers an overview of cancer stem cells and research on cornering cancer stem cells. Sometimes stem cells can turn malignant, so this article is not too positive in content, but an important awareness is created.

http://stemcells.alphamedpress.org/
 The International Journal of Cell Differentiation and Proliferation. "Stem Cells," Vol. 24, No. 8, 2006. The reader of this article may search for articles on stem cells from 1983 through the present. The articles enable people to read the latest advances in the field of stem cells, or scientists may be able to submit their own papers. This is a technical site but, for students interested in this topic, it would provide helpful informative data.

http://www.lifeissues.net/writers/irv/irv_19stemcellprocon.html
 Life Issues.net. "Stem Cell Research: Some Pros and Cons" by Dianne N. Irving, October 15, 1999. This article is written in a question/answer format:

> What is stem cell research?
>
> What are the major purposes of doing stem cell research?
>
> Are all kinds of stem cell research ethical?
>
> Is it legal to do stem cell research?

The answers are not highly technical and, therefore, readable to a high school student.

Books

Stem Cell Biology by Daniel R. Matshak, David Gottlieb and Richard L.
 Gardner (CSHL Press, 2001). 0879696737.
 This text features contributions from a number of the world's leading laboratories and offers an understanding of the biology of stem cells and their potential for clinical exploitation.

Stem Cell Research by Jennifer Viegas (The Rosen Publishing Group,
 2003). 0823936694.
 This text is for the middle or high school student. The book presents the story of the breakthroughs in working with embryonic stem cells and how these procedures, if implemented, may help to grow new tissues to repair injuries. The scientific community may be able to induce stem cells to become nerve and muscle cells to replace non-functioning cells and thereby eliminate some disabilities.

Stem Cell Handbook by Stewart Sell (Humana Press, 2004). 1588291138.
 This book explains the origin of stem cells and how they function, how they can cause illness, yet how they also may be used to cure or ameliorate disease.

The Stem Cell Controversy by Michael Ruse and Christopher A. Pynes (Prometheus Press, 2006). 1591020301.

This text consists of a collection of articles and essays on stem cell research. It offers different perspectives in the debate over the ethics of this research and helps the reader to understand science and social policy questions.

Tobacco Smoking

Historically, tobacco smoking was practiced by the Native American cultures and introduced to the world by sailors after European exploration of the Americas. Medical research has determined that tobacco smoking contributes to many health problems—lung cancer, emphysema, and cardiovascular disease. Tobacco smoke contains a stimulant, nicotine, but it also creates a chemical dependence. Since the extensive research about the ill-effects of this practice have had wide publicity, many countries have begun to restrict this activity by regulating advertising sales and prohibiting tobacco smoking in many public establishments. The latter has been done to reduce the effects of second-hand smoke.

http://en.wikipedia.org/wiki/Tobacco_smoking

The *Wikipedia* provides much information on methods of smoking, factors that influence smoking behavior—addiction, advertising, peer pressure, genetic connection, health effects, opinions on smoking, legal issues, and regulations. Many links are provided which further embellish the above topics.

http://www.cdc.gov/doc.do/id/0900f3ec802346d8

Centers for Disease Control and Prevention. "Smoking and Tobacco Use." This site offers several topics, including: "Health Topic: Smoking and Tobacco Use"—educational materials, research, and Surgeon General reports; "Global Tobacco Control"—prevention, youth and school personnel surveys; "Measuring Environmental Chemicals in Tobacco Products, Tobacco Smoke, and People;" "Tobacco Control Program, Guidelines and Data"—community prevention services, state reports, best practices; "Tobacco Free Celebrities"—with several people discussing their smoking cessations; "Tobacco Free Sports"—different initiatives; and "Tobacco and Women"—marketing to women and girls, health consequences, and reproductive outcomes.

http://www.kidshealth.org/teen/drug_alcohol/tobacco/smoking.html

This site presents data on the addictive qualities of smoking, how smoking affects one's health with photos of healthy and diseased tissues, what smoking does to skin, how it causes reduced athletic performance, and the fact that smoking is expensive. The site provides further links to diseases, infections, and Frequently Asked Questions with accompanying answers.

Journal Articles through the Web

http://www.findarticles.com/p/articles/mi_qa4020/is_200501/ai_n13640469

Journal of Public Health Policy. "Tobacco Industry Opposition to Designating Environmental Tobacco Smoke Through E-Codes" by Michael Givel, 2005. This article examines public policy importance of 1993 and the United States Department of Health and Human Services actions to require doctors and hospitals to report a new external cause of injury code for environmental tobacco smoke related to causes of death from lung cancer and heart disease.

http://www.findarticles.com/p/articles/mi_m0999/is_7268_321/
ai_67442824

British Medical Journal. "Why Journals Should Not Publish Articles Funded by the Tobacco Industry—For and Against" by Gavin Yamey et al., October 28, 2000.

Why they should not publish: The tobacco industry casts doubt on good research and discredits accepted scientific findings and uses public relations activities which are carefully orchestrated by the tobacco industry.

Why they should publish: Should censorship be used to silence the above distrust of the tobacco industry? Does censorship serve the interests of science, journalism, or a free society? Each of these viewpoints is further discussed in the article.

http://www.cancercouncil.com.au/editorial.asp?pageid=1927

New South Wales Public Health Bulletin; "Promoting Tobacco to the Young in the Age of Advertising Bans" by Greg Soulos and Stafford Sanders, Vol. 15, No. 5–6, May/June 2004. Many forms of tobacco advertising have been banned in Australia, yet the tobacco industry there has undermined this ban. The article discusses the promotional strategies adapted by the tobacco industry which have targeted young adults in recent years. The article further features smoking links with the fashion world, advertising in the media, promotion at youth music festivals, and smoking depicted in films.

Books

Tobacco Or Health?: Physiological and Social Damages Caused by Tobacco Smoking by Knut-Olaf Haustein (Springer, 2003). 3540440313.

This book offers the discussion of the consequences that tobacco smoking has on health and all the organ systems that are affected. Discussed as well are primary prevention measures.

Environmental Tobacco Smoke by Ronald R. Watson and Mark L. Witten (CRC Press, 2001). 0849303117.

This text offers observations on the effects of exposure to environmental tobacco smoke and on effects in pregnant women, newborns, youths, adults, and on the elderly. The discussion centers on the various maladies and diseases caused by smoking tobacco.

Stop Smoking and Chewing Tobacco for Life Changes by David L. Johnson and Carole A. Johnson (Infinity Publishing, 2000). 0741404818.

The authors describe techniques and strategies to help people overcome their tobacco addiction. This text uses a self-instructing, self-paced approach with emphasis on a person taking his/her own responsibility to learn skills to stop smoking and what to do if there is a relapse, and how to re-frame the setbacks.

Transracial Adoption

This process refers to placing a child who is of one race or ethnic group with adoptive parents of another race or ethnic group. In the United States, this term often means placing children of color or children from another country with Caucasian adoptive parents.

There are a number of reasons why this process occurs. There are fewer Caucasian children available for adoption. There are some prospective adoptive parents who wish to adopt children from their own ancestry. Others just wish to reach out to children who need them.

However, many experts in the field of adoption feel that at least one parent should be of the same race or culture as the adopted child so that child can have a strong cultural or racial identity.

http://transracial.adoption.com/

Adoption.com. "Transracial/Transcultural Adoption." This is a very informative site that includes directions for the adoption process. It offers the following issues to consider: adoption language, attachment and bonding, disabled parents, failed placement, siblings, single parents, how to inform family and friends, and adoption risks.

http://darkwing.uoregon.edu/~adoption/topics/transracialadoption.htm

The Adoption History Project. This interesting site provides a chronological history of transracial/transcultural adoption beginning in 1851 and concluding in 2000. There is also a discussion of organizations through which this process can proceed, information on adoption studies, and document archives—which is an extensive alphabetical listing of documents which include nature-nurture studies and psychopathology studies.

http://www.adoptivefamilies.com/transracial-adoption.php

Adoptive families. "Transracial Adoption: The Color of Life." This site offers information for those interested in personally pursuing this process. There is a Frequently Asked Questions link, plus data on adoption agencies, adoption attorneys, parents' support groups, links to domestic and/or international adoption, an online magazine, an opportunity to share adoption stories, and an archive of adoptive family articles which would be inspiring and helpful to those who have chosen this route to adopt a child.

Journal Articles through the Web

http://www.blackwell-synergy.com/links/doi/
   10.1111%2F1468–0424.00298

Gender and History. "Mother, Child, Race, Nation: The Visual Iconography of Rescue and the Politics of Transnational and Transracial Adoption" by Laura Briggs, Vol. 15, No. 2, pp. 179–200, August 2003. This article explores the images of thin children, either with or without mothers, and how these images created the desire to rescue these children. However, not part of the images were the explanations for poverty, famine, and other disasters that may have contributed to the devastating, but moving photos of needy-looking children.

http://www.questia.com/PM.qst?a=o&se=gglsc&d=5001339594&er=deny

Social Work. "Promoting Same-Race Adoption for Children of Color" by Leslie D. Hollingsworth, Vol. 43, 1998. This article offers the history of the transracial adoption controversy and discusses the current status of this issue (although written in 1998). However, it counters assertions used to oppose same race adoption policies for children of color. It is still a useful article because it summarizes the positions taken of various social work organizations regarding adoption and race, and offers recommendations for education, policy, research, and practice.

http://bjsw.oxfordjournals.org/cgi/content/abstract/29/5/779

The British Journal of Social Work. "Perspectives on 'Race' and Adoption: The Views of Student Social Workers" by Derek Kirton, Vol. 29, No. 5, 1999, pp. 779–796.

This article discusses the views of 835 student social workers on race and adoption. It was interesting to note that support for same race adoption was much stronger among minority ethnic student social workers than their white counterparts.

http://lawprofessors.typepad.com/family_law/2006/08/
  recent_news_and.html

Family Law Prof. Blog. "Recent News & Scholarship on Transracial Adoptions," August 18, 2006. These are articles from the *New York Times* indicating more Caucasian couples are now adopting black children, up 14 percent from 1998. Other articles indicate that racial preferences, even if this is an unconscious decision, play a role in Americans adopting internationally. A number of the articles are from various civil rights law journals, with various links to additional data.

Books

The Ethics of Transracial Adoption by Hawley Fogg-Davis (Cornell University Press, 2001). 0801438985.

The author describes her use of this topic as a case study to examine racial assumptions people bring to social life in America, including the way we build our families and interact with one another.

Transracial Adoptions: An Adoptive Mother's Documentary of Racism, Injustice by Joann Lang (Writers Club Press, 2002). 0595259502.

The adopted children, middle school students, have a chapter in this text. The author has written numerous articles on parenting, adoption, and race relationships.

In Their Own Voices: Transracial Adoptees Tell Their Own Stories by
Rita James Simon and Rhonda Roorda (Columbia University Press, 2000). 0231118295.

This is a collection of interviews conducted with black and bi-racial young adults who were adopted by white parents. The issues raised are: How does the experience affect their racial and social identities, choice of friends, marital partners, and life styles? The text also includes overviews and history and legal status of transracial adoption.

Entertainment

Entertainment Software Rating Board

Media Bias

Media Restrictions

MPAA Film Rating System

Entertainment Software Rating Board

The purpose of this board is to offer accurate and objective information about the content in computer and video games so those purchasing these products can make an informed decision about whether or not to buy them. The ratings have two basic components: *the ratings symbol* which suggests age appropriateness for the game, and *content descriptors* which indicate elements in a game that might have tagged a particular rating or may be of interest or concern.

http://www.esrb.org/ratings/ratings_guide.jsp

Game Ratings and Descriptor Guide. This site provides rating symbols with descriptions of each, plus ESRP (Entertainment Software Rating Board) content descriptors and a definition of each of those descriptors. This site also describes the ratings process, enforcement of rules, and Frequently Asked Questions.

http://www.answers.com/topic/entertainment-software-rating-board

Answers.com. This site offers information on the ESRB, an overview as to the process of the ratings system, the ratings, with thoroughly described definitions, the same thorough descriptions of content descriptors, the discontinued content descriptors, plus examples of products on the market today with their accompanying ratings. Also discussed are the controversies of the rating system offered by critics of the system.

http://acronyms.thefreedictionary.com/Entertainment+Software+Rating+Board

This site offers gaming industry news, an entertainment software directory, and an extensive listing of entertainment links to entertainment services, to software, to entertainment rights, and to the ESRB and its links, as well.

Journal Articles through the Web

http://archpedi.ama-assn.org/cgi/content/short/160/4/402

Archives of Pediatrics and Adolescent Medicine. "Content and Ratings of Mature-Rated Video Games" by Kimberly M. Thompson et al., April, 2006, Vol. 160, pp. 402–410. The objectives of this article are to discuss the depiction of violence, blood, sexual themes, profanity, and gambling in video games rated M (Mature) and to measure whether the content observed and the rating information provided on the game box agree. The site also discusses the design of the research process, the outcome procedures, and the results.

64   Encouraging and Supporting Student Inquiry

http://www.esrb.org/about/news/12062005,jsp.

Entertainment Software Rating Board Site. "ESRB Flunks National Institute for Media and the Family for Its Disservice to Parents and Their Children," December 6, 2005.

The ESRB gave a failing grade to the National Institute for Media and the Family (NIMF) for its flawed Video Game Report Card. Inaccuracies, incomplete and misleading statements, and flawed research were factors in receiving the failing grade. The ESRB felt that NIMF elevated its political and media agenda over its concerns for consumer welfare, especially those of children and teens.

http://www.delawareonline.com/apps/pbcs.dll/article?AID=/20060320/
   NEWS/603200332/1006

Delaware Online and *The News Journal.* "Bill Would Limit Sale of Video Games; Violent Games, Like Porn, Would be Illegal to Sell to Kids" by J.L. Miller, March 20, 2006. This is a scathing report on the video "Grand Theft Auto: San Andreas." The images were considered violent. There were scenes of prostitutes being killed and their money stolen, while other scenes depict gang warfare, pimping, and carjacking. The debate over this issue was how to prevent videos like this one from reaching children and still adhere to Constitutional guidelines and First Amendment protection.

Books

Media Ratings for Movies, Music, Video Games and TV: A Review of the Research and Recommendations for Improvements by Douglas A. Gentile et al. (Adolescent Medicine Clinics, 2005, a downloadable article from Proquest).

This digital document published by Proquest Information and Learning is concerned with environmental influences. In this case the article referred to media being critical for development of personality traits and behavior. Children's environment has been media saturated and, therefore, affects children's behavior. This article is part of a larger text.

Game Coding Complete by Mike McShaffry (Paraglyph, 2003). 1932111751.

This text offers pointers on memory management, scripting, debugging, production, scheduling, and testing. It is really a text for someone who wants to become a game programmer. The guidelines specified are those of the ESRB.

Masters of Doom: How Two Guys Created an Empire and Transformed Pop Culture by David Kushner (Random House Trade Paperbacks, 2004). 0812972155.

Doom is a video game in which the player navigates a dungeon and lays waste to everything and anything that crosses their path. However, the subject matter of the game raised serious questions about decency in products aimed at school-age children.

Media Bias

This topic is concerned with real or perceived bias of journalists and news producers within the mass media; in the manner in which events are selected and reported on and how they are covered. In some countries, there is government influence that reflects both overt and covert censorship. Types of bias include: ethnic or racial, corporate (advertising), class (class divisions), political (in favor of or against a political party, candidate or policy), or religious.

http://www.mediaresearch.org/biasbasics/biasbasics1.asp
"Media Bias Basics." According to this site it is believed that journalists tend to vote Democratic. They have supported every Democratic presidential candidate since 1964. Many journalists admit to being liberal or support liberal positions. The public also views the media as being liberal. What results is that often the sympathetic media might boost the votes for certain candidates. Yet many journalists deny the liberal bias.

http://www.newsroom.ucla.edu/page.asp?RelNum=6664
"Media Bias is Real, Finds UCLA Political Scientist" by Meg Sullivan, December 14, 2005. This article considers the issue that while the editorial page of the *Wall Street Journal* is conservative, the news pages are liberal. The author indicates that even though the Drudge report may have a right-wing reputation, it leans to the left. Also, coverage by public television and radio is conservative compared with much of the mainstream media. The author feels that the most centrist media outlet is the "News Hour" with Jim Lehrer and ABC's "Good Morning America" is a close second. Of the twenty outlets studied, eighteen scored left of center, with CBS "Evening News," the *New York Times*, and the *Los Angeles Times* ranking second, third, and fourth most liberal behind the news pages of the *Wall Street Journal*.

http://rhetorica.net/bias.htm
This article stipulates that there is no such thing as an objective point of view. Politicians are biased. They belong to parties and espouse policies and ideologies. Journalists often speak from political positions, even though journalistic ethics of objectivity and fairness strongly influence their writings. The article also highlights questions for detecting bias:

> With whom is the author or speaker identified—political, social or professional group?
>
> Who is paying for the message?
>
> What sources does the speaker/author use?

66   Encouraging and Supporting Student Inquiry

How does the speaker/author present arguments?

Does the speaker/author offer alternative points of view?

Journal Articles through the Web

http://www.opinionjournal.com/extra/?id=110005312

WSJ.com Opinion Journal from the *Wall Street Journal*; "High Bias" by Orson Scott Card, July 12, 2004. The author is a supporter of Fox News and feels that the other news channels like CNN and MSNBC reflect a liberal bias. He believes that the differences between Fox News and all other news media are: Fox News admits that on some issues they take sides, and Fox News allows the conservative side to be heard without contempt. The author cites several examples of biased reporting in the media.

http://www.sscnet.ucla.edu/polisci/faculty/groseclose/Media.Bias.8.htm

Quarterly Journal of Economics. "A Measure of Media Bias" by Tim Groseclose and Jeff Milyo, 2005. These university professors attempted to use computation analysis to see if the average article in the *New York Times* was liberal and/or the average story on Fox News more conservative. The authors counted the times the media outlets cited various think tanks and other policy groups. These figures were then compared with the number of times that members of Congress cited the same think tanks. Specific scores were assigned to these comparisons. The results showed a strong liberal bias in the *New York Times*. All of the research was limited to news stories, not editorials, book reviews, or letters to the editor.

http://mediamatters.org/items/200606020006

Media Matters for America. "Taranto Conspicuously Mum on the Status of His Media-Bias Theory," June 2, 2006. James Taranto is an editor at the OpinionJournal.com. He feels that "the mainstream media are generally biased in favor of liberals and Democrats, but this ends up helping conservatives and Republicans by breeding complacency on the Democratic side." *Media Matters for America*, a think tank, attempted to prove that the editor's theory of media bias could not be substantiated.

Books

What Liberal Media?: The Truth About Bias and the News by Eric Alterman (Basic Books, 2003). 0465001769.

This media columnist pursued an aggressive investigation into the conservative nature of the U.S. news. The author tries to dispel the notion put forth by Bill O'Reilly and Rush Limbaugh that liberals control the media.

South Park Conservatives: The Revolt Against Liberal Media Bias by Brian C. Anderson (Regnery Publishing, Inc., 2005). 0895260190.

The author, who is a political journalist, expresses the concept that for thirty years liberal bias has dominated mainstream media. He now feels that the era of liberal dominance is no longer.

Press Bias and Politics: How the Media Frame Controversial Issues by Jim A. Kuypers (Praeger Paperback, 2002). 0275977595.

The author charted the potential effects the press and broadcast media have on the messages put forth by political and social leaders when the latter discuss controversial issues. The author examined 800 press reports on race and homosexuality from sixteen different newspapers and he documented a liberal political bias in mainstream news. He feels this bias hurts the democratic process, and that the mainstream press in America is an anti-democratic institution.

Coloring the News: How Political Correctness Has Corrupted American Journalism by William McGowan (Encounter Books, 2003). 1893554600.

The author is a fellow at the conservative Manhattan Institute. He presents several cases in which, he contends, reporters and editors got stories wrong or chose to ignore worthy topics because of their liberal leanings and their fear of offending African-Americans, gays, or feminists. The author also cites biases in reporting about abortion, since he indicates that over 80 percent of journalists surveyed said they were pro-choice.

Media Restrictions

All forms of media, especially electronic media, have been subject to restrictions. Some of this media constitutes: computer and video games, television programs, motion pictures, theatrical plays, comics, books, magazines, concerts, and websites. The restrictions reflect issues of violence, profanity, sexuality, nudity, capital punishment, horror, and drug abuse. Those restricting viewing, reading or listening are often parents and/or guardians on the basis of religious teachings.

http://people-press.org/reports/display.php3?ReportID=241

The Pew Research Center for the People and the Press. "Support for Tougher Indecency Measures, But Worries About Government Intrusiveness: New Concerns About Internet and Reality Shows," April, 19, 2005. This article is based on a nationwide survey of 1500 Americans and concerns public opinion about government intervention and regulation of entertainment and how this reflects political and religious aspects regarding this control.

http://seattletimes.nwsource.com/html/artsentertainment/
  2003143107_abortion23html

The Seattle Times. "Mitzi's Choice: Staging a Controversy" by Misha Bersa, July 26, 2006. This article discusses a theatrical production about a woman's decision to consider abortion to terminate her pregnancy. Some media watchers believe that writers and producers are avoiding the abortion issue in the theater, television, and in film because it could become a hotly contested issue.

http://en.wikipedia.org/wiki/Public_outcry

This article in the *Wikipedia* is based on a mass movement referred to as *moral panic*. This panic is brought on by media coverage of social issues. The social issues could be: same-sex marriage, witchcraft, rock n' roll music, white slavery, day care abuse, and Communism.

Journal Articles through the Web

http://www.parentstv.org/PTC/facts/mediafacts.asp

Parents Television Council; Parents TV.org; Facts and TV Statistics. "It's Just Harmless Entertainment" Oh Really? From a survey by the Pew Research Center 75 percent of 1500 adults polled want tighter enforcement of government rules on broadcast content. The *Times Magazine* poll indicated that 53 percent of respondents want FCC (Federal Communications Commission) to place stricter controls on broadcast channels. The American Psychiatric Association indicated that exposure to media portrayals of violence increases aggressive behavior in children. This article cites many such statistics regarding children's media viewing.

http://www.opinionjournal.com/extra/?id=110007867
Opinion Journal from the *Wall Street Journal*. "Shut Up, They Explained: The Left's Regulating War against Free Speech" by Brian C. Anderson, January 25, 2006. This article is about the rise of alternative media—political talk radio in the 1980s, cable news coverage in the 1990s, and the blogosphere since 2000. According to the article, the author states that the liberal establishment is trying to smother the political discourse through the above outlets and that, therefore, this is an attack on free speech. This is a very one-sided article but important to read, nevertheless.

http://online.wsj.com/public/article/SB112777213097452525-
 zRQZ358IZKZDPMzNayOR6RUfXOw_20060926.html?mod=blogs
The Wall Street Journal Online. "China Tightens Grip on Internet with New Content, Media Rules: How Can Crackdown Track 100 Million Internet Users? Ban on Word 'Democracy'" by Geoffrey A. Fowler and Mei Fong, September 27, 2005. China is attempting to impose new regulations that will centralize all China-based web news and opinion under a state regulator. What will be prohibited would be content that "goes against state security and public interest." This prohibition is also imposed on television and other media.

Books

Propaganda, The Press and Conflict: The Gulf War and Kosovo by David R. Willcox (Routledge, UK, 2005). 0415360439.

This text analyzes the use of the press for propaganda purposes during conflicts, using both the First Gulf War and the intervention in Kosovo, as case studies. The five propaganda themes are: portrayal of the leader figure, portrayal of the enemy, military threat, threat to international stability, and technological warfare. Also discussed in this book is the academic debate of the role of the journalist in war coverage.

It's Not the Media: The Truth About Pop Culture's Influence on Children by Karen Sternheimer (Westview Press, 2003). 0813341388.

This text challenges the usual notion that media creates a toxic environment for America's youth, diverting us from the real reasons for problems affecting children today. The author contends that fear of social change and what it means to be a child growing up in today's media-saturated climate, is the reason for our media-bashing culture. She feels that the changes in media culture are much easier to see than the other complex social/societal, economic, and political changes over the last few decades.

The Media & Morality edited by Robert M. Baird, William E. Loges and Stuart E. Rosenbaum (Prometheus Books, 1999). 1573926817.

This book offers a framework for analyzing ethics in the media. Some of the issues raised are: Do the practices of media professionals have moral consequences? To whom are the media responsible—the public, advertisers, and/or stockholders? Who decides what may "harm" an audience? How do political agendas affect censorship and media profits?

MPAA Film Rating System

The Motion Picture Association of America (MPAA) is a trade organization of the six major film studios. This organization decides on the following classifications of films: G, PG, PG-13, R, and NC-17. This is a voluntary rating system in cooperation with the National Association of Theater Owners. These ratings are provided by a board of parents who view each film and then, after group discussion, assign a rating. This information is offered as a guide to parents to decide on the appropriate films for their children's viewing. The criteria considered are: theme, language, violence, nudity, sex, and drug use. Ten to thirteen parents serve on the rating board. "They work for the Classification and Rating Administration, which is funded by fees charged to producers/distributors for the rating of their films. The MPAA Chairman chooses the Chairman of the Rating Board, thereby insulating the Board from industry or other group pressure. No one in the movie industry has the authority or power to push the Board in any direction or otherwise influence it."[1]

http://www.gayalliance.org/content/view/597/54/
Written by GLAAD (Gay & Lesbian Alliance Against Defamation). "The Empty Closet." This site concerns the issue of a film about the discriminatory rating system which itself received a discriminatory rating. The film is about the MPAA rating system and the influence this system has had on American culture, specifically the representations in films of lesbian, gay, bisexual, and transgender (LGBT) people. The question raised is whether films with people who are either LGB or T face stricter scrutiny than films with heterosexual people. Evidently, this film attempts to confront the double-standard the MPAA places on films with gay content.

http://en.wikipedia.org/wiki/MPAA_film_rating_system
The *Wikipedia* discusses the current rating system, provides a history of the rating system, and offers details on the rating process, the effects of the ratings, and the comments and reviews of various critics of the system.

http://dictionary.laborlawtalk.com/MPAA_film_rating_system
Dictionary of Labor Law Talk. This site provides a historical discussion of the MPAA Rating System, the earlier (previous) rating system, and data about when the new rating system was implemented. Also presented are the rating process, effects of the ratings, and how some of the ratings discourage some age groups from viewing certain films. In addition, there is a discussion of the critics of the system and why they disagree with some of the ratings.

Journal Articles through the Web

http://findarticles.com/p/articles/mi_qn4196/is_20010423/ai_n10693820

Milwaukee Journal Sentinel. "Film Rating System Too Secretive" by Sharon Waxman, April 23, 2001. This article discusses the anonymity given to the raters, who are only known to the members of the MPAA. The author interviewed a rater who resigned from his job. The latter told the author about his criticisms of the possible indiscriminate ratings, why he felt the system was dysfunctional, and the solutions he offered to correct the problems.

http://findarticles.com/p/articles/mi_m1374/is_1_60/ai_59021329

Humanist. "Three Decades of Film Censorship . . . Right Before Your Eyes" by Chris Roth, January 2000. The thesis of this article is that the rating system can limit viewing of certain films, even though the system is not law. The author also discusses the misconceptions about the rating system. Mentioned, too, are circumstances that have occurred historically which have eroded the ratings codes.

http://www.pubmedcentral.nih.gov/articlerender.fcgi?artid=1435631

MedGenMed. "Violence, Sex, and Profanity in Films: Correlation of Movie Ratings with Content" by Kimberly M. Thompson and Fumie Yokota, July–September 2004. The objectives of this article were "to characterize available information about violence, sex, and profanity content of movies as a function of rating; quantitatively explore the relationships between content, rating, and economic information; compare the amount of violence in animated and non-animated G-rated films; and test for a trend of decreased stringency of rating criteria (ratings 'creep') as a function of time."[2] The authors felt that age-based ratings really did not provide good, accurate information on the depiction of violence, sex, profanity, and other content and that over time the ratings became less stringent.

Books

Controlling Hollywood: Censorship/Regulation in the Studio Era by Matthew Bernstein (Rutgers University Press, 1999). 0813527074.

This text offers a historical perspective on the rating system. There are ten essays that examine major turning points, crises, and contradictions that affected movie-making from the 1910s – 1970s. Legal cases are examined as well as groups that took a special interest in film entertainment (i.e., religious, social interest groups, and government bodies).

Hollywood v. Hard Core: How the Struggle Over Censorship Created the Modern Film Industry by Jon Lewis (New York University Press, 2002). 0814751431.

The author presents a history of the ratings guidelines and he analyzes the social, political, and financial motives that drive the ratings system.

Also discussed are disputed scenes, definitions of pornography and obscenity, and artistic content.

Turning Points in Film History by Andrew J. Rausch (Citadel Press, 2004). 0806525924.

The author discusses thirty-two pivotal moments in the history of the film medium that changed significantly the way movies were produced. The text also provides insights from noted film historians and filmmakers.

Notes

1. http://www.mpaa.org/Ratings_HowRated.asp
2. http://www.pubmedcentral.nih.gov/articlerender.fcgi?artid=1435631

Environment

Acid Rain
Global Warming
Nuclear Power
Ozone Depletion
Pesticides

Acid Rain

Acid rain refers to the deposition of acidic components in rain, fog, dew, or dry particles. It might also be called acid precipitation. This extra acidity in rain comes from the reaction of acid pollutants, mostly sulfur oxides and nitrogen oxides, with water in the air, which form strong acids (sulfuric and nitric acids). The sources from which these strong acids come are vehicles (cars, trucks, buses) and industrial and power generating plants. The greatest areas of acidity are in the Northeastern United States. This is because of the number of large cities with dense populations and the concentration of power and industrial plants. Also, the winds bring storms and pollution to the Northeast from the Midwest.

http://www.epa.gov/acidrain/

U.S. Environmental Protection Agency. "Acid Rain." This site mentions the damage done to lakes, streams, forests, plants, and animals that live in the aforementioned ecosystems. The site further describes the causes of acid rain, the effects of acid rain, how acid rain is measured, and what is being done to reduce acid rain.

Both societal changes and individual action are important steps to alleviating this problem. In 1990, Congress created the Acid Rain Program as part of the Clean Air Act Amendments. The main goal has been to reduce emissions of sulfur dioxide and nitrogen oxides. This is being done through energy efficiency and pollution prevention.

From this site, one may also locate information on acid rain where you live, and links to educational resources.

http://www.ec.gc.ca/acidrain/acidfact.html

Environmental Canada Website. This site provides various facts about acid rain:

1. What causes it?—the transformation of sulfur dioxide and nitrogen oxides into secondary pollutants which are transported into the atmosphere.
2. What is pH? —measures the amount of acid in liquid-like water.
3. Where is acid rain a problem? Since this is a Canadian site, the answer is Eastern Canada just as it is prevalent in the Northeastern United States and near urban areas.
4. Where do sulfur dioxide emissions come from?—industrial processes and burning of fossil fuels.
5. Would acid rain remain a problem without further controls?—Yes, in Southeastern Canada, an area the size of France and the United Kingdom combined, would receive harmful levels of acid rain, well above critical load limits for aquatic systems.

http://www.policyalmanac.org/environment/archive/acid_rain.shtml

This is a paper adapted from The Environmental Protection Agency. "What Is Acid Rain and What Causes It?" August 6, 2002. A precise term for acid rain is acid deposition, which has two parts: wet and dry. Wet deposition refers to acidic rain, fog, and snow and affects a variety of plants and animals. Dry deposition refers to acidic gases and particles. Wind blows these particles and gases onto buildings, cars, homes, and trees.

The article continues with information on measurement of acid rain, the effects of acid rain, and what society can do about acid deposition.

Journal Articles through the Web

http://www.sciencedaily.com/releases/2002/07/020718075630.htm

Science Daily. "Damage from Acid Rain Pollution Is Far Worse Than Previously Believed," University of Vermont, July 18, 2002. This article is based on a study which revealed that acid rain's damage to America's forests may be more widespread than previously thought. It can create conditions in trees which are similar to compromised immune systems in adults. Acid rain depletes calcium in high elevation red spruce trees, plus affects balsam fir, white pine, and eastern hemlock. A basic resultant problem is that it would alter the competition and survival of populations, and species, including animals at higher levels of the forest food chains.

http://www.findarticles.com/p/articles/mi_qa4038/is_200410/ai_n9459636

Journal of the American Water Resources Association. "Acid Rain Science and Politics in Japan" by Richard H. McCuen, October 2004. This is a pioneering work in environmental and Asian history, and an in-depth analysis of the influence of science on domestic and international environmental politics. Also discussed is the global struggle to create sustainable societies. The article points to three pollution related "sustainable crises" in modern Japanese history:

1. Copper mining in late nineteenth and twentieth centuries;
2. Post World War II domestic industrial pollution;
3. Present day global problem of transboundary pollution.

http://news.bbc.co.uk/2/hi/science/nature/2189151.stm

Science/Nature. BBC News, World Edition; "Forests Fall Silent with Acid Rain," August 12, 2002. The article purports that birds could disappear from North American forests because of acid rain. For example, acid rain affects the breeding habits of the wood thrush who live on the mountain slopes in the Eastern United States. There has been a drop in their numbers since 1960.

This article refers to a study done by a team at Cornell University who looked at the possible link between acid rain, soil acidity, and impaired breeding behavior.

Books

Crossing Borders, Crossing Boundaries by Leslie R. Alm (Praeger/Greenwood, 2000). 0275969169.

This text provides an analysis of the science-policy linkage that defined the acid rain debate in the United States. The book contains in-depth interviews with scientists about the communications challenges among the science, policy, and interest group communities that deal with the major environmental issues of acid rain.

Trashing the Planet by Dixy Lee Ray (Harper Perennial, 1992). 0060974907.

This book is for educators, public officials, scientists, and citizens. It was a best seller and provides an invaluable, sensible approach for understanding and saving the environment.

Effects of Acid Rain on Forest Processes by Douglas L. Godbold and Aloys Huttermann (Wiley-Liss, 1994). 0471517682.

This text offers a detailed analysis of acidification effects on forest soil and plant life. The findings were from the Solling Project, a long-term study on acid rain results in Germany's Black Forest and other European forests.

Markets for Clean Air: The U.S. Acid Rain Program by Paul L. Joskow et al. (Cambridge University Press, 2000). 0521660831.

This book presents a comprehensive in-depth description and evaluation of the first three years' experience with the U.S. Acid Rain Program. This program is the world's first large-scale use of a tradable emission permits system to achieve environmental goals. The book also quantifies emission reductions associated with this program.

Global Warming

This topic refers to the increase in average temperature of both the Earth's atmosphere and the oceans. Scientists attribute the increase to human activities. The latter points to the increased amounts of carbon dioxide and other greenhouse gases. These gases are the result of three major processes: 1) the burning of fossil fuels, 2) the clearing of land, and 3) agricultural activities. Historically, a Swedish chemist speculated about these processes as early as 1897.

The problems that can occur as a result of global warming are rising sea level and the amount of precipitation which can cause flooding, droughts, heat waves, hurricanes, and tornadoes. Also, there is evidence of glacial retreat in both the Arctic and Antarctic regions.

http://www.foxnews.com/story/0,2933,214419,00.html

FoxNews.com. "Al Gore Chastises U.S. Leaders for Lack of Action on Global Warming," September 19, 2006. Former Vice President Al Gore called global warming a "climate crisis" and he discussed the lack of attention and action by politicians. He also indicated that the Bush Administration edited official scientific studies to minimize the importance of the impact of global warming.

http://yosemite.epa.gov/oar/globalwarming.nsf/content/index.html

U.S. Environmental Protection Agency (EPA). This is the EPA's Global Warming site which is divided into the following sections:

1. Climate (What is the problem? And what do we know?)
2. Emissions (Greenhouse gases and how much do we emit?)
3. Impacts (How serious is it? How? In the future?)
4. Actions (What's being done? What can I do?)
5. Resource Center (Publications and tools)
6. News and Events
7. Aspects of problem based on where you live (World, U.S., EPA regions, Natural regions)
8. A Visitor Center (citizens, educators, public officials, coastal residents, health professionals, and meteorologists)

http://www.globalwarming.org/

This site is the project of the Cooler Heads Coalition. On this site are links to:

1. Gorey truths: 25 inconvenient truths for Al Gore.
2. A Skeptics Guide to "An Inconvenient Truth," Al Gore's documentary movie.

3. Scientists wake-up to European Union Kyoto failure.
4. Ocean cooling confounds climate models, August 14, 2006.
5. Not as bad as we thought—World Climate Report.
6. Jumping to conclusions: frogs, global warming and nature—World Climate report, January 11, 2006.

There are several other links on this site that refute some scientific evidence.

Journal Articles through the Web

http://www.realclimate.org/
RealClimate—Climate science from climate scientists. Sachs' *Wall Street Journal Challenge,* September 19, 2006. Jeffrey Sachs, who works at the Columbia Earth Institute, reported in *Scientific American* on the disconnect between the *Wall Street Journal* Editorial Board and the *Wall Street Journal*'s own reporters when the subject is climate change. The author urges the board to keep an open mind regarding discussions of global warming and to have representation from all points of view at a scientifically called meeting on this topic.

http://www.usatoday.com/news/opinion/editorials/2003-10-28-schulz_x.htm
USA Today. "Researchers Question Key Global-Warming Study" Editorial/Opinion by Nick Schulz, October 28, 2003. The author refers to a new paper in the journal, *Energy and Environment*, which critiques a scientific claim about climate change. There were claims that the late twentieth century was not unusually warm by historical standards. The author does express the importance of verifying facts to make informed decisions.

http://www.opinionjournal.com/extra/?id=110008220
WSJ.com Opinion Journal for the *Wall Street Journal* Editorial Page. "Climate of Fear," April 12, 2006. The subheading to this article is "Global Warming Alarmists Intimidate Dissenting Scientists Into Silence." The author mentions various climactic changes that occurred in 2006—hurricanes, heat wave in Paris, heavy snows in Buffalo, and others, and he wonders how a one-degree rise in global mean temperature in the last century can cause these weather problems. He feels there has been misunderstanding about the science of climate.

Books

Is the Temperature Rising? The Uncertain Science of Global Warming by
S. George Philander (Princeton University Press, 2000). 0691050341.
The author explains why it is so difficult to forecast the consequences

of global warming, yet he feels it is still important to do something about this issue rather than wait for even more scientific data than has already been revealed. He explains factors that contribute to global warming and to act on the problem now.

Global Warming: The Complete Briefing by John Houghton (Cambridge University Press, 2004). 0521528747.

The author explores the scientific basis of global warming and the impact of climate change on human society. He discusses the actions that governments, industry, and individuals can take to diffuse the effects of global warming.

Climate Change: Debating America's Policy Options by David G. Victor (Council on Foreign Relations Press, 2004). 0876093438.

This author provides a political approach by offering American policy options in climate change and also surveys the economic and social costs of changing climate conditions. He discusses three major points:

1. The ability of wealthy societies to adapt
2. Attention to be given to the Kyoto Protocol
3. Unilateral action to create a market for low-carbon emission technologies worldwide.

An Inconvenient Truth: The Planetary Emergency of Global Warming and What We Can Do About It by Albert Gore (Rodale Press, 2006). 1594865671.

The author has condensed the information on global warming. He has provided extensive photographs from NASA (National Aeronautics and Space Administration) which illustrate climate change around the world. A documentary movie, based on this book, was also produced.

Climate of Fear by Thomas Gale Moore (National Book Network, 1998). 1882577655.

This book calls into question the campaign waged by Vice President Al Gore and others about global warming. The author, an economist, indicated that a warmer climate would be, on balance, beneficial to people and the environment.

Meltdown: The Predictable Distortion of Global Warming by Scientists, Politicians, and the Media by Patrick J. Michaels (Cato Institute, 2004). 1930865597.

The author challenges the doom about global warming. This climatologist suggests that the warming would be modest and nature would adjust to it. He debunks stories of melting ice caps and glaciers.

Nuclear Power

The basic definition of nuclear power is electric energy generated using heat produced by atomic reaction. Nuclear energy is energy produced from the splitting of atoms. Nuclear fission is the splitting of an atomic nucleus, resulting in the release of large amounts of energy. This is the basic process a nuclear reactor uses to provide heat for the generation of electricity. Nuclear radiation is invisible particles or waves given off by radioactive materials such as uranium.

"How Nuclear Power Works." Nuclear power plants provide about 17 percent of the world's electricity. In the United States, nuclear power supplies about 15 percent of electricity overall, however, some states get more power from nuclear power plants than others. There are approximately 400 nuclear power plants around the world; the United States has more than 100.[1]

Uranium is a fairly common element on Earth. Uranium 235 has an interesting property because it is useful for both nuclear power production and for nuclear bomb production. To build a nuclear reactor what is needed is some mildly enriched uranium. This site[1] provides information on what happens inside a nuclear power plant.

http://en.wikipedia.org/wiki/Nuclear_power

Nuclear power releases energy for work including propulsion, heat, and the generation of electricity. Nuclear energy is produced when Uranium 235 is so concentrated that nuclear fission takes place. The United States produces the most nuclear energy, with nuclear power providing 20 percent of the electricity it consumes. The *Wikipedia* site provides information on the early years of nuclear power, different types of reactors, concerns about nuclear power—accident or attacks, health effects on populations, nuclear proliferation, and environmental effects—air pollution and waste heat in water systems.

http://web.mit.edu/nuclearpower/

"The Future of Nuclear Power." This was an MIT (Massachusetts Institute of Technology) study on how to determine if nuclear power is really an important option for the United States and the world to consider to meet future energy needs without giving off carbon dioxide and other atmospheric pollutants. The study group believed that nuclear power would increase efficiency and reduce greenhouse emitting gases. Yet, there are still unresolved problems: high costs, adverse safety, environmental and health effects, potential security risks with proliferation, and long-term management of nuclear wastes.

http://www.formal.stanford.edu/jmc/progress/nuclear-faq.html

"Frequently Asked Questions About Nuclear Energy" by John McCarthy. The author is an Emeritus Professor of Computer Science at Stanford

University. He discusses the importance of having adequate sources of energy in order to sustain human progress. There are energy sources in coal, oil, and natural gas, but these sources may well be depleted in years to come. He speaks of solar energy, but the cost is high. Nuclear energy might well be less expensive and it also does not put carbon dioxide into the atmosphere, which can cause problems. This is an excellent article, especially because of the many answers to the provocative questions posed.

http://www.uic.com.au/nip08.htm

"The Economics of Nuclear Power." This article compares costs of nuclear power with other forms of electricity generation. The issues raised are:

1. Nuclear power is cost competitive with other forms of energy, except where there is direct access to low-cost fuels.
2. Fuel costs for nuclear plants are a minor part of total energy costs; but capital costs are greater than those that use coal.
3. When comparing costs of nuclear energy, waste disposal costs are considered. This site offers charts and graphs.

Journal Articles through the Web

http://www.city-journal.org/html/15_1_nuclear_power.html

City Journal. "Why the U.S. Needs More Nuclear Power" by Peter W. Huber and Mark P. Mills, Winter 2005. The interesting thing about nuclear power is that small quantities of raw material can go a long way. Just a bundle of enriched uranium fuel-rods that could fit into a two-bedroom apartment would power New York City for a year. The authors argue for the development of renewable sources of power, like nuclear power over oil. A century ago, coal was the all-purpose fuel, then from the 1930s on it was oil. About 60 percent of fuel we use today is from coal, uranium, natural gas, and gravity—all making electricity. Yet, from an engineering standpoint, the authors see that nuclear power is now safe and sufficient and should be the choice for generating energy.

http://www.alaskajournal.com/stories/122604/loc_20041226003.shtml

Alaska Journal of Commerce. "Galena Opens the Door to Nuclear Project" by Tim Bradner, December 26, 2004. Galena, a city in Alaska, planned to install a small-scale nuclear power plant as a demonstration project. It was to be built by Japan's Toshiba Corporation. This was to be built outside of Alaska, encased in several tons of concrete, and not to be opened for thirty years, its operating life. Toshiba felt that this plant could provide electricity at one-fourth the cost of conventional fuel.

http://energypriorities.com/entries/2006/10/nuclear_power_no_hedge.php

Energy Journal; an online business resource. "Nuclear Power Is No Hedge Against Uncertain Gas Prices" by Denis Du Bois, October 3, 2006.

In the United Kingdom's energy markets, power producers are free to choose nuclear power over fossil fuels for their new plants. Yet, this article concludes that nuclear power is *not* a wise economic investment. Natural gas will be selected instead. However, nuclear power could be a hedge against rising gas prices and carbon emission fees. A study done by economists and engineers showed that nuclear power is less profitable and more financially risky than natural gas. Yet, long-term fixed price contracts could encourage nuclear plant construction. This all seems to be an economic, fiscal decision, rather than one based on efficiency.

Books

A Case for Nuclear-Generated Electricity: (Or Why I Think Nuclear Power is Cool and Why It is Important That You Think So Too) by Scott W. Heaberlin (Battelle Press, 2003). 1574771361.

The author is a registered professional nuclear engineer. He advocates the use of nuclear energy for producing electricity. He addresses the current cultural bias against nuclear technology. People are fearful about nuclear power and radioactive waste. But he demystifies nuclear energy and its potential future.

Nuclear Power Is Not the Answer by Helen Caldicott (New Press, 2006). 1595580670.

The author, a physician and activist, presents facts about problems related to the use of nuclear power. She indicates that large amounts of fossil fuel are burned during the nuclear-energy process and nuclear reactors use and pollute large amounts of water. Radioactive emissions do escape and enter the food chain and our bodies. Nuclear power plants are vulnerable to natural disasters and terrorists. She also comments on the fact that nuclear power is costly and dangerous.

Commercial Nuclear Power: Assuring Safety for the Future by Charles B. Ramsey (John Wiley & Sons, 2006). 0471291862.

The author describes the role nuclear power should and could play in meeting our electrical energy needs. He is concerned with increasing energy consumption needs and environmental consequences. The text examines nuclear plant operations, the potential for accidents, and how to avoid them.

Note

1. http://science.howstuffworks.com/nuclear-power.htm

Ozone Depletion

Approximately 90 percent of the Earth's ozone is in the ozone layer. The latter is a concentration of ozone molecules in the stratosphere. The immediate layer around the Earth is called the troposphere. The stratosphere is the next higher layer. Stratosphere ozone is a naturally occurring gas that filters out the sun's ultraviolet (UV) radiation. If the ozone layer is diminished, it allows radiation to reach the surface of the Earth. Overexposure to UV rays can lead to skin cancer, cataracts, and weakened immune systems. UV rays can also lead to reduced crop yields and disruptions in the food chain.[1]

http://www.beyonddiscovery.org/content/view.article.asp?a=73

This is a National Academy of Sciences site. Beyond Discovery. "The Ozone Depletion Phenomenon." The hole in the ozone layer keeps getting larger each year. Since the late 1970s much of the protective layer of stratospheric ozone above Antarctica disappears during September. This has resulted in what is referred to as the ozone hole. The Antarctic hole measures nine million square miles, almost the size of North America. The article is based upon the work of Dr. F. Sherwood Rowland who shared the 1995 Nobel Prize in Chemistry. He discussed the nature of ozone and how researchers discovered its role in the Earth's atmosphere and the consequences of its depletion.

http://www.ciesin.org/TG/OZ/oz-home.html

CIESIN Thematic Guides. "Ozone Depletion and Global Environmental Change." This guide helps to locate documents that pertain to ozone depletion, its causes, human and environmental effects, and policy responses. This article reflects the 1985 research that was conducted when the ozone hole was discovered over Antarctica and basically focused attention on the fact that humans have an important impact on the global environment.

http://info-pollution.com/common.htm

"Common Ozone Depletion Myths." There is much evidence for an environmental crisis, but there are also many anti-environmental myths about ozone depletion. This site offers many common myths about ozone depletion. Here are a couple of examples of myths with accompanying facts.

> *Myth:* The Antarctic ozone hole was there all along; it was discovered in the 1970s with the introduction of satellite equipment and when satellite measurements started.
>
> *Fact:* The hole was discovered using a ground based instrument that was used

since 1956—but there was no hole until 1976. Since then the hole has increased in size and intensity.

Myth: Spray cans deplete the ozone layer.

Fact: Spray cans (in the United States) have not used CFCs as propellants for about twenty years. CFCs are chlorofluorocarbons which are chemicals that have been used in great quantities in industry, for refrigeration and air conditioning and in consumer products.

Journal Articles through the Web

http://jxb.oxfordjournals.org/cgi/content/abstract/49/328/1775

Oxford Journals. *Journal of Experimental Botany.* "Ozone Depletion and Increased UV-B Radiation: Is There a Real Threat to Photosynthesis" by D. Allen, S. Nogues, N. Baker, Vol. 49, No. 328, 1998. This is a critical review of recent literature that questions earlier predictions that photosynthetic productivity of higher plants is vulnerable to increased ultraviolet B radiation as a result of ozone depletion. The authors feel that ozone depletion and the rise of UV radiation is not a direct threat to photosynthetic productivity of crops and natural vegetation.

http://www.ciesin.org/docs/011-464/011-464.html

Environment. "Common Threads: Research Lessons from Acid Rain, Ozone Depletion, and Global Warming" by Michael E. Kowalok, 1993. The author has indicated that the evolution of land life is believed to be tied closely to the formation of the protective ozone layer. He offers a historical perspective from the fascination with the upper atmosphere, from the late 1800s. He indicated that there is a normal daily creation and destruction of the ozone layer. Scientific concerns about the human-induced destruction of the ozone layer started with the impact of the supersonic transports (SSTs) and all the accompanying combustion products. The author discusses the various research papers presented by environmental groups, scientists, and government agencies.

http:www.newscientist.com/article.ns?id=dn4010

NewScientist.com News Service. *Journal of Geophysical Research.* "Earth's Ozone Depletion Is Finally Slowing" by Gaia Vince, July 2003. The author indicates that between 1997 and 2000 the average rate of ozone depletion slowed by 7 percent a decade. However, it will take about forty years before the depletion stops and recovery begins. The research was done by three NASA satellites and three international ground stations. This article provides some positive news that does contradict the latest data.

Books

Protecting the Ozone Layer; Science and Strategy by Edward A. Parson (Oxford University Press, 2003). 0195155491.

88   Encouraging and Supporting Student Inquiry

   This text discusses early stratospheric science, the American "ozone war," aerosol debates, efforts of ozone depletion, and cause of the ozone hole. Globally, environmental issues have taken center stage, with nations participating in controlling ozone depletion and with ozone depleting chemicals being reduced by 95 percent, positive changes are occurring.

Climate Change, Ozone Depletion and Air Pollution: Legal Commentaries with Policy and Science Considerations by Alexander Gillespie (Brill Academic Pub., 2005). 9004145206.

   This text provides a collection of material necessary to understand the legal debates on climate change, ozone depletion, and air pollution within scientific and policy contexts. This book assembles all the essential documents and resolutions generated by the various proponents of the above issues, analyzes them, and offers background material to make the issues understandable and relevant.

NASA and the Environment: The Case of Ozone Depletion by W. Henry Lambright (History Division, 2005). 0160749468.

   This is part of NASA's Monographs in Aerospace History, No. 38. The text chronicles the stages NASA went through in its efforts to study and provide information on the depletion of the ozone.

Note

1. http://www.epa.gov/ozone/science/q_a.html

Pesticides

The purpose of pesticide use is to prevent, destroy, or repel pests from encroaching on human food supply, on plants, on soil. "A pesticide may be a chemical substance or biological agent (virus or bacteria) used against pests including insects, plant pathogens, weeds, mollusks, birds, mammals, fish, roundworms, and microbes that compete with humans for food, destroy property, spread disease or are a nuisance. Pesticides are usually, but not always, poisonous to humans."[1]

The *Wikipedia* section on pesticides includes information on types of pesticides, history of its use, regulations, effects of use on the environment, on farmers, on consumers, residues in food, the dangers inherent in its use, and managing pest resistance.

http://www.epa.gov/pesticides/about/

U.S. Environmental Protection Agency (EPA). This site offers a comprehensive question/answer format about pesticides and their uses. The site considers what a pesticide is, whether household products contain them, the balance between risks and benefits of its use, and pest control devices. The site also provides many links to fact sheets, information sources, and about EPA's Pesticides Program.

http://www.pesticides.gov.uk/

Pesticides Safety Directorate (PSD) Home Page. PSD is an executive agency in the United Kingdom (UK). The goal of this agency is to ensure that pesticides used in the UK are safe for users, and the environment. The site defines what pesticides are and that its use in food would not be at harmful levels. PSD also supports efforts to reduce the environmental impact of pesticide use; PSD provides data on the correct and effective uses of pesticides in home gardens. This is an extremely informative site.

http://extoxnet.orst.edu/

The Extension TOXicology NETwork. This site, designed for the non-expert, provides a great deal of information on the topic of pesticides. The site contains various sections: Pesticide Information Profiles—for specific information on pesticides; Toxicology Information Briefs—a discussion of concepts in toxicology and environmental chemistry; Toxicology Issues of Concern, Fact Sheets, News About Toxicology Issues, Newsletters, Resources for Toxicology Information, and Technical Information.

The information provided on this site has been developed by toxicologists and chemists within the Extension service of land-grant universities, such as: University of California-Davis, Oregon State, Michigan State, Cornell, and the University of Idaho.

Journal Articles through the Web

http://aje.oxfordjournals.org/cgi/content/abstract/151/7/639

American Journal of Epidemiology. "Leukemia and Non-Hodgkin's Lymphoma in Childhood and Exposure to Pesticides: Results of a Register-Based Case-Control Study in Germany" by Rolf Meinert, et al., Vol. 151, No. 7, pp. 639–646, 2000. The authors of this paper presented results from a population-based case-control interview study of parents of children less than fifteen years old and conducted in West Germany from 1993–1997. There were cases of 1184 children with leukemia, 234 with non-Hodgkin's lymphoma, and 940 with a solid tumor. The essence of the results was that there was an increased leukemia risk for children living on farms and for an association between use of household pesticides and risk of childhood leukemia or lymphoma.

http://jama.ama-assn.org/cgi/content/short/294/4/455

The Journal of the American Medical Association. "Acute Illnesses Associated with Pesticide Exposure at Schools" by Walter A. Alarcon, M.D. et al., Vol. 294, No. 4, July 27, 2005. The context of this article is that pesticides are used on school property and some schools are at risk of pesticide drift exposure from neighboring farms, which leads to pesticide exposure among students and school employees. Before this study there was no information available on the magnitude of illnesses and risk factors associated with pesticide exposure.

The results of this study found that incidence rates among children increased significantly from 1998–2002. Most illnesses were associated with insecticides (35 percent), disinfectants (32 percent), repellents (13 percent), and herbicides (11 percent). The recommendations were to integrate pest management programs in schools, reduce pesticide drift, and adopt pesticide spray buffer zones around schools.

http://jeq.scijournals.org/cgi/content/abstract/30/3/1033

Journal of Environmental Quality, technical report on Surface to Water Quality. "Turf PQ, A Pesticide Runoff Model For Turf" by Douglas A. Haith, Vol. 30, 2001. This article concerns environmental assessments of golf courses and other turf systems. The concern is pesticide runoff. The study was done with mathematical modeling applications. The author studied fifty-two pesticide runoff events involving six pesticides measured in plot studies in four states.

Books

Pesticides: Health, Safety and the Environment by Graham Matthews (Blackwell Publishing, Inc., 2006). 1405130911.

This book examines how crop protection was achieved before pesticides were in use; how pesticides are registered for use now; pesticide application and concerns of operator safety; and what happens to pesticides in food and the environment. In addition, there is a chapter covering the future of pesticides with the growing use of crops that have been genetically modified to resist disease and attack by pests.

Saving the Planet with Pesticides and Plastic: The Environmental Triumph of High-Yield Farming by Dennis T. Avery (Hudson Institute, 2000). 1558130691.

This author takes the position that pesticide use is not harmful, will not harm the immune system or cause diseases. He feels that environmentalists, conservationists, and others are creating flawed paranoia about pesticide use.

This text was included because it so differed in concept and belief from most other materials on the hazards of pesticide use.

Silent Spring by Rachel Carson (Mariner Books, 40th anniversary edition, 2000). 0618249060.

This text was originally published in 1962 and presented the first look at widespread ecological degradation. The book created an environmental awareness on the poisons from insecticides, weed killers, and use of sprays in agriculture which left dangerous chemicals on our food sources. Carson felt that these chemicals were more dangerous than radiation and that the chemicals stayed in the systems of humans throughout their lives.

Chemical Pesticides: Mode of Action and Toxicology by Jorgen Stenersen (CRC, 2004). 0748409106.

The author provides answers as to why pesticides are toxic to the target organisms and not to others. In addition, the book offers information on legal matters and on potential environmental problems.

Note

1. http://en.wikipedia.org/wiki/Pesticides

Geography

Israeli-Occupied Territories

Persian Gulf

Puerto Rico Self-Determination

United States–Mexican Border Dispute

Israeli-Occupied Territories

These territories are those that were captured by Israel during the Six-Day War of 1967. The territories were in Egypt, Jordan, and Syria. The other names associated with these territories are: West Bank, Gaza Strip, East Jerusalem, the Golan Heights, and Sinai Peninsula. The latter was returned to Egypt as part of the 1979 Israel-Egypt peace treaty. There are a number of issues concerning these territories that make them controversial: the legality of Israel's policy of encouraging major settlement in the area; whether it is legitimate for Israel to annex portions of the territories; whether Israel can be an occupying power, by the rules of the Fourth Geneva Convention (which protects civilians during times of war in the hands of enemies and under occupation by a foreign power); whether an independent Palestinian state could be created in the territories.

The turmoil in this area was also reflected in the Lebanese/Hezbollah conflict during the summer of 2006. During this time, Israel and the militant group Hezbollah had violated laws of war during their battle. This was a determination by the human rights advocacy group, Human Rights Watch. This group noted that Israeli Defense Forces failed to distinguish between combatants and civilians. The battle ensued for thirty-four days and resulted in the deaths of 1000 people on both sides. This conflict was so significant that, months later, in January 2007, the Chief of the Israeli Armed Forces, Lieutenant General Dan Halutz resigned, even before an investigation into the conduct of the war, known as the Winograd Commission.

The Winograd Commission determined that Hezbollah's role in this conflict was very significant, that Hezbollah used portable anti-tank weapons which contributed to the majority of Israeli military casualties in this conflict. The Commission was originally appointed by the Israeli Prime Minister to stave off calls for a more formal inquiry, which would have caused the firing of officials. The Winograd Commission's interim report was presented in March 2007.

http://www.answers.com/topic/Israeli-occupied-territories

This is the site of the "world's greatest encyclodictionalmanacapedia." This site describes the areas in question; why the areas are strategically significant to Israel (water sources); religious and historic sites; political status of the areas; historical background; the meaning of the term "occupies" in this situation; and how this arrangement affects Arab Palestinians and Israeli law.

http://www.questia.com/PM.qst?a=o&d=79269562

"Prolonged Military Occupation: The Israeli-Occupied Territories Since 1967" by Adam Roberts. The author's discussion centers on a formal system of external control by a force (Israel) whose presence was not sanctioned by international agreement, and a conflict of both nationality and interest between the inhabitants and those who experience power over them.

http://www.hrw.org/reports/1989/WR89/Israel.htm

Human Rights Watch site, "Israeli-Occupied Territories." This article reflects the negative attitude of the administration of the first President Bush against the Israeli occupation. The concern involved the treatment of Palestinians in the occupied territories, which was considered unacceptable and, therefore, might weaken Congressional support for aid to Israel. Since the United States commitment to Israel for security and economic well-being is over $3 billion a year, this occupation takes center stage in any debate over the ramifications in the Middle East regarding this occupation.

Journal Articles through the Web

http://cosmos.ucc.ie/cs1064/jabowen/IPSC/php/art.php?aid=37542

The Nation. "Ferment Over 'The Israel Lobby'" by Philip Weiss, April 27, 2006. The topics addressed in this article are: United States politics—lobbying the United States Congress; political influence; Anti-Semitism and its political uses; Zionist tactics to suppress criticism of Israel. Comments are offered by a number of distinguished writers and academics: Noam Chomsky, Francis Fukuyama, Alan Dershowitz, and Charles Krauthammer, to name a few.

http://www.cnsnews.com/

CNS News.com (Jerusalem). "Hizballah Says Israeli Resignation Foreshadows Same in Lebanon" by Melanie Hunter, CNS News.com Senior Editor; January 18, 2007. A Lebanese (Hizballah) lawmaker predicted that the Lebanese government would quit, just as Israel's army chief did, because of the Hizballah victory in the summer of 2006. However, there are some people in Lebanon who refuse to see the conflict of 2006 as a victory. Many in Israel were calling for Prime Minister Ehud Olmert and Defense Minister Amir Peretz to resign because they mismanaged the war. The United States is backing Lebanon's Siniora government which is in a power struggle with Hizballah.

http://cosmos.ucc.ie/cs1064/jabowen/IPSC/php/art.php?aid=4668

Common Dreams. "Israeli Abuses the Worst in 35 Years—U.N. Report" by Thalif Deen, November 6, 2003. A United Nations (UN) committee that monitors human rights abuses of Palestinians concluded that the situation in the Israeli-occupied territories of Gaza and the West Bank was the worst ever since 2002. It was argued that Israel felt certain human rights treaties did not apply to the occupied territories and, therefore, Israel indicated it was not required to report to UN bodies on its practices.

Books

International Law and the Administration of Occupied Territories: Two Decades of Israeli Occupation of the West Bank and Gaza Strip by Emma Playfair (Oxford University Press, 1992). 0198252978.

The text consists of essays which emanated from a conference organized to draw attention to legal problems arising from the Israeli occupation of the West Bank. The contributors include internationally renowned experts on international and human rights laws and Palestinian lawyers, who promoted interests of indigenous Palestinians.

The Case for Peace: How the Arab-Israeli Conflict Can Be Resolved by Alan Dershowitz (Wiley, 2005). 0471743178.

The author feels that with Arafat's death and a new Palestinian leadership, prospects for peace are more encouraging. He endorses the "two-state" solution, Israel's withdrawal from Gaza and most of the West Bank, divided sovereignty over Jerusalem, and recognition of Palestinian refugees by Israel without an absolute "right of return."

Myths and Facts: A Guide to the Arab-Israeli Conflict, 2nd edition by Mitchell Geoffrey Bard (American-Israeli Cooperative Enterprise, 2002). 0971294518.

This is a pro-Israel account, but not necessarily one-sided. The text of twenty-five chapters breaks up the Arab-Israeli Conflict into easily readable pieces. Chapters include data on Jewish settlements, Jerusalem and human rights in the territories, arms balance, United States-Middle East policy, peace process, and Holocaust denial, and major documents that govern Israel and its relationship with Arab states and the Palestine Liberation Organization (PLO).

Persian Gulf

The Persian Gulf region has experienced wars and major petroleum spillages, and has been a significant area of focus in political and economic news. This region is located in Southwest Asia and is an extension of the Gulf of Oman between Iran (historically called Persia) and the Arabian Peninsula. Countries with coastlines on the Persian Gulf are Iran, Oman, United Arab Emirates (UAR), Saudi Arabia, Qatar, Bahrain, Kuwait, and Iraq.

From 1980–1988, the Iraq/Iran War consumed the region with each side attacking the other's oil tankers. In 1991, the Persian Gulf was enmeshed in the Persian Gulf War when Iraq invaded Kuwait. Iraq was pushed back in this skirmish. Environmentally, the Persian Gulf is rich with excellent fishing grounds, many coral reefs, abundant pearl oysters, and oil.

http://www.eia.doe.gov/emeu/cabs/pgulf.html

"Persian Gulf Oil and Gas Exports Fact Sheet." The Persian Gulf is also known as the Arabian Gulf. It is a 600 mile long body of water separating Iran from the Arabian Peninsula and is one of the most strategic waterways in the world because of its importance in world oil transportation. There have been and continue to be many territorial disputes between and among the Persian Gulf countries:

1. Iran/Iraq War, 1980–1988;
2. Iraq invasion of Kuwait in 1990;
3. The United Arab Emirates (UAE) and Iran over three islands—Abu Musa, Greater Tunb Island, and Less Tunb Island—all in the Strait of Hormuz.

Iran felt the islands were part of its kingdom, but the UAE regained sovereignty in 2001. This site also discusses the oil and gas reserves in the region.

http://en.wikipedia.org/wiki/Persian_Gulf

The *Wikipedia* section on the Persian Gulf. As with all the *Wikipedia* entries, this site offers a significant amount of background material. It provides geographical information, historical data, including the British residency, oil and gas issues, featured articles, current events, with frequent updated changes. All of the data is offered in many languages, as well.

http://www.pbs.org/wgbh/pages/frontline/gulf/

This site offers an in-depth analysis of the examination of the 1990–1991 Persian Gulf crisis. There is an oral history component presented by twenty major decision-makers, military commanders, Iraqis, and analysts. There are first-hand accounts of soldiers and pilots in the battlefield who were captured by the Iraqis and a discussion of weapons and technology: aircraft, ground systems, munitions, and space operations used in Operation Desert Storm.

http://gulf2000.columbia.edu/
The Gulf/2000 Project site developed at the School of International and Public Affairs (SIPA) at Columbia University in New York City. This site makes available data on the eight countries of the Persian Gulf region: Bahrain, Iran, Iraq, Kuwait, Oman, Qatar, Saudi Arabia, and the United Arab Emirates (UAE).

Journal Articles through the Web

http://www.1.va.gov/gulfwar/page.cfm?pg=6
United States Department of Veterans Affairs. "Gulf War Illnesses"; Journal article summaries; "Research on the Health Status of Gulf War Veterans," 1999. There are five articles provided cited here:

- "Lessons Learned from the Department of Veterans Affairs"
- "Gulf War Veterans' Health Registries, Who is Most Likely to See Evaluation?"
- "Illnesses Among United States Veterans of the Gulf War: A Population-Based Survey of 30,000 Veterans"
- "Mortality Among United States Veterans of the Persian Gulf War"
- "The Postwar Hospitalization Experience of United States Veterans of the Persian Gulf War"

http://www.iranian.ws/cgi-bin/iran_news/exec/view.cgi/2/2675
Persian Journal. "Slavery of Children and Women in Persian Gulf Countries" by Morteza Aminmansour, June 20, 2004. Women were lured with fake promises of lucrative job opportunities, but then forced into sexual exploitation. Women who resisted faced physical assaults. There has been a significant increase of forcing teenage girls (ages 13–17) into prostitution, especially in the United Arab Emirates, Kuwait, Oman, and Qatar. Girls as young as six are forced to work as maids in the United Arab Emirates and Saudi Arabia.

http://www.thenation.com/doc/20061009/lindorff
The Nation. "War Signals?" By Dave Lindorff, October 9, 2006. The author discusses the deployment of a major "strike group" of ships, the nuclear aircraft carrier *Eisenhower*, as well as cruisers, destroyers, and frigates headed for the Persian Gulf, off Iran's western coast. This article raises the issue of preparedness of the Bush Administration for a possible military strike on Iran. This has been a theoretical possibility in the past but, evidently, the movement of these vessels creates a more "active" situation.

Books

Jarhead: A Marine's Chronicle of the Gulf War and Other Battles by Anthony Swofford (Scribner, 2003). 0743235355.

The author provides the first Gulf War memoir by a frontline infantry marine. The marines are called "jarheads." He discusses accounts of boot camp (with physical abuse by his drill instructor), reflections on the myth of the marines, and remembrances of battles. His reason for writing this memoir is to perpetuate the memory of the Americans wounded or killed and the difficulties of American soldiers re-entering civilian life.

War in the Persian Gulf (Reference Library); From Operation Desert Storm to Operation Iraqi Freedom by Laurie Collier Hillstrom (U.X.L., 2004). 0787665622.

This text covers the pre-war events, Operation Desert Shield, the U.S. effort to prevent an Iraqi invasion of Saudi Arabia, and Operation Desert Storm, the conflict that brought about the Iraqi defeat and the liberation of Kuwait. This is a good book for high school students to understand this historical period.

In the Company of Soldiers: A Chronicle of Combat by Rick Atkinson (Henry Holt & Company, 2004). 0805075615.

This is written by a Pulitzer Prize winning author (*An Army at Dawn*). Here he looks at the strategies, personalities, and struggles of waging modern warfare. This focuses on the war in Iraq and reveals aspects of war not often discussed (difficulty getting gas masks, how to pack supplies into tiny kits, and dealing with dust storms).

Puerto Rico Self-Determination

Puerto Rico is also referred to as the Commonwealth of Puerto Rico. It is located in the northeastern Caribbean, east of the Dominican Republic and west of the Virgin Islands. It consists of a main island and smaller ones: Mona, Vieques, and Culebra.

The controversy surrounding this Commonwealth concerns the political relationship with the United States. Those who wish to maintain the status quo indicate that Puerto Rico entered into a voluntary association with the United States. Others feel that Puerto Rico is an unincorporated organized territory of the United States, subject to plenary powers of the United States, and yet others consider Puerto Rico a colony with the right to govern itself as an independent country.

http://veteransforpr.com/documents-navas.htm

This site is the American Veterans Committee for Puerto Rico Self-Determination. "Count All the Votes? How About Puerto Rico?" by William A. Navas, Jr., December 4, 2000. This article was written around the time of the national election of George W. Bush. 80 percent of registered voters went to the polls on November 7, 2000, but they were unable to vote for presidential candidates. Puerto Rico has been a territory of the United States for 102 years, but the residents may not vote for President. The author feels that voting for President should be a fundamental human right of self-determination. Yet, 200,000 Puerto Ricans have served in the military, with 1225 having died. It is the author's hope that true self-determination can be achieved by his people.

http://en.wikipedia.org/wiki/Puerto_Rico

The *Wikipedia* offers a very good summary of the background of Puerto Rico under U.S. rule, its pre-Columbian historical era, with the Spanish arrival, the demographics of the people (education, languages, religion), politics (its status and international law), economy, culture, sports, and ready-reference fact sheet. Maps are provided which show both the geography and geology of the island.

http://www.puertorico-herald.org/issues/vol2n08/GOP-SEN-QA.shtml

Puerto Rico Herald. "Answers to Frequently Asked Questions about Puerto Rico Self-Determination." Puerto Rico has the highest voter registration of any state (98 percent) and highest Election Day turn-out (80 percent), yet the people are denied voting representation in the national Congress. They are not shielded from various acts of discrimination. Puerto Rico has had territorial status longer than any other American territory without becoming independent (Philippines) or a state (Alaska, Hawaii). In

1993 only 48.6 percent of Puerto Rico's population favored Commonwealth status. The American taxpayer continues to subsidize Puerto Rico's Commonwealth at $43 billion a year.

This site evidently supports full self-government for Puerto Rico. On the site is also a discussion between being independent or becoming a free association. The latter would mean that the associated state would not have a guarantee of permanent ties with the United States.

Journal Articles through the Web

http://findarticles.com/p/articles/mi_m1282/is_n20_v49/ai_19973504

National Review. "Controversy-Defense of Puerto Rico's Right to Self-Determination" by Carlos Romero-Barcelo, October 27, 1997. The author is the Resident Commissioner for Puerto Rico in the U.S. House of Representatives. He speaks of the lengthy time Puerto Rico has remained a colony with its history of peace, commitment to democracy, and political tolerance. He also mentions the fact that Puerto Rican citizens have fought in two World Wars and in other conflicts. There was also the indication that every U.S. president since Truman (up until now) supported self-determination.

http://www.findarticles.com/p/articles/mi_m1282/is_n21_v49/ai_19987389

National Review. "Buying Statehood-Puerto Rico" by Ramesh Ponnuru, November 10, 1997. The article concerns the bill H.R.-856, the United States-Puerto Rico Political Status Act. The bill was sponsored by eighty-seven representatives and would have Puerto Ricans decide in a referendum about whether Puerto Rico should remain a Commonwealth, become the 51st state, or declare independence.

http://www.letpuertoricodecide.com/blog/archives/000018.php

"Let Puerto Rico Decide," Project of Citizen's Educational Foundation, United States, August 4, 2004—Status and Language. This blog discusses the issue of culture and language having little to do with Puerto Rico's political status. The issue is whether to become fully bilingual. Some feel that speaking English will dilute "Puerto Ricanhood." Yet, the U.S. Spanish-speaking population continues to grow. Thus, Puerto Ricans should not have to make a choice of language when confronting political status. However, when considering self-determination, there must be a voting process. If Puerto Rico chooses statehood, they will have the rights and responsibilities of any citizen living in the United States. Languages enrich a person and being bilingual would seem to enhance the Puerto Rican culture.

Books

Colonial Subjects: Puerto Ricans in a Global Perspective by Ramon Grosfoguel (University of California Press, 2003). 0520230213.

This book offers an approach to nationalism, colonialism, capitalism, and to citizenship.

Pay to the Order of Puerto Rico: The Cost of Dependence by Alexander Odishelidze and Arthur Laffer (Allegiance Press, 2004). 159467289X.

The authors support freedom for Puerto Rico and its people. They indicate that tax payer subsidies to Puerto Rico are costing every U.S. taxpayer $400 per person per year. The United States is not subsidizing the Government of Puerto Rico but providing tax breaks for many U.S. leading corporations and drug companies that have operations in Puerto Rico. Despite the subsidies the percentage of Puerto Ricans below poverty level is just under 50 percent. This is in sharp contrast to the poorest state in the United States and Puerto Ricans remain subjects, not full participants in the democratic process.

America's Colony: The Political and Cultural Conflict Between the United States and Puerto Rico by Pedro A. Malavet (New York University Press, 2004). 0814756808.

The author critiques Puerto Rico's current status as well as the treatment by the U.S. legal and political systems. The Puerto Ricans are presently the largest group of U.S. citizens living under territorial status. Malavet argues that Puerto Rico experiences U.S. imperialism which compromises the island's sovereignty and Puerto Ricans' citizenship rights. He analyzes alternatives to Puerto Rico's present status and what would be the best course of action.

United States-Mexican Border Dispute

This dispute has been a focus in the news for both political and economic reasons. Data from the *Jurist*, a University of Pittsburgh School of Law Journal, reported on October 9, 2006, that Mexico may ask the United Nations to intervene in the U.S. border fence issue. Evidently, legal experts are trying to determine the legality of the U.S. Secure Fence Act of 2006. The Mexican Foreign Secretary Luis Ernesto Derbez said, "It was a shame the United States Government was using the creation of a border fence for short term political gain, rather than addressing the real concerns between the neighboring countries."[1] The Mexican Government requested that President George W. Bush veto the bill which would construct a 700 mile fence. Mexico feels the border fence would harm U.S. relations with Mexico.

There is an Anti-Immigration Movement which is linked to racist hate groups. The Movement wants to prevent illegal immigration along the United States–Mexican border. This Movement was inspired by the Minuteman Project, which has chapters in at least eighteen states. These groups have been accused of vigilantism since they urged members to bring baseball bats, mace, pepper spray, and machetes to patrol the border. The Department of Homeland Security does not want to enlist any civilian volunteers to patrol the nation's borders.

The Southern Poverty Law Center, a group that monitors activities of extremist and hate groups and is supported by private donations, tracks this Movement's activities and launched an e-newsletter about the increase in extremism and anti-immigration sentiment. For further information, see The Southern Poverty Law Center-Intelligence Project site, http://www.splcenter.org/intel/intpro.jsp.

In order to pursue ongoing information about this topic the following two sites would be most helpful: NPR.org, http://www.npr.org/templates/story/story.php?storyId=6381764; and *Jurist Legal News and Research*, http://jurist.law.pitt.edu/jurist_search.php?q=us%20and%20mexico%20border

http://www.adl.org/PresRele/Extremism_72/4255_72.asp

Anti-Defamation League (ADL). "ADL Says Armed Anti-Immigration Groups in Arizona Share Ties to White Supremacists," April 2005. Extremist groups along the Arizona-Mexican border use radical tactics, that is, armed vigilante action to promote their anti-immigration stance. The anti-immigration groups are associated with both white supremacists and anti-Semitic groups. One of these groups calls itself "Ranch Rescue" and its mission is referred to as "Operation Hawk."

http://news.yahoo.com/2/ap/20061010/ap_on_re_la_am_ca/
   mexico_us_border_fence

Yahoo News. "Mexico May Take Fence Dispute to U.N." by Jenny Barchfield, Associated Press Writer, October 9, 2006. The Mexican Government sent a note to Washington criticizing its plan for the 700 miles of fencing along the border with Mexico. However, the President of Mexico, Calderon, also denounced the plan but felt it was a bilateral issue that should not come before the international group (United Nations). Mexico's Foreign Secretary, Derbez, believes this is a political ploy by the Bush Administration before the mid-term election.

http://news.bbc.co.uk/1/hi/world/americas/5040372.stm

BBC News. "Web Users to 'Patrol' U.S. Border." Texas will enlist web users in its fight against illegal immigration by offering live surveillance footage of the Mexican border on the Internet. This would enable viewers to call authorities, free of charge, if they spot illegal crossings. The cameras will cost $5 million to install and be located on sections of the 1000 mile border.

Journal Articles through the Web

http://www.watsoninstitute.org/news_detail.cfm?id=16

The Watson Institute for International Studies-Brown University. This article that emanated from the Institute indicated that before September 11, 2001, United States/Mexico trade tripled between 1993–2000 from $85 billion to $263 billion, making Mexico America's second most important trading partner. Therefore, the Mexican President Vincente Fox, wanted to keep borders open for migrant labor and the creation of a North American community. After September 11, border patrols are back significantly with a new U.S. policy debate over immigration, homeland defense, and security.

http://www.siouxcityjournal.com/articles/2005/07/15/news/latest_news/
  d550344d83d9c1a78625703f00130779.txt

Sioux City Journal. "Border Security to Top Agenda as United States, Mexican Border Governors Meet in Northern Mexico," October 17, 2006. Governors of California, Texas, and six Mexican border states planned to work together to fight drug violence in border communities. Texas allocated over $5 million for law enforcement at the border. They plan to share information on gangs and install emergency response equipment in case of terrorist attack, chemical spill, or natural disaster.

http://www.journalstar.com/articles/2004/03/07/nation/10046371.txt

JournalStar.com, Lincoln, Nebraska. "Bush, Fox Spat," October 17, 2006. President George W. Bush had pledged to exempt frequent Mexican visitors from security checks at the U.S. border. This meeting took place before the 2004 election and was seen as a political maneuver to gain favor with the Hispanic/American community. Immigration issues were foremost on President Vincente Fox's mind. He was hoping that illegal immigrants from Mexico, and already working in the United States, would be granted temporary visas.

http://www.cato.org/dailys/08-15-01.html

Cato Institute publication. "House Vote Erects Roadblock to United States–Mexican Trade" by Daniel T. Griswold, August 15, 2001. The U.S. House of Representatives voted to keep Mexican-owned trucks off U.S. highways. It was an effort by the House to protect the Teamsters union from competition and to protect American consumers and producers from lower prices. NAFTA (North American Free Trade Agreement), enacted in 1993, was supposed to open the border to trucking. This ban on cross-border trucking imposes a real cost on both countries, wastes time and manpower to offload trucks, and disrupts business planning.

Books

Operation Gatekeeper: The Rise of the "Illegal Alien" and the Making of the U.S.–Mexico Boundary by Joseph Nevins (Routledge, UK, 2001). 0415931053.

Operation Gatekeeper was launched in 1994 for the United States to gain control of the United States–Mexican border. The author discusses how the effort has failed to significantly reduce unauthorized immigration, contributed to hardships, and death. At issue is how to keep third world immigrants out of developed nations.

Illegals: The Imminent Threat Posed By Our Unsecured U.S.-Mexico Border by Jon E. Dougherty (Nelson Current, 2004). 0785262369.

The author is an investigative journalist who has looked into how indiscriminate immigration is affecting culture and society. He interviewed Border Patrol Agents, local residents, citizen enforcement groups, and immigrants themselves. The author examined the dangers of our "reckless attitude" toward admittance. He felt everyone is threatened by drug lords and terrorism, and political and social turmoil on the U.S.–Mexican border.

Immigration's Unarmed Invasion: Deadly Consequences by Frosty Wooldridge (Authorhouse, 2004). 1418463868.

Over 2000 immigrants are apprehended daily in a specific 260 mile stretch of the Arizona border. Between 1970 and 2000, over 50 million immigrants have come to the United States illegally. The book explains how this illegal immigration affects Americans and why we must regain control by enforcing our laws so that America does not decline into second rate status. The author is also concerned about overpopulation.

Whatever It Takes: Illegal Immigration, Border-Security and the War on Terror by J.D. Hayworth (Regnery Publishing, 2006). 089526028X.

The author is a conservative Arizona congressman. He is very concerned that illegal immigrants take advantage of health and education benefits. He also feels illegal immigrants are hastening the downfall of the Social Security System, and taking jobs away from American workers. This is an irate approach to the illegal immigration problems, but important to include in this listing to have another perspective on this troubling situation.

Note

1. http://jurist.law.pitt.edu/paperchase/2006/10/mexico-may-seek-un-intervention-in-us.php

History

Apartheid in South Africa

Cyprus Dispute

Genocide

Holocaust Revisionism

Roswell UFO Incident

Unidentified Flying Objects (UFOs)

White Supremacy

Apartheid in South Africa

South Africa was colonized by the English and Dutch in the seventeenth century. The Dutch descendents (Boers and Afrikaners) were dominated by the English. Around 1900 the Boer War was fought over diamonds found in the Dutch areas of Transvaal and the Orange Free State. The National Party in the1940s, after independence from England, invented apartheid to obtain control over the economic and social system. The goal was to effect white domination and extend racial separation and political repression. This form of racial discrimination was instituted officially in 1948. Prohibitions were many, including no marriage between non-whites and whites, and "white only" jobs. The population was divided into three categories: white, black (African), or colored (mixed descent). Dissent, disruptions, and states of emergency existed until 1990 when F. W. deKlerk became president and lifted the ban on the leading anti-Apartheid group, the African National Congress. He also released Nelson Mandela from jail. In 1993, both deKlerk and Mandela received the Nobel Peace Prize for the termination of the Apartheid regime.

http://www.un.org/av/photo/subjects/apartheid.htm
"Human Rights—Historical Images of Apartheid in South Africa." This site gives a clear, short historical account of the Apartheid situation in South Africa, with accompanying photos and side bar descriptions of each of the photos. These photos are part of the United Nations photo archive collection.

http://africanhistory.about.com/library/bl/blsalaws.htm
This site presents a review of Apartheid legislation in South Africa. The Nationalist Government in South Africa enacted laws in 1948 to define and enforce segregation. Summarized at this site are all the major laws enacted from 1949 through the 1970s. Related articles are also provided from the Apartheid era which furthers the discussion of this period of time in South Africa.

http://www.hrw.org/reports/2000/safrica/Sarfio00–01.htm
This site discusses the Armaments Corporation of South Africa (Armscor) which was given the task in 1968 to develop and produce armaments. Today it is housed with the Ministry of Defense to deal with its expanded activities. Armscor was formed because South Africa was hit by an international arms embargo during the Apartheid era. It needed to circumvent the sanctions. By 1994, South Africa was the tenth largest arms producer in the world.

Journal Articles through the Web

http://www.jcu.edu.au/aff/history/articles/limb.htm

The Electronic Journal of Australia and New Zealand History. "An Australian Historian at the Dawn of Apartheid: Fred Alexander in South Africa, 1949–1950" by Peter Limb/University of Western Australia. This article summarizes Australia's relations with South Africa during the Apartheid era. There was military involvement and conflict over Apartheid. The article reviews the relationship of these two areas from the 1600s through Apartheid. The historian, Fred Alexander, interacted with the Afrikaners. He was very critical of the Apartheid movement and wrote of the growing signs of assertive African nationalism. He continually spoke of constitutional change and racial segregation in South Africa in various radio talks and he discussed the intensity of the black resistance led by the African National Congress.

http://www.findarticles.com/p/articles/mi_m1282/is_v37/ai_3968314

National Review. "Relatively Speaking—Apartheid in South Africa" by Brian Crozier, October 4, 1985. The author speaks of his abhorrence of the situation in South Africa with the ban on mixed marriages, ban on black unions, and on black ownership of property, yet he feels that Botha's reforming government was discontinuing these procedures. However, the author also feels that separate developments and communities would not be so bad—like having separate homelands for Basques in Spain and France or making Northern Irish Protestants a minority in a united Ireland.

http://www.africaaction.org/docs03/rep0302.htm

Africa Policy E-Journal. "South Africa: Apartheid Reparations Update," February 24, 2003. This article contains information on various reparations lawsuits against U.S. companies for complicity in slavery and the slave trade. The essence is that corporations and banks were aiding and abetting Apartheid. Complaints named seven banks and thirteen international corporations from Germany, Switzerland, Great Britain, the United States, the Netherlands, and France. In these law suits, South Africans expressed their commitments to Apartheid's victims, to protection of human rights, and to the rule of law.

Books

The Making of Modern South Africa: Conquest, Segregation and Apartheid by Nigel Worden (Blackwell Publishing, Inc., 2000).
0631216618.

This is the third edition in which the author presents an introduction to the key themes and debates that are central to understanding South Africa. The book examines the major issues of South Africa's history—from colonial conquests of the eighteenth and nineteenth centuries through the establishment of racism, segregation and Apartheid, reform resistance, and repression of the 1980s to the present.

Kaffir Boy: An Autobiography—The True Story of a Black Youth's Coming of Age in Apartheid South Africa by Mark Mathabane (Free Press, 1998). 0684848287.

The young writer makes the reader feel intensely about the horrors of Apartheid. He grew up in a shanty town outside Johannesburg and endured the hopelessness of poverty and violence of sadistic police and gangs. The author taught himself to read English and play tennis, and through Stan Smith, the tennis star, obtained a tennis scholarship through a South Carolina college. He is now a freelance writer in New York.

No Future Without Forgiveness by Desmond Tutu (Image, 2000). 0385496907.

Desmond Tutu and Nelson Mandela were the two most significant people who worked through the struggles to end Apartheid in South Africa. Tutu was the Archbishop of Cape Town throughout the 1980s and was awarded the Nobel Peace Prize in 1984. He became Chair of the Truth and Reconciliation Commission in 1995. This Commission was an attempt by South Africans to come to terms with the violations of human rights through offering amnesty and forgiveness rather than punishment and dismissal. The book is Tutu's personal memoir as Chair of this Commission.

Long Walk to Freedom: The Autobiography of Nelson Mandela by Nelson Mandela (Black Bay Books, 1995). 0316548189.

Much of this book was written secretly while Mandela was imprisoned for twenty-seven years. Mandela discusses his ambivalence toward his lifetime of devotion to public works, since it cost him two marriages and kept him distant from a family life he would have cherished. The book reveals his struggles, setbacks, renewed hope, and ultimate triumphs.

Cyprus Dispute

This refers to the conflict between Greek Cypriots and Turkish Cypriots and the Republic of Cyprus and Turkey over Cyprus, which is an island in the eastern Mediterranean Sea. The Cyprus dispute has involved not only Turkey and Greece, but the United Kingdom, the United Nations, and recently the European Union.

Since 1974, the island has been divided into the internationally recognized Republic of Cyprus in the South and the Turkish Republic of Northern Cyprus (recognized only by Turkey) in the North.

http://en.wikipedia.org/wiki/Cyprus_dispute

The *Wikipedia* site has a wealth of information on this issue. There is much historical content with the background prior to 1960. There is the constitutional breakdown from 1960–1974, followed by peace-making efforts. The United Nations has a plan for reunification. Also presented are the issues from the perspectives of the Republic of Cyprus and the Turkish Republic of Northern Cyprus.

http://www.foreignminister.gov.au/releases/2004/fa046_04.html

Statement of Minister for Foreign Affairs, Australia, the Honorable Alexander Downer. "Progress in Cyprus Dispute," April 2, 2004. The author was pleased with the UN Secretary General's plan to settle the Cyprus dispute. The plan was presented to the leaders of the Greek Cypriot and Turkish Cypriot communities and the Greek and Turkish governments. The UN Secretary General's plan calls for a federal government composed of two constituent states, each largely running its own affairs. The reason why there was interest by Australia in this effort is that Australia has maintained a police presence on Cyprus since 1964 and they have a Special Envoy to Cyprus. Alexander Downer was hoping that the two communities would seize this opportunity to achieve a lasting, peaceful settlement.

http://www.ntvmsnbc.com/news/380120.asp

MSNBC site. "US Backs Efforts to Resolve Cyprus Dispute: Bryza" by Matthew Bryza. The Senior State Department official, Byrza, praised the willingness of the Turkish Cypriot President and the Greek Cypriot leader to resume contacts. He indicated that it was the policy of the United States to support the United Nation's endeavors and to end isolation of the Turkish Cypriots, as well. He also felt that it was the duty of the European Union (EU) to also make progress on this issue.

Journal Articles through the Web

http://www.ecmi.de/jemie/download/Focus2-2002_Oguzlu.pdf

Journal on Ethnopolitics and Minority Issues in Europe. "The EU as an Actor in the Solution of the Cyprus Dispute: The Questions of 'How'?"

by H. Tarik Oguzlu, February 2002. The author has indicated that despite optimism of the international community, the accession process of the Republic of Cyprus with the European Union (EU) has only perpetuated the conflict. The author further argued that the dangers of EU membership of a divided Cyprus would far outweigh the benefits. He feels the EU should adopt a new approach—the active support of the European countries to the EU membership of a loosely centralized federal Cyprus.

http://www.findarticles.com/p/articles/mi_qa3923/is_200505/ai_n14717701

Dispute Resolution Journal. "Letters from Cyprus: Notes from a Deeply Divided Island" by Edward Costello, May–July 2005. The author serves on the American Arbitration Association panel and went to Cyprus for six months. He offered his impressions of life in Cyprus. The day to day life seems to be dominated by the fact of partition. There are only a few places where one can cross the Green Line between Turkish and Greek communities. There is a buffer zone staffed by UN peacekeepers. The author also speaks of a psychological separation, not just a physical one. Religion has been another factor in the separation of the communities. Most of the citizens of the Republic of Cyprus belong to the Greek Orthodox Church. Islam is the main religion of most citizens of the Turkish republic. There is also a small group of Maronite Catholics who live in Southern Cyprus.

http://sdi.sagepub.com/cgi/content/abstract/36/2/175

Sage Publications, *Security Dialogue.* "Assessing the Conflict Resolution Potential of the EU: The Cyprus Conflict and Accession Negotiations" by Doga Ulas Eralp, Vol. 36, No. 2, pp. 175–192, 2005. This article shows the changes in the roles the EU has played on the island of Cyprus within the context of accession negotiations. The author describes the consequences of EU involvement on UN-led negotiation efforts. He feels the EU has not been terribly effective in its foreign policy making efforts on behalf of the Cyprus dispute situation. The EU has produced inefficient policies. The EU needs more vision-building in the process of helping to settle the dispute.

Books

Cyprus: A Troubled Island by Andrew Borowiec (Praeger Publishers, 2000). 0275965333.

The author reports that there was never a "Cypriot Nation"--only Greeks and Turks living in Cyprus, and separated by the hostility reflecting the traditional animosity between their motherlands. The author traces the history of Cyprus from Antiquity through Ottoman and British colonial rule and post-independence. He speaks of the break of the communities in 1963, United Nations intervention in 1964, and the Athens' coup in 1974. The author pays much attention to the two separate economic and political entities on the island.

Imagining the Modern: The Cultures of Nationalism in Cyprus by
Rebecca Bryant (I.B. Tauris & Co., 2004). 185043462X.

This book poses the argument that the two conflicting styles of nationalist imagination led to the violence in Cyprus in 1974. This book demonstrates how the conflict emerged through Cypriot's encounters with modernity under British colonialism. The author further describes how Muslims and Christians in Cyprus were transformed into Turks and Greeks.

Embracing Cyprus: The Path to Unity in the New Europe by Pauline
Green and Ray Collins (I.B. Tauris, 2002). 1860648401.

When Turkish forces invaded the island in 1974 and the Archbishop Makarios was toppled as president, few people saw Cyprus as part of the drive to create a new Europe. Yet, the authors feel there is a growing view among Greek and Turkish Cypriots that the solution to Cyprus' problem lies within Europe, that the Cyprus dispute can only be resolved by embedding Cyprus within Europe.

Genocide

The following basic definition of genocide is from the *Wikipedia*: "Genocide is a term defined by Article 2 of the Convention on the Prevention and Punishment of the Crime of Genocide as 'any of the following acts committed with intent to destroy, in whole or in part, a national, ethnic, racial, or religious group, as such; killing members of the group; causing serious bodily or mental harm to members of the group; deliberately inflicting on the group conditions of life, calculated to bring about its physical destruction in whole or in part; imposing measures intended to prevent births within the group; and forcibly transferring children of the group to another group.'"[1]

http://en.wikipedia.org/wiki/Genocide

The *Wikipedia* site offers much information on this topic, including data on the prosecution of genocide at the Nuremberg Trials, in the former Yugoslavia, in Rwanda and Darfur. The site further provides information on genocide in history and stages of genocide with accompanying efforts to prevent it. The term genocide was coined by Ralph Lemkin, a Polish-Jewish legal scholar, in 1943 during the period of the Holocaust. The term was found in his book, *Axis Rule in Occupied Europe*. It is a work of legal analysis of Nazi German rule in countries that were occupied during World War II.

http://www.ess.uwe.ac.uk/genocide.htm

"Web Genocide Documentation Center." This site contains resources on genocide, war crimes, and mass killing. There are many links to areas of genocide in the world, including Armenian genocide, Third Reich, Cambodia, East Timor, Jewish Holocaust, Kosovo, Macedonia, Poland-Third Reich, Rwanda and Burundi, Sierra Leone, Yugoslav Wars, plus information on Euthanasia, Nazi occupation policies and war criminals.

http://www.genocidewatch.org/

"Genocide Watch." This site has articles by the founder and Chair of the International Campaign to End Genocide, Gregory H. Stanton, President of Genocide Watch—founded in The Hague, Netherlands, May 1999. There are links to the International Campaign to End Genocide Member Organizations; What is Genocide; the Eight Stages of Genocide; Genocides and Politicides since 1945 with stages in 2006; Documents about Genocide from 1998–2006; Genocide Emergency in Darfur, Sudan; Judgment on Genocide in Sudan; Genocide Warning in Chad, in Ethiopian Anuak, in Zimbabwe; Genocide Watch in Burma (Myanmar), in Uzbekistan; and Data on the Cambodian Genocide Project, plus the Armenian Genocide Denial.

Journal Articles through the Web

http://www.ideajournal.com/articles.php?id=38

Idea Journal. "Report of the International Commission of Inquiry on Darfur: A Critical Analysis" by Eric Reeves, Vol. 10, No. 1, October 14, 2005. This report offers a compelling picture of massive criminality in the Darfur conflict and establishes the blame on Khartoum's regular military forces and the Janjaweed militias' allies. The author also speaks of the scale of atrocities, the killing, displacement, and rapes that have targeted only the African tribes.

http://findarticles.com/p/articles/mi_hb3376/is_200001/ai_n8114843

Prooftexts: A Journal of Jewish Literary History. "Gender, Genocide and Jewish Memory" by Sara R. Horowitz, January 2000. This is the study of women in the Shoah (an emergent area of inquiry). The article reflects the concern of gender-based differences. It focuses on the experiences of or writing of women and their representations in postwar reflections. However, the author feels ideas about gender are important to Jewish representations of genocide and atrocity. She points to ways that women and men under atrocity are depicted in classic rabbinic texts, in their depiction in ghetto diaries, and in Holocaust fiction.

http://arts.monash.edu.au/eras/edition_1/harris.htm

Monash University, *ERAS Journal.* Edition 1 "Defining Genocide: Defining History?" by Deborah Harris (Melbourne University, 2001). The author discusses the debate on the appropriate definition of genocide. Scholars attempt to understand the most extreme of crimes. She feels that the specific definition of genocide has the "power to influence how the history of genocide is written." The article examines the strengths and weaknesses of the many approaches to understanding genocide. The author's definition of genocide is a "one-sided attempt by a state or other authority to destroy a specific victim group, as that group and membership in it are defined by the perpetrator."

Books

Genocide in International Law: The Crimes of Crimes by William A.
   Schabas (Cambridge University Press, 2000). 0521787904.

The author gives detailed attention to the concept of protected groups, the dimension of genocide, problems of criminal prosecution, and the issues of international judicial cooperation such as extradition. He also explores the duty to prevent genocide and the consequences that might have on the emerging law of humanitarian intervention.

The Specter of Genocide: Mass Murder in Historical Perspective edited
   by Robert Gellately and Bon Kiernan (Cambridge University Press,
   2003). 0521527503.

This book appears to be a good starting point for those who wish to learn more about the complexities of the genocide debate. The editors, who are historians at Clark and Yale Universities, have selected a number of academics who present theories and case studies focusing on the fifty-five years since the United Nations genocide convention was adopted.

A Century of Genocide: Utopias of Race and Nation by Eric D. Weitz (Princeton University Press, 2005). 0691122717.

The author is a history professor at the University of Minnesota. He offers a comparative study of four of the past century's genocidal regimes: Stalin's Soviet Union, Nazi Germany, Cambodia under Pol Pot, and Bosnia in the 1990s. He blames much of the genocides on the growth of nationalism and racism. This work raises many questions about the human capacity for violence.

Note

1. http://en.wikipedia.org/wiki/Genocide

Holocaust Revisionism

The essence of this issue is that those who are Holocaust revisionists believe that the genocide of the Jews during World War II did not occur. These people reject the ideas that the Nazi government targeted Jews and/or those of Jewish ancestry, homosexuals, the gypsies, and others for extermination, or that six million Jews were systematically killed or that tools of mass extermination, such as the gas chambers were used in extermination camps to kill the Jews. These Holocaust deniers also feel that the issue of the Holocaust is a Jewish conspiracy used to advance the interest of the Jews at other peoples' expense. The discussion of the Holocaust issue has remained illegal in many European countries because it is thought to be motivated by an anti-Semitic agenda.

The Iranians hosted a conference of Holocaust deniers in Tehran in December 2006. This conference was backed by Iranian President Mahmoud Ahmadinejad, who has referred to the Holocaust as a "myth." The organizers of this conference, the Foreign Ministry's Institute for Political and International Studies, indicated they wanted to provide a forum to discuss "questions" about the Holocaust. They were not seeking to deny the actual occurrence of the Holocaust, but to offer a scientific atmosphere for scholars to provide their opinions.

http://en.wikipedia.org/wiki/Holocaust_denial

The *Wikipedia* site provides extensive background information on Holocaust deniers—their claims and examples of such claims, citing different cases. The site also provides public reactions to Holocaust denial, laws against this denial, other genocide denials, and notable Holocaust deniers and revisionists.

http://www.zundelsite.org/english/basic_articles/nutshell.html

"Holocaust Revisionism in a Nutshell" by Bruce Hagen. This site professes to render the Holocaust revisionists and deniers as holocaust "diminishers." The latter question what they feel are major exaggerations in the Holocaust. The revisionists do not deny that many Jews suffered during World War II and had property confiscated, that many died of disease or starvation, and that there were some atrocities. The revisionists feel there were atrocities on all sides: Hiroshima and Nagasaki were bombed, as was Dresden. In addition, the revisionists also claim there were no gas chambers and that the testimonies by survivors were false and preposterous.

http://www.nizkor.org/

The Nizkor Project—This Project is dedicated to twelve million Holocaust victims who suffered and died. The site offers research guides on the concentration camps, special features including Questions and Answers on the Holocaust, techniques of Holocaust deniers, the Trial of Adolph Eichmann, and people who were prominent as both deniers and those who suffered. There is also a special section of all the concentration camps, on the Nuremberg Trials, and on organizations in various countries dedicating themselves to the perpetuation of the Holocaust memory.

Journal Articles through the Web

http://www.questia.com/PM.qst?a=o&d=5002321331&er=deny

The Atlantic Monthly. "Holocaust on Trial: A Controversial British Writer, David Irving, has Instigated a Libel Suit Against an American Historian (for Denying the Holocaust)" by D.D. Guttenplan, Vol. 283, February, 2000. The author appears to be a Holocaust denier, himself. He has indicated that what people seem to believe about the Holocaust is not true. He indicates that most stories are fabrications, like Allied propaganda during World War I. He also indicated that Dachau concentration camp did have a gas chamber but it was never used and there were no gas chambers at Belsen.

http://www.questia.com/PM.qst?a=o&d=5000715635&er=deny

The Australian Journal of Politics and History. "Forgetting the Fuhrer: The Recent History of the Holocaust Denial Movement in Germany" by Anthony Long, Vol. 48, 2002. In the 1970s, Holocaust denial became the propaganda of the far right. Most works written, among them Arthur Butz's *The Hoax of the Twentieth Century* and Richard Harwood's *Did Six Million Really Die?,* are still considered important works by many on the far right. Such works claim that the crimes were never committed. This article examines several German Holocaust deniers since 1988, plus events that shaped the nature of Holocaust denial in Germany during this period.

http://www.adl.org/Braun/dim_14_1_deniers.asp

Dimensions: A Journal of Holocaust Studies, published by the Anti-Defamation League's Braun Holocaust Institute. "Deniers, Relativists and Pseudo-Scholarship" by Deborah E. Lipstadt. The author claims that deniers are motivated by racism, extremism, and virulent anti-Semitism. In denying the Holocaust, the deniers mix truth with falsehood and half-truths. When deniers say that war is evil, they are talking generally about World War II. Some deniers feel Hitler was a man of peace, forced into the war by the aggressive Allies and that the Germans were the true victims of the war. They suffered the bombings, starvation, invasion, and being dislocated after the war. The author makes note of the fact that the deniers charge of genocide was a Jewish invention, that the Germans transferred populations (deportations) to resolve social, economic, and labor problems.

This is an excellent, and rather lengthy article, but important to read to understand the Holocaust deniers within the total context of historical perspectives.

http://www.ynetnews.com/articles/0,7340,L-3354347,00.html

Ynetnews.com. "Iran Exiles Slam Holocaust Deniers," January 19, 2007. More than 100 Iranian activists worldwide signed a statement condemning the conference in Tehran that questioned the occurrence of the Holocaust. They indicated that the Iranian government "distorted the facts," even though they have diverse views on the Israeli-Palestinian conflict. Most of the signers have Muslim backgrounds.

Books

Denying History: Who Says the Holocaust Never Happened and Why Do They Say It? by Michael Shermer and Alex Grobman (University of California Press, 2002). 0520234693.

This book explores the motivations behind the claims of the Holocaust deniers. The authors conducted interviews with the deniers, read their works, monitored their websites, attended their conferences, debated with them, and traveled through Europe to conduct research at the concentration camps. The authors try to understand the motives of the deniers and refute their points.

Holocaust Denial by John C. Zimmerman (University Press of America, 2000). 0761818227.

This author examines the underlying arguments of Holocaust deniers. He delves into their methodology, use of sources, and their reasoning process. This text enables the reader to evaluate the legitimacy of the deniers' arguments.

Selling the Holocaust: From Auschwitz to Schindler: How History Is Bought, Packaged, and Sold by Tim Cole (Routledge, 2000). 0415928133.

The author reflects on the public representation of the Holocaust in literature, art, and film. He focuses on three people: Anne Frank, Adolph Eichmann, and Oskar Schindler, and three sites: Auschwitz, Yad Vashem (Israel's Holocaust Museum in Jerusalem), and the United States Holocaust Memorial Museum in Washington, D.C. He fears that the Holocaust has turned into a "virtual" history where people become viewers through media, rather than fully understanding the Holocaust from its actual locations.

The Holocaust on Trial by D.D. Guttenplan (W.W. Norton & Company, 2002). 0393322920.

This is an account of a landmark trial dealing with the controversy over Holocaust denial. In 1977, David Irving, a British historian, wrote a book, *Hitler's War*. This was a work of revisionist claims about the Holocaust. Irving indicated that Hitler was barely aware of the Holocaust. In 1994, an American historian, Deborah Lipstadt, refuted Irving's findings, so Irving sued her for libel. In this book, Guttenplan notes the number of empirical facts as evidence on both sides of the argument, the lack of "witnesses, memories, and testimony" which is an aspect of historical truth.

Roswell UFO Incident

This incident occurred in 1947 in the desert outside of Roswell, New Mexico. On July 3, 1947, a business owner and his wife spotted a bright saucer-shaped object with glowing lights move across the sky at approximately 400–500 m.p.h. The husband believed the object was about 20–25 feet across. Then a ranch owner noticed much unusual debris on his pastures and showed them to his sheriff thinking the debris might be connected to military operations. A commander of a bomb group issued a press release indicating that a crashed disk had been recovered. A nurse was contacted at an army base hospital who said autopsies were performed on non-human (alien) bodies. But the nurse was abruptly transferred to England after that and could not be reached. Subsequent to all the testimonies about the incident, all the witnesses were either transferred to other locations or disappeared. There is suspicion of a government cover-up.

http://www.doomsdayguide.org/UFO/ufo_roswell.htm
This site provides links which examine the various aspects of the Roswell UFO incident: *The Daily Record News* article, July 8, 1947; the UFO incident updated, plus a timeline; the UFO crash in photos; the U.S. Air Force report; cause of the crash; Roswell UFO testimony; autopsy film investigation, and the cover-up.

http://www.americaslibrary.gov/cgi-bin/page.cgi/es/nm/ufo_1
UFO Museum and Research Center. This site describes the efforts of people to contact government agencies about the UFO incident, only to be rebuffed. It seems that the military had been watching a UFO on radar for four days prior to its crash down. Yet, the military tried to convince the news media that what had crashed was a weather balloon. There were a number of efforts by the military subsequent to this incident that were attempts to thwart the investigation and to prevent news reports from getting into the media.

http://www.answers.com/topic/roswell-ufo-incident
Answers.com. "Roswell UFO Incident." The original incident in 1947 was forgotten until 1978 when a reporter interviewed Jesse Marcel, who was involved in the original recovery of all the debris from the crash. Marcel was convinced of a cover-up. Other witnesses and their reports emerged over the next several years, including accounts of a large military operation that recovered alien craft and aliens. There were as many as eleven crash sites. In all of these incidents, witnesses were continually intimidated. This site offers a very thorough accounting of all the events that occurred at the crash site and thereafter.

Journal Articles through the Web

http://www.roswellfiles.com/Articles/RoswellNews.htm

The Roswell Daily Record. "RAAF Captures Flying Saucer on Ranch in Roswell Region," July 8, 1947. This article not only discusses the incident, but also offers links to each of the witnesses, to government reports, and to Freedom of Information Act papers. All of these sources further establish the events that occurred on that day in July and the following "cover-ups" by the military and government.

http://www.findarticles.com/p/articles/mi_qn4182/is_20060516/ai_n16412434

Journal Record (Oklahoma City). "Roswell UFO Festival Takes Off, June 30–July 3" by the *Journal Record* Staff, May 16, 2006. This article was about the 12th Annual Roswell International UFO Festival. People attending this Festival were hoping to seek the truth from UFO researchers about the Roswell UFO incident.

http://www.findarticles.com/p/articles/mi_m2843/is_2_27/ai_98252925

Skeptical Inquirer. "Bait and Switch on 'Roswell: The Smoking Gun'—Special Report—Television Documentary: The Roswell Crash: Startling New Evidence" by David E. Thomas, March–April 2003. This article highlights a new documentary on the Sci Fi Channel. The promotion on this program declared that archeologists from the University of New Mexico, working under top secret conditions, planned to uncover physical evidence to prove whether the Roswell crash was science fiction or fact. However, it seemed that the promotion for the program was an over zealous attempt to get viewers, since the evidence offered and the people interviewed were not credible. Perhaps the "UFO incident" was a hoax. There seems to be no believable evidence to prove that the incident was in fact a crash of a truly alien spacecraft, a weather balloon, or many government cover-ups. Even though the interviews by the "witnesses" were credible, no substantial evidence proves these people saw what they suspected was a UFO.

Books

The Roswell UFO Crash: What They Don't Want You to Know by Kal K. Korff (Dell, 2000). 0440236134.

On the 50th Anniversary of the crash, the author tries to examine one of the most baffling cases of all time. He does uncover information never before published—military records, formerly classified projects, and correspondence. He examined the testimony of all the people who originally witnessed the event. He feels the incident could have been a major military personnel cover-up.

*Roswell UFO Crash Update: Exposing the Military Cover-Up of the Cen-

tury by Kevin D. Randle (Inner Light-Global Communications, 1995). 0938294415.

The author offers disturbing evidence of death threats to witnesses, removal of alien bodies, one extra-terrestrial kept alive at a secret location for a period of time, and scientific findings hidden away for secrecy purposes. This seems to be the inside story of the most famous crash case of all time, written by a full time investigator.

Roswell: Inconvenient Facts and the Will to Believe by Karl T. Pflock and Jerry Pournelle (Prometheus Books, 2001). 1573928941.

Pflock was a former Defense Department official and a CIA intelligence officer. This is a well-documented, well-illustrated case against the 1947 crash being that of an alien spacecraft. He identifies the weak points in supporters' arguments, picks apart ambiguous evidence, re-examines critical testimony, and has decided that it was just wishful thinking that an alien spacecraft crashed. He feels what happened was that a government project called Project Mogul, that involved a weather balloon was the incident in question and that the balloon had gone astray.

Unidentified Flying Objects (UFOs)

This phenomenon is commonly cited as UFOs or flying saucers. They have been identified as possible or actual spacecrafts. Oftentimes, a UFO has actually been a meteor, or disintegrating satellite, a bird or flocks of birds, an aircraft, or a weather balloon. Some descriptions have been glowing wheels, colored balls of light, or disk or crescent-shaped objects. The U.S. government has records of thousands of UFO sightings, including photos and interviews with people who have claimed to have seen them. The reliability of such reports depends on the number of independent witnesses to the object(s).

There are two specific areas of the United States that have been considered to be connected to the UFO phenomenon: Roswell, New Mexico, a topic covered in this section, and Area 51, a remote location in Southern Nevada. Area 51 is owned by the U.S. Department of Defense and the U.S. Air Force. Area 51 contains an airfield that is believed to be where enemy aircraft and weapons systems are analyzed. Some activities attributed to the UFO phenomenon at Area 51 are the examination and storage of crashed alien spacecraft and the study of the occupants of those spacecraft, and the development of time travel technology.

http://en.wikipedia.org/wiki/UFO

Sightings of UFOs date back to ancient times; however, reports of such objects became more frequent after a widely publicized sighting in 1947. The *Wikipedia* site offers a history of past accounts of sightings, research into UFO categorizations, physical evidence of events, various explanations and opinions about sightings by astronomers, or whether reports were hoaxes. The site also reports on conspiracy theories, plus the use of UFOs as themes in film and television productions.

http://www.daviddarling.info/encyclopedia/U/UFOS.html

The Encyclopedia of Astrobiology Astronomy and Spaceflight. This site offers a brief introduction to early sightings, as far back as 1896–1897 with a sighting of "mystery airships." This was during the time when an American astronomer, Percival Lowell, was advocating the existence of an advanced race on Mars. Then, in 1947, Kenneth Arnold saw a "flying saucer." However, this "sighting" and others may have been natural phenomena, unusual clouds, illusions, hoaxes, balloons, or prototype aircraft. This website has many related articles, some skeptical accounts.

http://www.defenselink.mil/faq/pis/16.html

United States Department of Defense-UFOs. The U.S. Air Force began investigating UFOs in 1948 under a program called Project Sign. Then this program name was changed to Project Grudge and changed again in 1953 to Project Blue Book. The latter was terminated in 1969. The conclusions of Project Blue Book were:

1. No UFO reported was considered a threat to national security.
2. No evidence about sightings represented technological developments or principles that were beyond the range of present-day scientific knowledge.
3. No evidence that sightings are extraterrestrial vehicles.

All this documentation is now in the Military Reference Branch of the National Archives and Records Administration in Washington, D.C.

Journal Articles through the Web

http://www.iranian.ws/cgi-bin/iran_news/exec/view.cgi/2/5135
Persian Journal. "UFO Sightings Over Iranian Nuclear Installations," December 26, 2004. Iranians had complained about UFOs at very low altitudes around their nuclear installations, all around their country. The Iranian Air Force assumed they were U.S. spy crafts and the Iranian Air Force was directed to shoot them down.

http://findarticles.com/p/articles/mi_m1430/is_n7_v16/ai_14932640
Omni. "Soviet Saucers-Unidentified Flying Objects in Southern Russia" by James Oberg, April, 1994. In the fall of 1967, the Soviet Union reported many sightings: Cossacks on horseback in the evening sky, pilots on commercial airliners, and military interceptors chased them, and astronomers in the Caucasus Mountains noted their crescent shapes. Then the reports ceased in the controlled media, but appeared in the underground Russian press. Some reports indicated there was a cover-up of illegal space-to-earth nuclear weapons. The author indicated many of the sightings were missile warheads in low orbit.

http://www.findarticles.com/p/articles/mi_m2843/is_5_25/ai_77757756
Skeptical Inquirer. "UFO Believers Sighted in Nation's Capitol!—Unidentified Flying Objects" by Joel Achenbach, September, 2001. A group of believers in UFOs held a news conference in Washington, D.C. on May 9, 2001. They referred to a program called the Disclosure Project, which was an attempt to have the government admit that UFOs are piloted by aliens. Some witnesses told they saw aliens—dead and alive—at the scenes of crashed saucers. There was nothing presented at the news conference that could be considered forensic evidence. Some of the subplots of this meeting were: people believed the Bush Administration wanted to build a missile defense shield as part of its covert war with aliens, and that the oil industry wanted to suppress a secret energy source.

Books

Night Siege: The Hudson Valley UFO Sightings by Dr. J. Allen Hynek (Llewellyn Publications, 2002). 156718362X.

The Hudson Valley Siege occurred New Year's Eve, 1982. Over 7000 sightings were recorded of boomerang-shaped craft or crafts moving silently in the sky over New York and Connecticut between 1982 and 1995. The data in this text was gathered from witnesses. About 900 people wrote out witness forms. However, after an investigation the authors concluded there was no conventional explanation.

The Phoenix Lights: On the Evening of March 13, 1997, A Formation of UFOs Flew Over Phoenix, Arizona. They Were Witnessed by Commercial Pilots, Air Traffic Controllers by Lynn D. Kitei and Paul Perry (Hampton Roads Publishing Company, 2004). 1571743774.

During the night of March 13, 1997, thousands of Arizona residents witnessed a mile-long, v-shaped formation of lights in the sky. This came to the attention of major news outlets. Dr. Kitei had been witnessing this phenomenon for months, so she was pleased to have her observations validated by thousands of people statewide.

UFO Briefing Document: The Best Available Evidence by Don Berliner and Whitley Streiber (Dell, 2000). 044023638X.

This text contains a compilation of compelling and authenticated UFO cases ever recorded. This data is from the government's secret files, spanning a half-century of eyewitness testimony, documented sightings, and unexplained phenomena. The authors believe there has been a major government cover-up.

White Supremacy

This issue concerns the ideology that white people are superior to all other races. This belief is often thought to encompass anti-black racism and anti-Semitism; however, it also focuses on discrimination against Asians, Arabs, Hispanics, Native Americans, and Australian Aboriginals. White supremacists also believe that whites should rule over all other races. This ideology is often associated with ethnic cleansing and total racial separation.

There are a number of white supremacist organizations. Among them are the American Nazi Party, Aryan Brotherhood, Aryan Nations, and the Ku Klux Klan.

http://www.tgia.net/Links/Information_Sites/White_Supremacy/white_supremacy.html

This site has links to the Anti-Defamation League, Gangs and Extremist Groups, Hate Crimes: The State Laws (MSNBC), Hate Watch (Combating Bigotry Online), Southern Poverty Law Center, plus many racist sites, including American Front, American Nazi Party, Aryan Nations, Christian Defense League, Holocaust Revisionist, Jew Watch, National Socialist Movement, and many Ku Klux Klan links, as well.

http://www.geocities.com/white_truth/

This is a White Supremacy site. The issues and concerns raised here involve white survival. The data offered indicate that other races are multiplying faster than the white race. There is also a concern that every race needs a homeland, that multiculturalism and diversity are good; however, the comments on this site reflect the fear that whites are being phased out and being brainwashed about the richness of diverse cultures.

http://www.publiceye.org/eyes/whitsup.html

Public Eye Organization—Political Research Associates. "White Supremacy in the 1990s" by Loretta Ross. The author contends that the progress made by the Civil Rights Movement in the 1960s is slowly eroding, that there have been many incidents of anti-Semitism, homophobia, and violence against women. Her concern is that intolerance is gaining as the white supremacist ideologies are becoming part of our life. This article reveals the strategies of white supremacist organizations. The author's goal is to create an awareness of this situation.

http://en.wikipedia.org/wiki/White_supremacy

The *Wikipedia* site offers a thorough introduction and overview of this topic: the history of the movement from the eighteenth century forward, contemporary white supremacist ideologies, contemporary white supremacist groups, violent actions, lists of white supremacists by country, and a listing of all the white supremacist organizations.

Journal Articles through the Web

http://jbs.sagepub.com/cgi/content/abstract/33/2/179
   Journal of Black Studies. "An African-Centered Perspective on White Supremacy" by Mark Christian, Vol. 33, No. 2, pp. 179–198, 2002. This article reveals the nature of white supremacy as it is operated in the United States and the United Kingdom. The existence of white supremacy marginalizes African people within both societies.

http://www.bizjournals.com/phoenix/stories/2006/09/25/daily52.html
   The Business Journal of Phoenix. "White Supremacist Group Distributes Flyers in Scottsdale" by Mike Sunnucks, September 29, 2006. The white supremacist group that is distributing flyers opposes immigration and accuses the media, business, and political establishments of being antiwhite. This group calls for racial segregation and supports a boycott of Home Depot because of the Hispanic day laborers who congregate near the stores looking for contracting work. The group, called the National Vanguard, has a chapter in Tempe, Arizona, and espouses negative views toward Hispanics, blacks, Jews, and gays.

http://cosmos.ucc.ie/cs1064/jabowen/IPSC/php/art.php?aid=440
   Counter Punch. "Israel and White Supremacy" by Aaron Michael Love, October 15, 2002. The author speaks of "Zionist Apartheid" which he feels is a war on people of color and, therefore, can be related to the historical psyche of White America. The author questions why Americans, especially those in the political, business class and some sectors of the white class, should love Israel so much.

Books

The Rural Face of White Supremacy: Beyond Jim Crow by Mark Schultz
   (University of Illinois Press, 2005). 0252029607.
   The author studied the daily experiences of people in a rural county in Georgia and was pleasantly surprised to find the ease with which the races interacted, much more so than in urban areas. He found interracial relationships that included mixed housing, midwifery, church services, meals, and common-law marriages.

White Supremacy and Racism in the Post-Civil Rights Era by Eduardo
   Bonilla-Silva (Lynn Rienner Publishers, 2001). 1588260321.
   The author feels that a racial structure is in place in the United States. He describes a contemporary system that operates in a covert, subtle, institutional, and superficially non-racial manner. The system labels the post-civil rights ideology as color-blind racism.

Lift High the Cross: Where White Supremacy and the Christian Right Converge by Ann Burlein (Duke University Press, 2002). 082232864X.
   The author explores the links between white supremacist organizations and groups representing the religious right.

People

Salvador Allende

Yasser Arafat

Cesar Chavez

Hugo Chavez

David Duke

Galileo Galilei

Malcolm X

Martin Luther King, Jr.

Salvador Allende

Salvador Allende was President of Chile from 1970–1973. He was removed from power by a coup in 1973 and he died during this skirmish. He had developed a democratic socialist program, which he felt would aid the poor and downtrodden. However, his short term as president was marked by strikes, lockouts, and much civil unrest.

The United States had unsuccessfully attempted to prevent Allende from taking office. When that proved ineffective, the United States imposed sanctions. The United States objected to Allende's socialist ideology and his friendship with Cuban President Fidel Castro.

Allende's supporters considered him a martyr who died for the cause of socialism. He felt he could enact his socialist political theory by following a democratic path. Yet, his opponents criticized his nationalization of private industry, the resultant supply shortages and extraordinary inflationary economic situation, and his autocratic style.

http://en.wikipedia.org/wiki/Salvador_Allende

The *Wikipedia* provides a succinct overview of Salvador Allende, his life and legacy. The outline of Allende at this site is as follows: Allende's early life, the election, his presidency, coup, foreign involvement in Chile during Allende's administration, U.S. involvement in Chilean affairs, viewpoints of both the liberals and conservatives, and accusations of racism.

http://www.fas.org/irp/world/chile/allende.htm

Intelligence Resource Program. This site records highlights of Allende's leftist regime. American intelligence, specifically the Central Intelligence Agency (CIA), had influenced elections in Chile back to 1958, but not the election of a physician, Salvador Allende.

Allende quickly socialized the Chilean economy by taking over the copper mines, foreign firms, banks, and large estates. The latter were turned over to resident workers. He raised salaries and wages. Allende's Popular Unity government opened up diplomatic relations with Cuba, China, North Korea, North Vietnam, and Albania. The article also provides background of the coup in 1973.

http://www.cnn.com/SPECIALS/cold.war/Kbank/profiles/allende/

This site offers information on Allende's life, his presidency, and how that affected the Chilean economy and government, plus information on the coup. This article is a concise encapsulation of Allende as a person, a leader, and as a failed bureaucrat.

Journal Articles through the Web

http://www.ajph.org/cig/content/full/93/12/2014

American Journal of Public Health. "Voices from the Past: Salvador Allende: Physician, Socialist, Populist, and President" by Sara K. Tedeschi et al., Vol. 93. No. 12, December 2003. This article offers the background into Allende's life, beginning in medical school when he was attracted to writings of Marx, Lenin, and Trotsky. He became a student activist. In 1933 he became one of the founders of the Chilean Socialist Party. Allende published a book, *The Chilean Socio-Medical Reality*, which focused on health problems of the poor, working conditions of the working class, material on infant mortality, tuberculosis, sexually transmitted diseases, and other diseases. Allende felt the country needed social change. This led to his presidential candidacy.

http://topics.nytimes.com/top/reference/timestopics/people/a/
salvador_allende_gossens/index.html?query=ASSASSINATIONS

New York Times, November 13, 2006. This journal site contains three articles on Allende. One may click onto each one.

1. "Documents Shed Light on Assassinations of Chilean in United States"
2. "Chile is Planning Ceremony to Bury Allende"
3. "Santiago Journal; With a Thunderclap, Leftist Breaks Chile's Silence"

http://query.nytimes.com/gst/fullpage.html?sec=health&res=
9COCE6DA1731F934A2575ACOA966958200

New York Times. "Leftist Journal Concludes Allende Killed Himself" by Shirley Christian, November 13, 2006. This information was reported in Chilean news magazine, *Analisis*. This article appeared after Allende's remains were exhumed from an unmarked grave and brought to Santiago for burial. The author indicated that the original claim of assassination, or death, in battle during the coup, was political and useful in opposing the sixteen year military regime that followed the fall of Allende.

Books

Salvador Allende Reader: Chile's Voice of Democracy edited by James D. Cockcroft (Ocean Press, Australia, 2000). 1876175249.

This anthology was published on the 30th anniversary of Allende's election as President of Chile in 1970. This is the first collection, in English, of Allende's speeches and interviews. Allende addressed such questions as: What support did his government have? and Why did the United States actively participate in his overthrow?

My Invented Country: A Memoir by Isabel Allende (Harper Perennial, 2004). 0060545674.

The author is the niece of Salvador Allende. She explores two life-changing moments:

1. The assassination of her uncle on September 11, 1973, which caused her to go into exile and in doing so gave her the impetus to become a literary writer, and

2. Terrorist attacks on September 11, 2001 on her adopted homeland (U.S.).

The latter was an acknowledgment that she had indeed really left her native homeland.

The Last Two Years of Salvador Allende by Nathaniel Davis (I.B. Tauris & Co., Ltd., 1999). 186064399X.

The author was Ambassador to Chile for two years prior to the coup and for a short time thereafter. He provides historical context on a "dark chapter" in American foreign policy. This text recounts U.S. alleged involvement in the assassination of Salvador Allende.

Yasser Arafat

(Several different spellings of Arafat's name are presented here, depending on those used by the various authors.)

Yasser Arafat was considered a controversial and polarizing figure during his career. He was Chairman of the Palestine Liberation Organization (PLO, 1969–2004), President of the Palestinian National Authority (PNA, 1993–2004). He also was a co-recipient of the 1994 Nobel Peace Prize with Shimon Peres and Yitzhak Rabin, as a result of the 1993 Oslo Accords (called for implementation of Palestinian self-rule in the West Bank and Gaza Strip over a five-year period). Yet, there was a breakdown of the Accord. Arafat's Fatah movement was responsible for many deadly attacks against Israeli civilians between 2000–2004.

Arafat has been hailed as both a heroic freedom fighter by his supporters and a terrorist among his opponents. Yasser Arafat died on November 11, 2004.

http://en.wikipedia.org/wiki/Yasser_Arafat
This site provides much information on Arafat's early life, the Palestinian Authority and peace negotiations, Arafat's political survival and controversy, his financial dealings, and his illness and death. In addition, the *Wikipedia* offers many links which embellish the content outline provided.

http://www.honestreporting.com/articles/45884734/critiques/
   Yassir_Arafat_1929–2004.asp
"Media Critiques." This site provides significant data about Arafat's engagement with the Fatah and PLO, his conflicts in Jordan, Lebanon, and Tunisia, his many terrorist activities in which he was involved, or which he directed, so others would serve the cause of Palestinian legitimacy.

http://www.ict.org.il/articles/yasir_arafat.htm
This site offers a psychological profile of Yasser Arafat. It describes his emotional stability, his need for independence, his need to demonstrate excellence and superiority, his interpersonal relations, his exaggerations, his embodiment as the symbol of the Palestinian revolution, and his ability to survive as long as he did.

Journal Articles through the Web

http://www.guardian.co.uk/israel/Story/0,2763,1348450,00.html
Guardian Unlimited. "Yasser Arafat" by David Hirst, November 11, 2004. Arafat grew up near the Wailing Wall in Jerusalem and saw firsthand the Zionist's struggle to wrest control of the traditionally Muslim administered Wall. Under British rule, there was a major struggle for Palestinian control and this served as an impetus for Arafat to become involved in the

conflicts. He experienced many military victories and reverses, as well. These are all discussed in this article, which provides background material on Arafat's struggles, legacy, and ultimate downfall.

http://www.opinionjournal.com/editorial/feature.html?id=110005863

Opinion Journal from the *Wall Street Journal* editorial page. "A Gangster with Politics; After Arafat, What's Left of the Palestinian Cause? Not Much" by Bret Stephens, November 7, 2004. The author indicated that the Palestine Liberation Organization (PLO), under Arafat, brought its estimated fortune to $14 billion through extortion, pay-offs, illegal arms dealing, drug trafficking, money laundering, and fraud. The author further indicated that even though Arafat might have been considered a gangster, he was also one of the twentieth century's "great illusionists." Arafat had at times rallied much of the world to his side. The author concludes with concerns that there is little to unite the Palestinians after Arafat's death. (He died four days after the article was published.) Stephens felt that no one could possibly step into Arafat's place as a leader.

http://www.findarticles.com/p/articles/mi_m1282/is_14_54/ai_88990523

National Review. "And a Thief, Too: Yasser Arafat Takes What He Likes" by Rachel Ehrenfeld, July 29, 2002. President George W. Bush had called for a change in leadership of the Palestine Liberation Organization (PLO), but no change would be likely. The author reveals the corruption in the PLO and the fact that it was probably the wealthiest of all terrorist organizations. (The latter was expressed by Britain's National Criminal Intelligence Service.) Much of the money went to fund terrorist training, not to alleviate the suffering of the Palestinian people.

Books

Yasir Arafat: A Political Biography by Barry Rubin and Judith Colp Rubin (Oxford University Press, 2005). 0195181271.

The authors trace Arafat's life from his student days in Cairo, Egypt, to head of a violent nationalist movement and eventually to be a leader respected by the Palestinian people. The authors considered Arafat a bad leader and a worse peace partner.

Arafat:The Biography by Tony Walker and Andrew Gowers (Virgin Books, Ltd., 2005). 1852279249.

The authors review hundreds of interviews with senior Israeli and Palestinian officials, including Arafat himself, which help to separate the man from the myth. These interviews indicate that Arafat became many things to many people; he was a terrorist, a Nobel Peace Prize winner, and pariah to the George W. Bush administration.

Arafat's War: The Man and His Battle for Israeli Conquest by Efraim Karsh (Grove Press, 2004). 0802141587.

The author is a Middle East scholar and makes a case that Yasir Arafat never intended to fulfill any peace commitments. The book focuses on the decade since the signing of the Oslo Accords (1993). Arafat unleashed much violence on Israel. The author tends to place the blame for failure to achieve peace on the Palestinian side, and makes little mention of Israeli settlement-building.

The Mystery of Arafat by Danny Rubinstein (Steerforth Press, 1995). 1883642108.

The author, a journalist, offers an analysis of Arafat. He addresses Arafat's childhood and education, his travels, ascetic image, and the problems he experienced guiding the Palestinian Authority. Arafat attempted to shift attention away from unifying Arabs toward the nationhood of Palestinians. Arafat laid the framework for recognition of his people by the world and by their neighbors in the Middle East. This text presents a positive picture of Arafat, the leader.

Cesar Chavez

Cesar Chavez was a Mexican American labor activist. He led the United Farm Workers and was a major advocate for migrant farm workers. This advocacy effort focused national attention on the deplorable working conditions of these laborers. Eventually, improvements were made so their lives were more tolerable. Both social and economic justice for the migrant farm workers were the two major goals Chavez was hoping to accomplish.

http://www.chavezfoundation.org/

On this site is an announcement of a petition for a national Cesar E. Chavez holiday to focus on Chavez's life and work. The Cesar Chavez Foundation was gathering signatures on petitions to ask the U.S. Congress to designate March 31 (Chavez's birthday) as Cesar Chavez Day. The Foundation feels this commemoration would help to ensure Chavez's legacy.

http://en.wikipedia.org/wiki/Cesar_Chavez

The *Wikipedia* site offers a concise encapsulation of Cesar Chavez's life as one of the greatest Mexican American civil rights leaders. On this site is a picture of a U.S. Postal Service stamp which was issued in 2003 to commemorate Chavez. The stamp depicts Chavez in the foreground, with fields behind him where the migrant farm workers toiled. This site offers information on Chavez's early life, his career as a labor leader, his legacy, and a timeline of his many accomplishments.

http://clnet.ucla.edu/research/chavez/bio/

This site offers a full narrative of Chavez's life from his birth in 1927 through his own work as a farm laborer, his service in the U.S. Navy at the end of World War II, and his efforts to foster a better life for migrant farm workers. Chavez's United Farm Workers Union practiced the principles of non-violence adhered to by Mahatma Gandhi and Martin Luther King, Jr. Chavez led several peaceful strikes and boycotts to bring attention to the plight of the farmers. Chavez worked tirelessly for the migrant workers until his death on April 23, 1993.

The two prestigious posthumous awards he received were the Aztec Eagle, Mexico's highest award presented to those of Mexican heritage who made major contributions outside of Mexico, and the Presidential Medal of Freedom, the highest civilian honor in the United States. President Bill Clinton bestowed this honor on Chavez at a ceremony at the White House, attended by Chavez's wife and six of their eight children.

Journal Articles through the Web

http://www.findarticles.com/p/articles/mi_m1571/is_16_18/ai_85523447

Insight on the News. "Activists Lobby for Chavez Holiday—*California Journal*: News from the Golden State—Cesar E. Chavez, United Farm

Workers" by Ellen Sorokin and Cheryl Wetzstein, May 6, 2002. This article is about the genesis of a campaign by community leaders and politicians in California to create a paid federal holiday to commemorate Cesar E. Chavez. Many local governments were divided on this issue. Up until this campaign effort, California was the only state that made Chavez's birthday, March 31, a paid holiday for state employees. Texas, Colorado, Arizona, and New Mexico now also recognize a holiday in Chavez's name.

http://news.rgj.com/apps/pbcs.dll/article?AID=/20060401/NEWS/ 604010327/1002

Reno Gazette Journal. "School Kids March on Birthday of Cesar Chavez" by Alex Newman, April 1, 2006. Approximately 150 Latino middle and elementary school children participated in this march. Some labor representatives also joined them. There were signs protesting a bill in Congress which was seeking harsh penalties for illegal workers. Many of the students were new to the United States and did not speak English.

http://www.questia.com/PM.qst?a=o&d=5002565350&er=deny

Western Journal of Communication. "Martyrs for a Just Cause: The Eulogies of Cesar Chavez" by Richard Jensen et al., vol. 67, 2003. The Martyrs were a group of college students whose interests were focused on needs of fellow human beings. These students did volunteer work for the United Farm Workers. They also helped in picketing during boycotts. Some Martyrs were killed during their volunteer work, but these Martyrs provided leaders of various social movements with examples of appeals to others to support various causes. Chavez eulogized the Martyrs and spoke of their bravery.

Books

Remembering Cesar: The Legacy of Cesar Chavez edited by Ann McGregor (Quill Driver Books, 2000). 1884956114.

This is a collection of stories, anecdotes, and essays on Cesar Chavez by those who knew him best. There are about forty-five contributors, among them are: Edward James Olmos, Henry Cisneros, Martin Sheen, and Coretta Scott King, wife of Martin Luther King, Jr.

The Words of Cesar Chavez edited by Cesar Chavez and Richard J. Jensen (Texas A&M University Press, 2002). 1585441708.

Cesar Chavez proposed cooperation and community, love, mutual respect, and non-violent approaches to achieve good working and living conditions for migrant farm workers. Chavez was also a deeply religious man and, therefore, believed in the dignity of all. This text consists of Chavez's collected speeches and writings.

The Fight in the Fields: Cesar Chavez and the Farmworkers Movement by Susan Ferriss et al. (Harvest, HBJ Book, 1998). 0156005980.

Ferriss is a journalist who reported on Chavez, the farmworkers, and their successful nationwide grape and lettuce boycotts. The author also discussed the injustices of California's agribusiness. This text is a companion volume to a PBS documentary which traces Chavez's life and all the events and people that had a significant influence on his activism.

Hugo Chavez

Hugo Chavez is the current President of Venezuela. He was re-elected to this post twice. His goals are to help the poor by combating illiteracy, disease, poverty, and malnutrition. His lofty aims are considered controversial both in his own country and elsewhere in the world. Those who oppose him consider him autocratic and feel he has not managed his economy sufficiently to aid his people. Despite concerns by some people about his methods for governing and handling the economy of Venezuela, *Time* magazine, in 2006 considered him to be one of its magazine's most influential people. *Time* selects a person, couple, group, idea, place, or machine that has done the most to influence events of the year regardless if the influence was good or bad.

http://en.wikipedia.org/wiki/Hugo_Chavez

The *Wikipedia* site offers data on Chavez's political rise, coup attempts, foreign relations, the impact of his Presidency—Chavez's many policies regarding domestic issues and labor concerns, his relationship with the media, his personal life, and a section on Chavez's interviews and speeches.

http://www.cbn.com/cbnnews/news/05053/a.aspx

"Hugo Chavez vs. America" by Dale Hurd. The author expresses concern about Chavez's alliance with Cuba, which has been paid for by oil profits and may well forge a group of anti-American states across Latin America. Venezuela has one of the largest oil reserves in the world and Venezuela owns Citgo, the United States' fourth largest oil supplier. Chavez has gained favor with the poor by setting up social programs, funding neighborhood food programs, and a proliferation of low-cost medical clinics.

http://abcnews.go.com/Nightline/International/story?id=1134098&page=1

ABC News International. "Hugo Chavez Interview: Venezuela President on Rocky Relations with Washington" (Interview with Ted Koppel). Ted Koppel was told by Chavez that he felt the United States was planning to invade his country. He described himself as a patriot and revolutionary. Chavez indicated he is revolting against inequality, injustice, and immorality. Chavez also indicated that the George W. Bush administration had no respect for the sovereignty of Venezuela.

Journal Articles through the Web

http://www.globalresearch.ca/index.php?context=viewArticle%code=
   LEN20060618&articleId=2665

"*Wall Street Journal* Gives Hugo Chavez a Mixed Review" by Stephen Lendman, June 18, 2006. The author commented on the *Wall Street Journal* coverage of Chavez. The latter referred to Chavez as a "revolutionary hero nearly on a par with Che Guevara and Fidel Castro," using Venezuela's oil riches to assist Castro's regime. The author feels this article has not reported entirely fairly or accurately on Chavez. The *Wall Street Journal* did not indicate some of the good programs Chavez provided for his poor countrymen, for example, free health care, and that he has no secret prisons or illegal political prisoners, and does not practice torture. The *Wall Street Journal* does speak of the Bolivian circles—which run counter to the hostile commentary on Chavez from high level administration officials. These circles, or groups, around the United States, are pro-Chavez. Thus, the author indicates that the *Wall Street Journal* was not in character by reporting on both aspects of the Chavez government—the good and the bad, rather than focusing only on the bad aspects.

http://www.citizen-journal.net/gmhome/archives/00000274.htm

The Citizen Journal, Conservative Political Forum. "Hugo Chavez: Pat Robertson Was Right" by Erik Rush, October 24, 2006. Pat Robertson had indicated that if Chavez thought the United States was planning to assassinate the Venezuelan President, they should go ahead with that plan. Robertson later apologized for his statement at the urging of the U.S. State Department. The House Committee on Homeland Security Sub-Committee indicated that Chavez trains those from Middle Eastern and Asian nations to pose as Latinos and enter the United States carrying Venezuelan passports. However, these people are really terrorists, according to the Sub-Committee mentioned above. The Committee felt this action could be considered an act of war.

http://www.iranian.ws/iran_news/publish/article_18370.shtml

Persian Journal (Iranian culture journal). "Iraq Will Stop Iran; Bolivia Will Stop Chavez" by Scott Sullivan, October 17, 2006. The author presents all the data regarding Iran's coming isolation, since the U.S. elections would indicate Iran stay out of Iraqi affairs, and the possibility of the United States gaining Syrian support with Iranian losses in Iraq. The latter could possibly mean the ouster of the Iranian President. Also, there is now a rivalry between Khamenei of Iran and Ahmadinejad, the Iranian President.

In Venezuela, Chavez has suffered the defeat of two of his favorite candidates to lead Mexico and Ecuador. In Bolivia, Evo Morales wants Chavez to build military bases on Bolivia's borders with Brazil, Paraguay, Chile, Peru, and Argentina. There appears to be so much intrigue between leaders of all these countries that it sometimes is difficult to sort out the legitimacy of all the claims of friendship, appeasement, or disloyalties.

The author believes that the U.S. State Department is upholding an anti-U.S. foreign policy, especially with the President of Iran and with Chavez, the President of Venezuela, both of whom may be possibly heading for defeat.

Books

Hugo Chavez: The Bolivian Revolution in Venezuela by Richard Gott (Verso; New Ed. Edition, 2005). 1844675335.

The author presents a fairly detailed look at Chavez's life. The author appears biased towards Chavez. Gott has spent a lot of time in Venezuela and personally interviewed Chavez. Gott feels that to understand Chavez, one needs to know about Simon Bolivar, the nineteenth century revolutionary, who wanted to liberate parts of South America from Spanish rule. Chavez wants to unite the people of Latin America so they can deter power from the North.

Venezuelan Politics in the Chavez Era: Class, Polarization, and Conflict by Daniel Hellinger and Steve Ellner (Lynne Rienner Publishers, 2004). 1588262979.

This text provides both historical and current information on Venezuelan politics. It contains a collection of articles from authors who provide objective viewpoints. Evidently, the poor are supporters of Chavez's programs in land reform and health care, but the upper and middle class minority are those protesting Chavez's presidential programs.

Chavez: Venezuela and the New Latin America edited by Hugo Chavez David Deutschmann, and Javier Salado (Ocean Press, 2004). 1920888004.

Chavez expresses a very nationalistic vision for Venezuela. He also wants a united Latin America. He writes of the military coup against his government in April 2002, his country's new democratic constitution, and discusses his relations with Cuba and the United States.

David Duke

David Duke, former Louisiana Republican state representative, was a former Imperial Wizard of the Knights of the Ku Klux Klan. Because of Duke's membership and position in the Ku Klux Klan, he has been accused of being a white supremacist. He speaks against racial integration and for white separatism. He ran unsuccessfully for several high profile offices in Louisiana, and twice for President of the United States. He also served a long prison sentence for tax evasion and fraud charges.

http://en.wikipedia.org/wiki/David_Duke

This *Wikipedia* site on David Duke discusses his life and various political campaigns, his affiliations with the Ku Klux Klan and other white separatist organizations, his publications, his public appearances, and his incarceration.

http://www.adl.org/special_reports/duke_own_words/duke_intro.asp

This is the Anti-Defamation League site which is set up to assist law enforcement in fighting extremism and terrorism. "David Duke: In His Own Words." This site provides information about Duke's own political organization which he formed after resigning from the Ku Klux Klan. His National Association for the Advancement of White People (NAAWP) was established to advocate for "white rights." Duke also formed a group called NOFEAR (The National Organization for European American Rights) to "defend the civil rights of European Americans." The site offers Duke's quotes on: blacks, the Ku Klux Klan, on segregation, on Jews, on the Holocaust, on immigration, on homosexuals, and on the Anti-Defamation League.

http://www.cnn.com/2004/ALLPOLITICS/01/23/elec04.h.duke.ap/

CNN.com. "David Duke Considering Run for Congress," January, 23, 2004. This site relays the message of Duke's hope to run for Congress from Louisiana, after his release from jail. The plea agreement for tax evasion and mail fraud, in 2002, would have permitted him to run for office.

Journal Articles through the Web

http://www.nysun.com/article/29380

The New York Sun. "David Duke Claims to be Vindicated by a Harvard Dean" by Eli Lake, December 6, 2006. Eli Lake, a reporter for the *New York Sun*, discusses a paper co-authored by a Harvard Kennedy School of Government Dean, about the influence of the "Israel lobby." The Palestine Liberation Organization (PLO) mission to Washington, D.C., distributed the paper. The paper in question, "The Israel Lobby and United States Foreign Policy" by Stephen Walt and John Mearsheimer of the University of Chicago, claims that journalists, think tanks, lobbyists, and Jewish officials have manipulated America to invade Iraq. The authors of the paper took umbrage with Duke and indicated that Duke twisted, manipulated, and "spun" the words to meet his own needs. This is an interesting article to absorb and debate.

http://www.thenation.com/doc/20060410/blumenthal

The Nation. "Republicanizing the Race Card" by Max Blumenthal, March 23, 2006. David Duke spoke at a white nationalists' conference. His comments, "The Jewish supremacists not only want to control Israel, they want to control America, Europe, and the whole world," were expressed to people in a hotel lobby prior to his speech which he delivered at the conference. The site recorded Duke's discussion of his days before prison and his sense of accomplishment on welfare reform, anti-immigrant advocacy, and white supremacy.

http://apr.sagepub.com/cgi/content/abstract/22/2/190

American Politics Research. "Racism, Cynicism, Economics, and David Duke" by Susan E. Howell (University of New Orleans), Vol. 22, No. 2, pp. 190–207, 1994. This article explains support for David Duke in three statewide Louisiana elections. This support reflects the impact of racism, cynicism toward government, and economic factors. Racial attributes assumed the most influential factor in Duke's support.

Books

Jewish Supremacism: My Awakening to the Jewish Question by David Duke (Free Speech Press, 2003). 1892796058.

This is a book for those wishing to understand anti-Semitism from a perspective of a white supremacist. This is also a good resource to help the reader fully understand David Duke's politics and philosophy and to determine, through discussion and debate, Duke's positions on many issues.

A Race Against Time: Racial Heresies for the 21st Century edited by Jared Taylor and George McDaniel (New Century Foundation, 2003). 0965638324.

This text is a collection of essays from *American Renaissance* magazine, which covers race relations from a scientific, historical, philosophical, and current perspective.

Troubled Memory: Anne Levy, the Holocaust, and David Duke's Louisiana by Lawrence N. Powell (University of North Carolina Press, 2000). 0807825042.

This text is about a Holocaust survivor whose mission was to defeat the political menace of neo-Nazi, Ku Klux Klan leader, David Duke. The author traces the Levy family's travels from the Warsaw Ghetto posing as Aryans, to New Orleans. Anne Levy wanted to honor the suffering of those who experienced the Holocaust by confronting racist hatred in contemporary times. Levy evidently played a role in Duke's defeat during his 1991 campaign for governor of Louisiana.

Galileo Galilei

Galileo Galilei was born in 1564 in Pisa. He was a physicist, astronomer, and a philosopher. He developed the telescope and was considered the Father of Modern Astronomy, Physics, and Science. Galileo believed in the Copernican System which resulted in his losing favor with the Catholic Church. At that time (mid 1600s), the Inquisition was a permanent institution of the Catholic Church. The Church used this forum to deal with heresies. The belief in the Copernican System, in which the Sun was considered the center of the universe, was considered a heresy. Since Galileo supported this system, he was told by Pope Paul V (who he had befriended) not to defend or discuss the Copernican theory. The Pope, who served from 1605–1621, suggested that Galileo treat the theory as a mathematical proposition. Eventually, Galileo had to face the Inquisition, was found guilty of heresy, and was placed under house arrest in his home near Florence, where he died in 1642.

http://en.wikipedia.org/wiki/Galileo_Galilei

As with other individuals, the *Wikipedia* provides an in-depth biographical sketch of Galileo's life. This site also offers information on Galileo's scientific methods, his astronomical contributions, data on his controversy with the Catholic Church, provides some of his writings, and also how popular culture has used Galileo's name.

http://www.newadvent.org/cathen/06342b.htm

This site offers information from the *Catholic Encyclopedia* on CD-ROM. This site provides a lengthy description of Galileo's life and his aptitude for mathematical and mechanical pursuits. Even though most people remember Galileo chiefly as an astronomer and his invention of the telescope, he made his most significant contributions in the field of dynamics—the function of the pendulum which enabled him to construct an astronomical clock. He also dealt with the centers of gravity, the laws of projectiles, and laws of motion.

http://www.law.umkc.edu/faculty/projects/ftrials/galileo/galileo.html

Famous Trials—The Trial of Galileo Galilei, 1633. This site offers a chronology of the Galileo trial, scriptural references, admonition, depositions, his defense, papal condemnation, his recantation, selected images and maps, and information on key trial figures.

Journal Articles through the Web

http://bjsm.bmj.com/cgi/content/extract/40/9/806

British Journal of Sports Medicine; pp. 806–807, 2006. This article deals with balance in sport, but refers to the scientific book Galileo wrote,

The Little Balance, which described Archimede's method of finding the specific gravities of substances using a balance.

Galileo had started, but not completed, his medical education, when he began teaching mathematics in Florence and then in Siena.

http://www.findarticles.com/p/articles/mi_qa4015/is_200301/ai_n9199980

Georgia Journal of Science. "Galileo's Condemnation: The Real and Complex Story" by Emerson Thomas McMullen, 2003. The author discusses what he considers the real reasons for Galileo's difficulties with the Catholic Church—not the war between science and religion or his advocacy of Copernicanism. The author considers the fact that Galileo angered his friend, Pope Urban VIII, who became Pope in 1623, two years after Pope Paul V died in 1621. This was because of Galileo's advocacy of atomism, which undermined the Church's scientific understanding of the Eucharist—when the bread and wine turn into the body and blood of Jesus Christ. Galileo felt that the qualities of the bread and wine change, which was against Church dogma. The Church stipulated that the substance of bread and wine changed, but the quality did not.

http://www.physicsnews1.com/

Universal Physics Journal, October 24, 2006. This journal is dedicated to the verification and improvement of Classical Physics—founded by Galileo and Isaac Newton. The premise is that man's understanding of common everyday events meets with the approval of a logical, impartial, distant, and non-accelerating observer. The many articles included in this section address gravitation and motion, mutual forces, reaction forces, the nature of time, and Galileo's Law of Constant Acceleration. Included in this section, as well, are a definitions page, plus a question and answer area.

Books

Galileo, Science, and the Church, 3rd edition, by Jerome J. Langford (St. Augustine's Press, 1998). 1890318256.

This text has been described as the classic account of the circumstances, issues, and consequences of Galileo's tragic confrontation with theologians. This book is cited in much of Galileo's literature. It is used in university courses and has a section with a survey of the most important advances in Galileo studies.

Dialogue Concerning the Two Chief World Systems by Galileo, Albert Einstein (Introduction) and Stillman Drake (Translator) (Modern Library, 2001). 037575766X.

With the publication of the original text, Galileo was brought to trial before the Inquisition. Galileo used the dialogue form to demonstrate the truth of the Copernican System, which proved for the first time that the Earth revolves around the Sun.

Galileo in Rome: The Rise and Fall of a Troublesome Genius by William

R. Shea and Mariano Artigas (Oxford University Press, 2004). 0195177584.

This text promotes the notion that Galileo contributed to his own fate. Evidently, many of Galileo's supporters suggested he tone down his rhetoric in his theories to protect himself, but he chose not to and, therefore, incurred the wrath of the Catholic Church. This text provides a new understanding of the political and religious institutional forces of seventeenth century Rome.

Malcolm X

Malcolm X, also known as Detroit Red and Al-Hajj Malik El-Shabazz, was a Black Muslim minister and the national spokesman for the Nation of Islam. He founded the Muslim Mosque and the Organization of Afro-American Unity. In his early years he was a burglar and drug dealer, but he became a black nationalist leader and a man who espoused equality as a human rights activist. Malcolm X was assassinated in February 1965. There are various theories about his death, including the involvement of the U.S. government, the Federal Bureau of Investigation (FBI), and the Central Intelligence Agency (CIA).

http://en.wikipedia.org/wiki/Malcolm_X
  This site provides much information on the life of Malcolm X, his involvement with the Nation of Islam, his marriage, meeting Fidel Castro, his politics, and his assassination. The *Wikipedia* also offers research sites, articles, and reports of this controversial figure.

http://www.brothermalcolm.net/
  This site is an 80th birthday commemoration: "Malcolm X; A Search for Truth." Included on this site are the following sections and links: Introduction, Index, Chronology, Family, Speeches, Photographs, Bibliography, Webliography, Study Guide, Conferences, Radical Black Tradition, and the Legacy of Malcolm X. This is an excellent research site for those working on a project of this charismatic leader.

http://www.colostate.edu/Orgs/MSA/find_more/m_x.html
  "Malcolm X—An Islamic Perspective." The content is adapted from the pamphlet *Malcolm X: Why I Embraced Islam* by Yusuf Siddiqui, with quotes taken from *The Autobiography of Malcolm X as Told to Alex Haley*. This site offers a timeline, Malcolm X's early life, a section on the Nation of Islam, The Change to True Islam, The Effect of the Pilgrimage, Malcolm's New Vision of America, The Oneness of Man Under One God, After the Pilgrimage, and Malcolm X's Legacy.

Journal Articles through the Web

http://jbs.sagepub.com/cgi/content/abstract/33/2/145
  Journal of Black Studies. "Malcolm X and/as Critical Theory: Philosophy, Radical Politics, and the African American Search for Social Justice" by Reiland Rabaka, Vol. 33, No. 2, pp. 145–165, 2002. This article examines Malcolm X as a critical theorist. The author suggests that Malcolm X was a major contributor to the Africana tradition of critical theory. This is a scholarly article that deals with Malcolm X's social and political philoso-

phy which offers a new paradigm for developing an Africana theory of contemporary society.

http://www.democracynow.org/article.pl?sid=05/02/21/1458213

Democracy Now! "The Undiscovered Malcolm X: Stunning New Info on the Assassination, His Plans to Unite the Civil Rights and Black Nationalist Movements & the 3 'Missing' Chapters From His Autobiography," February 21, 2005. This is an interview with Manning Marable, a Professor at Columbia University, who had spent a decade working on a new biography of Malcolm X. Marable, the historian, viewed the missing chapters mentioned in the title, had access to Malcolm X's family and documents which divulge information on the involvement of the New York City police, the FBI (Federal Bureau of Investigation), and possibly the CIA (Central Intelligence Agency) in Malcolm X's assassination. This was a very enlightening article on information surrounding the death of Malcolm X.

http://www.columbia.edu/cu/ccbh/pdfs/Souls.The_Unfinished_Dialogue.pdf

Emerge. "The Unfinished Dialogue of Martin Luther King, Jr. and Malcolm X" by Clayborne Carson, February 1998. The author discusses the contrasting ideas of both men regarding the future direction of black politics. Their opposing positions divide African Americans. Carson indicates that contemporary black young people are torn between racial integration and racial separation and Martin Luther King, Jr.'s call for nonviolence and Malcolm X's radical insistence on any means to gain a foothold in society.

Books

The Autobiography of Malcolm X: As Told to Alex Haley (Ballantine
   Books, reissue, 1987). 0345350685.
   Even though this is a 1987 re-issue, this text is a classic memoir. Malcolm X discusses his transformation from a bitter young criminal to an articulate political activist. He also analyzes white racism and he emphasizes self-respect for African Americans. Malcolm X also brings black culture alive.

Making Malcolm: The Myth and Meaning of Malcolm X by Michael Eric
   Dyson (Oxford University Press, 1996). 0195102851.
   The author provides the reader with a view of Malcolm X as a symbol of self-discipline and self-esteem, and as a leader in combating "economic corruption" of poor African American communities. The author sees Malcolm X's legacy to build bridges with Latinos, gays, feminists, environmentalists, and others who seek equality and "economic democracy,"

Malcolm X Speaks—Selected Speeches and Statements edited by George
   Breitman (Pub Group West, 1990). 0802132138.
   This text contains major speeches given by Malcolm X during the last

eight months of his life. His vision was to abolish racial inequality in the United States. He moved away from the Black Muslims, who were militaristic, and became more non-aggressive in his efforts to achieve acceptance of blacks into society.

Malcolm X: By Any Means Necessary by Walter Dean Myers (Polaris, 1999). 059066221X.

This text is for young adults and offers a wealth of information on Malcolm X's life. Myers organized Malcolm X's life into four stages: his childhood, his adolescence, the time he worked under Elijah Mohammad, and finally when Malcolm X broke off his relationship with the Nation of Islam.

Martin Luther King, Jr.

Martin Luther King, Jr., like his grandfather and father before him, served as a pastor. Martin, Jr. was a strong worker for civil rights for the African American people. He had served on the Executive Committee of the NAACP (National Association for the Advancement of Colored People). He also served in a leadership capacity in the first black (negro) non-violent demonstration in contemporary times in the United States. This was the bus boycott of 1955, which lasted for 382 days. During this time, King was arrested and his home was bombed. In 1957 he served as president of the Southern Christian Leadership Conference, and between then and 1968 he wrote five books, many articles, and led a number of protests. At the peaceful March on Washington, D.C., he delivered his "I Have a Dream" speech. Martin Luther King, Jr. was ultimately awarded five honorary degrees, named Man of the Year by *Time* magazine in 1963, and at the age of thirty-five was the youngest man to have received the Nobel Peace Prize. He turned over the prize money to the Civil Rights Movement. His life was cut short on April 4, 1968 when he was assassinated.

http://en.wikipedia.org/wiki/Martin_Luther_King,_Jr.
This website offers a comprehensive look at Martin Luther King, Jr.'s life, including his civil rights activism, his various challenges, his assassination with allegations of conspiracy, awards and recognition he received, a bibliography of books he wrote, his legacy, and many links to conduct further research into King's life and career.

http://www.enchantedlearning.com/history/US/MLK/
This is an interesting curriculum-focused site on Martin Luther King, Jr. There are links to African American biographies. There are provocative questions and activities, and there are also timeline quizzes, and word-search puzzles. Many of the activities are also geared toward reluctant learners/readers.

http://www.lib.lsu.edu/hum/mlk/
This site consists of reference sources from the Louisiana State University Libraries. It offers a biographical sketch on Martin Luther King, Jr., links to the King Center, the Martin Luther King, Jr. Home Page, history of the commemoration of Martin Luther King, Jr. Day, and King's writings.

http://www.gale.com/free_resources/bhm/bio/king_m.htm
This is a Thomson/Gale website that provides an extensive narrative of King's life, his family background, his educational pursuits, the Montgomery Bus Boycott, the sit-ins in which King was involved, and a lengthy bibliography.

Journal Articles through the Web

http://www.stanford.edu/group/King/additional_resources/articles/palimp.htm

Palimpsest: Editorial Theory on the Humanities, University of Michigan Press, 1993, by Clayborne Carson. This site represents articles by the Staff of the King Papers Project. Carson reflects on the religious and intellectual influences that shaped Martin Luther King, Jr.'s public presentation. He felt that King used his writings, speeches, and sermons to express his ideas, but more importantly to influence his multiracial audience.

http://topics.nytimes.com/top/reference/timestopics/people/k/martin_luther_jr_king/index.html?inline=nyt-per

New York Times. This site represents several articles, available in PDF format, on Martin Luther King, Jr. These articles, from the *New York Times* Archive, reflect various important events in King's life—his March on Washington, winning the Nobel Peace Prize, his assassination, and information on King's papers being saved from auction.

http://history1900s.about.com/od/martinlutherkingjr/a/mlkquotes.htm

20th Century History. This is an interesting site that presents numerous quotes from Martin Luther King, Jr. Many of the quotes offer students an opportunity to write a thesis paper on Martin Luther King, Jr. Each of the quotes might be adapted as theme statements from which to develop a study of King.

Books

The Autobiography of Martin Luther King, Jr. by Martin Luther King, Jr. and Clayborne Carson (Warner Books, 2001). 0446676500.

Carson, a historian, documentarian, and Director of the King Papers Project, wove together King's books, articles, personal letters, and unpublished manuscripts, to present a picture of King's quest for social justice. Carson felt that King incorporated the philosophies of Locke, Rousseau, Gandhi, and Thoreau into his teachings. This posthumous autobiography is a skillful representation of Martin Luther King, Jr.'s legacy in human rights activism.

Martin Luther King, Jr., (new and updated edition): Spirit-Led Prophet, A Biography by Richard Deats (New City Press, 2003). 1565481852.

From this text readers will become acquainted with King's spiritual side. The author highlights events that influenced King's approach to peaceful change. Martin Luther King, Jr. wanted a "beloved community" founded on morality, respect, and equality.

Why We Can't Wait by Martin Luther King, Jr. (Signet Classics, re-issue edition, 2000). 0451527534.

This text recounts the 1963 Birmingham campaign which launched the Civil Rights Movement and demonstrated the effectiveness of non-violent direct action. King discussed how the sit-ins and prayer marches provided for the American people a window of understanding of the plight of racial injustice.

Politics

Anarchism

Black Separatism

Communism

Fascism

Feminism

Gays in the Military

Gun Politics

People for the Ethical Treatment of Animals (PETA)

Public vs. Private School Education

USA Patriot Act (H.R. 3162)

Anarchism

Anarchism refers to a political theory which aims to create anarchy—which refers to the absence of a sovereign. This means that anarchism reflects a society in which individuals freely cooperate together as equals. Therefore, there would be no hierarchical control. Those who are anarchists do not believe that dominance and power are necessary for a society, nor do they believe that this form of political theory will lead to chaos or disorder.

http://www.geocities.com/CapitolHill/1931/
This site is an anarchist FAQ (frequently asked questions) web page. There is much information that will help to dispel myths about this political theory. The following sections are offered: What is anarchism? Why do anarchists oppose the current system? What are the myths of capitalist economics? What do anarchists think would cause ecological problems? What do anarchists do?

http://en.wikipedia.org/wiki/Anarchism
This site provides information on the origins of this political theory (before the nineteenth century), different schools of anarchist thought, anarchism as a social movement (organized labor, Russian Revolution), issues in anarchism (capitalism, globalization, communism, gender), recent developments, criticisms of anarchism, and cultural phenomena.

http://www.spunk.org/texts/writers/meltzer/sp001500.html
"Anarchism: Arguments for and Against" by Albert Meltzer. The Table of Contents of this site reflects the following topics: tenets of anarchism, class struggle, role of an anarchist in an authoritarian society, Marxist criticism of anarchism, social-democratic critique of anarchism, liberal-democratic objection to anarchism, fascist objection to anarchism, and the average person's objection to anarchism. This site is helpful because it provides different perspectives on this political theory.

Journal Articles through the Web

http://www.questia.com/PM.qst?a=o&d=5002415222&er=deny
Monthly Review. "Anarchism and the Anti-Globalization Movement" by Barbara Epstein, Vol.53, September 2001. The author offers a description of a contemporary anarchist activist. This would be someone who proposes a decentralized organizational structure for government, with groups that work together on an ad hoc (for one particular purpose) basis. Decision-making is done by consensus. There is suspicion of authority, with hostility toward corporations and to capitalism.

http://www.socialanarchism.org/mod/magazine/display/128/index.php
Social Anarchism; A Journal of Theory and Practice. "Anarchism and the Question of Human Nature" by Thomas Martin, Issue 37, June 28,

2006. The author contends that human nature has biological roots and though individuals enjoy free will, most drives and emotions are hard-wired. Hard-wired deals with evolutionary theory; contemporary anarchists must come to understand this in order to deal with how people can communicate with one another.

Anarchists need to consider whether human nature is peaceful or violent. This is important to anarchists who believe that rule is by consensus and, therefore, aggression is not part of the equation. Morality is learned behavior. This is also important to note in an anarchist society. In our prevalent society, there is a trade-off between equality and freedom, but anarchists believe that society does not require some authority to deal with equality and freedom. This article does stretch the intellectual capacity of the reader and may be well-suited to a mature high school student.

http://www.mises.org/story/2127

Ludwig von Mises Institute Journal. (The Mises Institute is a research and educational center of classical liberalism, libertarian political theory and Austrian School of Economics). "Can the State Improve a Hobbesian World?" by Edward Stringham, September 13, 2006. The author poses the issue that perhaps civil society can be attained without a government as we know it. The author wrote this article from the perspective of an economist. He describes a model where people can have social interaction, in a market economy, with a regular government model. He feels that market participants find ways to cooperate and not cheat. The author cites a number of economists who reflect both sides of the issue: anarchists vs. representative government, and how each encourages or discourages economic success.

Books

Anarchism: A Very Short Introduction by Colin Ward (Oxford University Press, 2004). 0192804774.

The author considers anarchism from different perspectives: theoretical, historical, and international and discusses key anarchist thinkers. He evaluates important ideas—blanket opposition to incarceration, and no compromise within political decision-making. He questions whether anarchy can function well as a political force.

No Gods No Masters; An Anthology of Anarchism by Daniel Guerin (Editor, French anarchist) (AK Press, 2005). 1904859259.

This is a first English translation of the editor's anthology. The text includes unpublished documents, letters, debates, manifestos, reports, plus the history, organization, and practice of the political theory of anarchism, its advocates and activists.

Chomsky On Anarchism by Noam Chomsky and Barry Pateman (AK Press, 2005). 1904859208.

Chomsky, a linguist, has been a critic of capitalism, domestic repression, and government propaganda. This book contains a collection of Chomsky's essays. They show his involvement with the anarchist community, his commitment to political organizations devoid of hierarchies, and his hope for a world without rulers.

Black Separatism

This is a movement that promotes a separate homeland for black people, especially for African-Americans. The issues that black separatists deal with are their perspective that whites are racist oppressors of blacks, and it is not possible for blacks to advance economically within a society dominated by whites. The Nation of Islam has also promoted a separate black state in America. Many of the adherents of this movement encourage instituting all black schools and businesses which would be directed by black politicians and police.

http://en.wikipedia.org/wiki/Black_separatism
This site mentions two outspoken figures who have called for African-Americans to return to Africa—Martin Delaney in the nineteenth century and Marcus Garvey in the 1920s. Both felt that blacks should move to Liberia. Another individual, Benjamin Singleton, wished to form separatist colonies in the American West. Two black leaders who had opposing views on black separatism were Martin Luther King, Jr. who wanted to remove segregation and Malcolm X who was a black separatist.

http://faculty.smu.edu/twalker/blkpower.htm
"Black Separatism: Deloria's Prescriptions to African-Americans" by Theodore Walker, Jr. The author relates that in Vine Deloria, Jr.'s works he offers historical and social parallels, contrasts, and similarities between Native American and African-American struggles. Deloria wrote a book *The Red and the Black* which urged African-Americans to "retribalize" and in doing so include economic, political, and legal goals. Deloria also referenced CORE (Congress on Racial Equality), an organization which in 1969 wrote a Community Self-Determination Act which would create a black owned and black controlled Community Development Corporation (CDC). This would help to eliminate black poverty in their ghettos and give them power and control in their communities. Deloria felt that whites would never accept blacks as equals.

http://www.answers.com/topic/separatism
Answers.com. This site offers definitions of separatists, separatism, political and administrative separatism, and separatist movements around the world with countries dismembered by separatist movements, motivations for separatism, degrees of separation, ethnic/racial separatism, religious separation, and gender and sexuality.

Journal Articles through the Web

http://www.slate.com/id/1080/
Slate, online journal. "Racial Integration" by Franklin Foer, November 23, 1997. The author indicates that the National Association for the Ad-

vancement of Colored People (NAACP), once an advocate for integration, has begun to question that concept. Even the Southern Christian Leadership Conference, which supported integration, is not satisfied with government policies. The author offers a historical accounting of black separatism from the nineteenth century through the Civil Rights Movement. The author does speak of the renewed interest in black separatism and the roots for its revival.

http://www.city-journal.org/html/11_1_whats_holding_blacks.htm

City Journal. "What's Holding Blacks Back" by John McWhorter, Winter 2001. The author, an African-American, had become disillusioned about black America and that even though there was an increase in the black middle class, interracial marriages and relationships, and blacks in significant positions in society, whites were still oppressing blacks. He expounded on seven issues that he felt were obstacles to blacks achieving progress within the "white" establishment. Yet, he also further indicated that these were myths.

1. Most blacks are poor; however, middle class blacks outnumber poor ones.
2. Black people earn 61 percent of what whites do; this figure is distorted by the number of single black welfare mothers.
3. There is an increase in racist church burnings; however, even though 80 black churches burned from 1990–1996, seven times that many white churches burned.
4. The CIA (Central Intelligence Agency) created inner cities by pouring drugs into them; this is not true.
5. Racism is rampant because more black men are incarcerated than white men. The War on Drugs actually was supported by the Congressional Black Caucus to help prevent blacks from assuming a life of crime.
6. Racial profiling is racism. Sometimes more blacks are detained, yet this number has decreased.
7. There is excessive police brutality against blacks, but this may be due to under training of police officers about dealing with tense situations.

http://www.opinionjournal.com/editorial/feature.html?id=110004295

Opinion Journal from the *Wall Street Journal* editorial page. "Yo, Howard! Why Did Dean Have to Embrace the Confederate Flag?" by Shelby Steele, November 13, 2003. The author was referring to Howard Dean's (At the time, Dean was a hopeful candidate for U.S. President.) comment about 'guys with Confederate flags in their pick-up trucks.' The author felt this was a repressed desire for white supremacy. He believes Dean was playing identity politics, to go after voting blocs of different groups. The author believed Dean was indicating that each ethnic group has the right to pursue power in the name of their race. Steele further commented on the conflict between democracy and peoples connections to their own racial group.

Books

Race: The Reality of Human Differences by Vincent Sarich and Frank Miele (Westview Press, 2005). 0813343224.

Sarich is an anthropologist and Miele, an editor of *Skeptic* magazine. They devote a number of chapters on DNA-based research into origin and differentiation among homo sapiens which indicates there are differences among people and differences can correlate to a concept of race, but not a justification for discrimination. Yet, the text challenges the existence and value of "color blindness."

Losing the Race: Self-Sabotage in Black America by John H. McWhorter (Harper Perennial, 2001). 0060935936.

McWhorter believes that African-Americans are sabotaging themselves when they align themselves with victimhood. He feels that black separatism and anti-intellectualism prevents black Americans from achieving success in our multiracial society.

The Covenant with Black America edited by Tavis Smiley (Third World Press, 2006). 0883782774.

This is a collection of essays that are aimed at helping African-Americans improve their lives from health and education to crime reduction and economic success. Each chapter outlines a key issue, lists resources, and indicates how the African-American community can progress socially, politically, and economically.

Authentically Black: Essays for the Black Silent Majority by John H. McWhorter (Penguin Group, 2004). 1592400469.

The author raises provocative issues on black America. He feels that blacks have distorted the meaning of what it is to be black and how this is reflected in topics ranging from rap music to reparations to portrayal of African-Americans on television to racial profiling.

Communism

This is a doctrine, a form of government, a political movement, which concerns itself with freeing the proletariat. The latter refers to a certain class in society which earns its money from its labors and does not receive any profit from specific capital. In other words, the proletariat is the working class.

In a true communist society, there is no specific class. There are a number of varieties of communism: Maoism, Trotskyism, Council communism, Anarchist communism, and Christian communism. Karl Marx might be considered the creator of the communist ideal.

http://en.wikipedia.org/wiki/Communism

This site gives an overview of both early communism and the emergence of modern communism (Marxism, Stalinism, Trotskyism, and Maoism). There is a narrative of the Cold War years and communism after the collapse of the Soviet Union. There is also a section of criticism of communism.

http://www.gmu.edu/departments/economics/bcaplan/museum/musframe.htm

This site houses the Museum of Communism, Bryan Caplan, Curator. The site offers background of the roots of communism—from the works of Karl Marx, which also reflected the traditions of Czarist absolutism. There is a section on Marxist origins of communism and another area on Czarist origins of Communism. The Czarist system was overthrown in 1917. The section on the History of Communism includes information on Lenin, Stalin and Trotsky, Mao, the Stalin of China, Stalin and Hitler dividing Europe, communism during World War II, post-war communist victories, Khrushchev in Russia, Deng, the Khrushchev of China, the fall of communism, and successes and failures.

http://www.anu.edu.au/polsci/marx/classics/manifesto.html

Manifesto of the Communist Party, 1848. The many sections of this site include: Bourgeois and Proletarians, Proletarians and communists, socialist and communist literature, Preface to the 1872 German edition, Preface to the 1882 Russian edition, Preface to the 1888 English edition, Preface to the 1890 German edition, and Notes on the Manifesto and various translations of it.

Journal Articles through the Web

http://www.americanpopularculture.com/journal/articles/spring_2005/aiello.htm

Americana; *The Journal of American Popular Culture, 1900–Present.* "Constructing 'Godless Communism': Religion, Politics and Popular Culture, 1954–1960," Vol. 4, No. 1, Spring, 2005. Since the American culture is imbued with religion, this concept brought about issues of anti-communism. America was engaged in a religious battle with an anti-religious enemy, rather than a political battle with a movement that believed in a collective ideal.

There was American opinion that communist philosophy was basically atheistic. It appeared that the increase of Americans participating in religion, may have been a response to communism's rejection of God. There were also a number of evangelicals, for example, Billy Graham, who helped to revive religious fervor. This is a lengthy article which explores the reasons for fear of communism, the importance of religiosity and how the latter managed to heighten the communist philosophy as a godless movement, that was anathema to the Christian faith.

http://home.flash.net/~comvoice/index.html

Communist Voice, a magazine of revolutionary theory, September 4, 2006. This magazine opposes market capitalism and the state capitalist regimes (Cuba, China, Russia) which the staff feels are not really socialist or communist. The magazine endorses revolutionary communism. There are sections that contain recent newsworthy articles, past articles classified by subject, where the magazine stands on rebirth of communism, and also, how to subscribe to the magazine.

http://www.findarticles.com/p/articles/mi_mOICK/is_1_15/ai_75578161

Aerospace Power Journal. "The Collapse of Communism" by Glenn Leinbach, Spring 2001. This is the review of a book *The Collapse of Communism* by Lee Edwards, which is a contributory volume of essays written by academics. Two themes evolve in the collection: 1) Western observers were surprised by the instability of the Soviet Union and how quickly it dissolved, and 2) Edwards discusses the former and current defenders of communism and indicates the fallacies in these peoples' views on this form of government.

Books

We Now Know: Rethinking Cold War History by John Lewis Gaddis (Oxford University Press, 1998). 0198780710.

The author, a professor of history at Yale University, believes the Cold War was inevitable. Gaddis researched many declassified and previously unavailable documents to reconsider the clash between the American government and the Soviet empire.

America, Russia, and the Cold War, 1945–2002 updated by Walter LaFeber (McGraw-Hill Humanities, 2002). 0072849037.

LaFeber, a recently retired professor of history at Cornell University, studied materials from both published and private sources and focused on United States/Soviet diplomacy to explain the causes and consequences of the Cold War. This updated edition was written after the attacks of September 11, 2001, and LaFeber includes an analysis of the world following the World Trade Center attacks. The newest chapters focus on reasons for terrorism, changes in the Islamic world, America's response and the close relationship that developed between the United States and Russia.

On Denial: Historians, Communism & Espionage by John Earl Haynes and Harvey Klehr (Encounter Books, 2003). 1893554724.

The authors accuse revisionists of downplaying and distorting evidence of communist espionage and subversion in the United States. They discuss new information about Stalin's crimes and American communists' subservience to Moscow. The authors also re-visit major Cold War controversies—Moscow's financial subsidies to the American Communist Party and the espionage cases against the Rosenbergs and Alger Hiss.

Fascism

Fascism is a type of right-wing ideology. This ideology believes in a revolution against materialism, individual rights, political pluralism, and representative government. This movement also promotes racial superiority and genocide to achieve this end. Fascism elevates masculinity and the power of violence.

http://en.wikipedia.org/wiki/Fascism
The *Wikipedia* site provides information on the roots of Fascism, various definitions, Italian Fascism, how it is different from and similar to Nazism, how this movement deals with religion, an analysis of Fascism and gender roles, and links to critics and those who are proponents of this ideology.

http://www.rense.com/general37/char.htm
"Fourteen Defining Characteristics of Fascism" by Dr. Lawrence Britt. The author studied the fascist regimes of Hitler in Germany, Mussolini in Italy, Franco in Spain, Suharto in Indonesia, and Latin American regimes. The characteristics that the author found which were common to all these regimes were:

1. Powerful and continuing nationalism.
2. Disdain for human rights.
3. Identification of enemies.
4. Supremacy of the military.
5. Sexism.
6. Controlled mass media.
7. Obsession with national security.
8. Religion and government intertwined.
9. Protection of corporate power.
10. Suppression of labor power.
11. Disdain for intellectuals and the arts.
12. Obsession with crime and punishment.
13. Much cronyism and corruption.
14. Fraudulent elections.

http://www.econlibrary/LIBRARY/Enc/Fascism.html
The Concise Encyclopedia of Economics. "Fascism" by Sheldon Richman. A good example of a Fascist economy is the regime of Benito Musso-

lini, the Italian dictator. Fascism is between capitalism and communism in economic terms. Under Fascism there could be private property and profit motive for productivity, as long as these roles did not conflict with the interests of the State. Under Mussolini, economic decisions were made by councils of workers and employers in the trades and industry. Since strikes were illegal, the aforementioned arrangement seemed to prevent them.

Journal Articles through the Web

http://www.jsonline.com/story/index.aspx?id=494615

Milwaukee Journal Sentinel. "Feingold Decries Creation of Term 'Islamic Fascism'; Bush Description Flawed, Insulting, Critics Say" by Craig Gilbert, September 11, 2006. Senator Feingold felt that President George W. Bush should not refer to the U.S. fight against al-Quaida as "Islamic Fascism." Feingold thought the term was insulting and further distances the United States from achieving friendship with the Muslim world. Muslims feel it stigmatizes their religion. The President of the Arab-American Institute, James Zogby, felt that when Bush linked Hitler and Mussolini, there was no understanding of Fascism and Islam.

http://www.findarticles.com/p/articles/mi_qa3686/is_200512/ai_n16350379

Canadian Journal of History. "Fashion Under Fascism: Beyond the Black Shirt/Nazi Chic? Fashioning Women in the Third Reich" by Kristin Semmens, December 2005. The author writes about both regimes integrating pleasure with persecution. Women wear blonde hair in braids, wear traditional dirndl skirts, sporty trousers, and stylish hats. The author reported on the work in two books: *Fashion Under Fascism: Beyond the Black Shirt* by Eugenia Paulicelli (Oxford, 2004) and *Nazi Chic? Fashioning Women in the Third Reich* by Irene Guenther (Oxford, 2004). After reading these books, Semmens felt that much could be learned about a nation's insecurities through fashion.

In the book, *Nazi Chic?* . . . there was an indication that the German fashion industry was purged of Jews. Women could not wear cosmetics. There was a shortage of clothing and necessities during the Nazi occupation. In the *Fashion Under Fascism* text there was also a shortage of apparel, but the fascist government did not promote peasant costume so the "couture" was not as strict as in Germany.

http://www.publiceye.org/eyes/whatfasc.html

PublicEye.org. This is an online magazine of Political Research Associates. "What Is Fascism? Some General Ideological Features," 1996. In this article there is an indication that Fascism has many forms. It must be seen in its historical context. Fascism arose in early twentieth century Europe as a form of counter-revolutionary politics. This happened because of the devastation of World War I and the Bolshevik Revolution. Both events caused much social upheaval.

Books

The Anatomy of Fascism by Robert O. Paxton (Vintage, 2005). 1400033918.

The author focuses on the literature about Fascism. His material is from Mussolini in Italy and Hitler in Germany. The author indicated that Fascism arose because of World War I and the destructiveness of power. Paxton chronicles Mussolini's and Hitler's rise to power, their global influence, and their eventual fall from power.

Fascism: A Very Short Introduction by Kevin Passmore (Oxford University Press, 2002). 0192801554.

This author relates that Fascism is both revolutionary and reactionary. He addresses the origins of Fascism as a result of the political and social crisis of the late nineteenth century, then the actual fascist movements in Italy and Germany. He shows how Fascism used propaganda and popular culture to promote itself. Passmore also relates information on the new arrival of the extreme right in Austria, Italy, France, and Russia.

Fascists by Michael Mann (Cambridge University Press, 2004). 0521538556.

The author focuses on the six countries where Fascism became the most dominant: Italy, Germany, Austria, Hungary, Romania, and Spain. Mann provides insights into the sources of European Fascism. He feels that the youth culture played a big part in this destructive ideology.

Feminism

Feminism is a movement that seeks justice for women. This movement also wishes to end all forms of sexism. Feminism is a quest for social justice in many different arenas: the human body, class, work, disability, the family, human rights, popular culture, reproduction and reproductive rights, science, and sexuality.

http://plato.stanford.edu/entries/feminism-topics/
   This is a rather inclusive site offering information on the definition of feminism related to beliefs and feminist movements, the diversity of women, and anti-sexism. There are a number of links to: Feminism and Class, Feminism and Disability, Feminism and Human Rights, Feminism and Race/Ethnicity, Feminism, Sex, and Sexuality.

http://feminism.eserver.org/
   Feminism and Women's Studies site. This site offers links to eight other areas dealing with feminism. The component on activism explores feminist activism, in particular, and the manner in which organizations are using feminism in the real world. The section on Gender and Sexuality explores issues in this area, related to feminism specifically. There is also a section on women's health topics and links to websites relevant to feminism, and, in addition, to women's studies programs at colleges and universities. Another section offers sites that record benchmarks in the history of women's studies, plus a collection of links discussing issues about working women.

http://www.feminist.org/
   Feminist Majority Foundation Online. This site offers a number of areas that highlight feminism and feminist principles: Feminist news and events, Helping Afghan Women, Sports and Education—Title IX, Feminists Research Center, National Center for Women and Policing, Student Activism, 911 for Women, Women's Health, Feminist Career Center, Global Feminism, Reproductive Rights, and Feminist Arts, Literature, and Entertainment.

http://womenshistory.about.com/od/feminism/Famous_Feminists_
   and_the_History_of_Feminism.htm
   This site has many articles on the History of Feminism, Famous Feminists, and sections on Cultural Feminism, Radical Feminism, *MS* magazine, and quotations from a number of significant feminists, such as Betty Friedan, Adrienne Rich, and Rachel Speght, an early feminist.

Journal Articles through the Web

http://www.city-journal.org/html/13_1_why_feminism.html
   City Journal. "Why Feminism is AWOL on Islam" by Kay S. Hymowitz, Winter 2003. The author initially mentions feminism's core moral

insight which is that women should have the same rights and dignity as men. She is, therefore, wondering why women have not spoken up more loudly about the deplorable conditions for women in the Islamic world. The author reveals these conditions: Afghan girls being barred from school, stoned for adultery, or beaten for showing an ankle or wearing high-heeled shoes, not permitted to leave their homes without being accompanied by a male relative, and even denied medical help because the only available doctors were male. An issue which answers the author's query as to why feminists are not reacting more toward Islamic women's enslavement is that feminists would need to recognize that free men and women need the same things and those things they already have in the West, so certain freedoms would mean an end to feminism as it is known today.

http://www.findarticles.com/p/articles/mi_m2294/is_n11–12_v35/
   ai_19280189

Sex Roles: A Journal of Research. "Feminism and Women's Sense of Humor" by L.R. Franzini, December 1996. The author has done a study of feminists and whether they really lack a sense of humor, as has been thought in the past. The author feels that only men think feminists are without humor since feminists have hidden this trait in order to appear traditionally feminine. The author also relates categories of humor: by or about women, which ridicules a person or social system with no change to be made; it may be self-deprecatory. Female humor may reveal hopelessness, but feminist humor may be hopeful. Feminist humor comes from a determination that males dominate society and, therefore, are oppressive toward women and exploit them. The content of feminist humor aims at changing women's behavior and women's relations with men. It is a survival mechanism. This is an interesting and insightful article.

Books

Feminism Is for Everybody: Passionate Politics by bell hooks (South End
   Press, 2000). 0896086283.
   The author speaks of her vision of a community of those committed to equality, mutual respect, and justice. She feels the most challenging issues feminists face today are reproductive rights, violence, race, class, and work.

Women's Voices, Feminist Visions: Classic and Contemporary Readings
   by Susan M. Shaw and Janet Lee (McGraw-Hill Humanities, 2005).
   007311250X.
   This is an anthology of over 105 selections. Each section/chapter includes at least one essay on a global feminist perspective. There is a mix of essays featuring minorities. The issues of race and sexuality are important topics. The representation of authors reflects a number of significant authors from the feminist movement.

Listen Up, 2nd edition: Voices From the Next Feminist Generation edited
   by Barbara Findlen (Seal Press, 2001). 1580050549.

According to the "voices" of the women in this collection, violence, rape, shame, and self-hate are very much part of the lives of girls and women. According to the contributors, young feminists are as angry, self-expressive, and political as their forebears.

Manifesta: Young Women, Feminism, and the Future by Jennifer Baumgardner and Amy Richards (Farrar, Straus and Giroux, 2000).
0374526222.

This book is recommended for high school, college and public libraries. Today's young women, from women rock stars and athletes to female entrepreneurs and inventors, have the responsibility to carry on with women's liberation. The authors encourage young women to fulfill feminism's promise of justice, equality, and sexual freedom for all.

Gays in the Military

The U.S. Armed Forces do not permit a sexually active, *openly* gay service member to remain in the service of his/her country. Many other countries have abandoned their anti-gay policies particularly as a result of mental health professionals indicating that a homosexual orientation is normal, natural, fixed, and unchosen. Those countries which permit gays to serve in their armed forces are: Austria, Australia, Belgium, Canada, Denmark, France, Germany, Ireland, Israel, Japan, The Netherlands, Norway, Spain, Sweden, and the United Kingdom.

http://www.religioustolerance.org/hom_mili.htm

ReligiousTolerance.org. "Gays in the U.S. Military; 'Don't Ask; Don't Tell'." This site offers quotations from notable politicians and statesmen, provides an overview of the issue, information on hate crimes law, reports of harassment, the pressure to dispose of the "Don't Ask, Don't Tell" policy, plus an opinion poll.

http://www.planetout.com/news/roundups/package.html?sernum=328

Planet Out. Com. "Gays in the Military." In 1993 President Bill Clinton signed into law the lifting of the U.S. military's ban on gay and lesbian personnel policies which now simply states, "Don't Ask, Don't Tell, Don't Pursue, Don't Harass." This site offers information on harassment, the discharging of gay soldiers, and the ramifications of the lifting of the ban for homosexuals to serve in the U.S. military. There is also information on the Servicemembers Legal Defense Network (SLDN) that had filed a suit against the ban in federal court. The SLDN did report a drop in gay discharges since 2002. The assumption is that the Iraqi War probably contributed to the decrease.

http://en.wikipedia.org/wiki/Don't_ask,_don't_tell

The *Wikipedia* site offers a history of the "Don't Ask, Don't Tell" legislation, introduced by President Bill Clinton and signed by him in 1993. There is also information on public opinion, statistics, criticism, and the situation outside the United States.

Journal Articles through the Web

http://www.gaymilitary.ucsb.edu/

Center for the Study of Sexual Minorities in the Military. *Armed Forces and Society*, September 25, 2006; This site has a number of articles. "Scholars Debate Combat Motivation of U.S. Soldiers; Disagreement Over Significance of Emotional Bonding Among Troops;" "West Pointer Wins First-Ever Military Award for Challenging Gay Ban" indicating that the original policy violates military values; "Lawmakers, Professional Groups,

Dispute Pentagon Document Calling Gays Mentally Ill; Report Card Gives Military Failing Grades on Treatment of Gay Troops." Some members of Congress sent a letter to then Secretary of Defense Donald Rumsfeld, to review a Pentagon Instruction that classified homosexuality as a mental disorder, along with mental retardation, impulse control disorders, and personality disorders. There are over twenty articles of this ilk on this site.

http://www.questia.com/PM.qst?a=o&d=5002538926&er=deny

Parameters. "Don't Ask, Don't Tell: Is the Gay Ban Based on Military Necessity?" by Aaron Belkin, Vol. 33, 2003. This article discusses the difficulties President Clinton faced in trying to get his policy passed, despite the opposition by the Joint Chiefs of Staff and prominent members of Congress. Many felt the new policy needed to be revisited and evaluated.

http://www.findarticles.com/p/articles/mi_m1589/is_2000_Feb_1/ai_59086781

The Advocate."More Military Maneuvers—Gays in the Military" by Chris Bull, February 1, 2000. President Clinton agreed with his wife, Hillary Rodham Clinton, when she proposed that the original "Don't Ask, Don't Tell" policy should be removed in order to have a more liberal policy that would permit gays to enlist and serve openly. There was a furor when Republicans said President Clinton and Vice President Al Gore should not advocate for a new policy without first consulting military leaders. The criticism appeared to be the result of new endeavors by a growing number of gay voters and gay sympathizers. The author indicated that these voters had become more politically mature and were more vocal than previously.

Books

Don't Ask, Don't Tell: Debating the Gay Ban in the Military edited by Aaron Belkin and Geoffrey Bateman (Lynne Rienner Publishers, 2003). 1588261468.

The book reflects the proceedings from a conference held in December 2000. The text is divided into eight sections: an introduction; historical review; inquiry into whether or not the ban preserves soldiers' privacy; inquiry into whether or not the ban helps unit cohesion; a discussion of the military of foreign militaries; a look at the cost, both financial and human, of the ban; a pair of talks by two openly gay servicemen; and lastly, an inquiry into the future of the "Don't Ask, Don't Tell" policy.

Officially Gay: The Political Construction of Sexuality by the U.S. Military (Queer Politics, Queer Theories) by Gary L. Lehring (Temple University Press, 2003). 1592130356.

This text traces the U.S. military's century-long attempt to identify and exclude gays and lesbians. The author also traces how the military historically constructed definitions of a homosexual identity that relied on religious, medical, and psychological "data" that defined homosexuality as evil, degenerate, and unstable which would make them a risk to national security. The latest statement was paraphrased from the book description.

Marching to an Angry Drum: Gays in the Military by Carl G. Mitchell (Writers' Club Press, 2002). 0595001440.

The author's reflections cover the difficulties encountered by gays and lesbians who have to lead a double life while they serve in the military. The author reveals how the prejudices against gays serving in the U.S. Armed Forces destroys lives not only through combat, but also through the hostility of purges and open intolerance.

Gun Politics

Gun politics is a term used to designate the policy debates around freedom or restriction of people having private ownership of, and the ability to use, firearms. There is the concern that gun policies might influence crime, deflect issues of using firearms for self-defense, and how the individual and the federal government can agree on policies that do not infringe on individual rights, yet have the government assert controls.

http://en.wikipedia.org/wiki/Gun_politics

This site provides information on gun policies in specific countries, the many different positions on restrictions of gun ownership and regulations, a general discussion of arguments for the power balance between government and the individual, self-defense, domestic violence, statistics, and external links to both pro gun control and pro gun rights.

http://www.opensecrets.org/news/guns/

"Gun Control vs. Gun Rights, The Issue." This article opens with the contents of the Second Amendment to the U.S. Constitution which stipulates the protection clause "the right of people to keep and bear arms." The gun control advocates feel that this right to bear arms does not extend to military-style firearms. This group also wants mandatory child safety locks, background checks on gun purchasers, the number of guns a person may own, and to raise the age limit for gun ownership. The Gun Rights Group, which is led by the National Rifle Association, feels that the above requirements infringe upon rights of citizens and that the other issues have not been proven effective or of benefit to the public.

http://columbia.thefreedictionary.com/Gun+politics

This is a *Columbia Encyclopedia* site. This site discusses the various interpretations of gun control and legislative efforts of states about this issue. Also mentioned is the Brady Bill which contained stipulations on gun ownership. This bill, named after James Brady, an advisor to President Reagan, was passed after the assassination attempt on President Reagan. Brady was severely wounded during this gunfire incident. The site reviews the several attempts by Congress to address gun control following a number of school shootings.

Journal Articles through the Web

http://www.davekopel.com/Religion/Religious-Roots-of-the-American-Revolution.pdf

Journal on Firearms & Public Policy. "The Religious Roots of the American Revolution and the Right to Keep and Bear Arms" by David B. Kopel, Vol. 167, 2005. The author is editor-in-chief of this journal. This article is an excerpt from a book he is writing on religious attitudes towards self-defense. The article examines the religious background of the American Revolution and how various religious beliefs of the colonists developed so the American people eventually came to the conclusion that overthrowing King George and Parliament was a sacred obligation. These same religious attitudes which impelled the colonists to armed revolution were the component of the idea of the right to keep and bear arms. In addition, using arms to resist tyranny was seen as a religious duty.

http://www.davekopel.com/2A/LawRev/WhatStateConstitutionsTeach.htm
Northern Kentucky Law Review. "What State Constitutions Teach About the Second Amendment" by David B. Kopel, Vol. 29, No. 4, 2002. The author indicated that state constitutions serve as an aid to interpreting the federal *Bill of Rights*. The Right to Arms provisions are found in forty-four state constitutions. He further indicated that state arms guarantees have been created or amended by special conventions, state legislatures, and referenda. In each state where people had the opportunity to vote directly, they voted for the right to bear arms overwhelmingly. The author examines each of the state constitutions that contain an arms right guarantee. However, he also analyzes whether bearing arms means in military service or for other purposes such as personal or family defense or for sporting events.

http://www.thejournalnews.com/apps/pbcs.dll/article?AID=/20061217/
NEWS01/612170348/1018/NEWS02
The Journal News. "Handgun Owners Irate Over Having Names Published ONLINE" by Jorge Fitz-Gibbon, December 17, 2006. This article describes the anger of many readers with the decision of this journal to run a list of pistol permit holders in Westchester and Rockland Counties in New York State. More than 30,000 licensed handgun owners were posted online. The readers were concerned that their homes might be targeted for theft, even though home addresses were not published. Then the New York State Rifle and Pistol Association posted the addresses and phone numbers of newspaper staff members. This latter list was eventually pulled from the paper. The journal indicated it received the lists through the Freedom of Information Law since state pistol permits are public records.

Books

The Politics of Gun Control by Robert J. Spitzer (CQ Press, 3rd edition, 2003). 1568029055.
   The author focuses on three key culture shocks that he felt influenced and shaped the politics of gun control in America: the shooting at Columbine High School, the gun issue presented in the 2000 election, and the 9/11 terrorist attacks. The author also reveals other issues on the gun control debate: the concealed-carry laws, liability laws filed against gun manufacturers, NRA (National Rifle Association) funding of Republican campaigns, and the assault weapons ban.

Disarmed: The Missing Movement for Gun Control in America by Kristin A. Goss (Princeton University Press, 2006). 0691124248.

The author has based her book on material from historical archives, interviews, and original survey evidence. She feels that the power of the so-called gun lobby has played an important role in preventing a true gun-control campaign.

Women & Guns: Politics and the Culture of Firearms in America by Deborah Homsher (M.E. Sharpe, 2001). 0765606798.

The author reviews the experiences of women on the American frontier and folkloric male frontier heroes. She met with women hunters. She addresses self-defense and the women who advocate for concealed-carry laws. The author had also interviewed women who participated in gun sports and militias, and African-American women who lived in neighborhoods where guns are everywhere.

People for the Ethical Treatment of Animals (PETA)

When one speaks of animal rights, the concern is that animals live their lives free from exploitation and suffering. Those who support animal rights believe that animals have an inherent worth which is separate from their usefulness to humans. This is a social movement which challenges society's view that non-human animals exist only for human use.

http://www.peta.org/about/WhyAnimalRights.asp

"Why Animal Rights?" Much of the information on this site is reflected in the above paragraph. This site is the Home Page for PETA (People for the Ethical Treatment of Animals). Included on this site are PETA's stands on animal rights, PETA's milestones, PETA in the headlines, PETA's *Animal Times* publication, PETA's recent victories, and how to become active in this organization/movement.

http://en.wikipedia.org/wiki/People_for_the_Ethical_Treatment_of_ Animals

The *Wikipedia* site provides much information on PETA, the largest animal rights organization in the world. It was founded in 1980, is based in Norfolk, Virginia, and is funded by its one+ million members. There are affiliates outside the United States in Canada, France, the United Kingdom, Germany, India, Italy, the Netherlands, Spain, South Africa, and Taiwan. The site provides data on the movement's philosophy and activism, its campaigning, undercover investigations, its policy on euthanasia, conflicts with other activists, and cultural influences.

http://www.activistcash.com/organization_overview.cfm/oid/21

ActivistCash.com. "People for the Ethical Treatment of Animals." This site provides an opposing viewpoint on this movement. The site considers this movement to be a radical one and reflects on the hypocritical nature of its philosophy. The site informs the reader about PETA planting firebombs in restaurants, destroying butcher shops, and torching research labs. This site indicates that PETA is not an animal welfare organization since it euthanized (killed) more than 10,000 animals from 1998–2003, exploits sick people and how food from animals created epidemics and infections. This site also tells how PETA distorts religious teachings, indicating the Jewish tradition of kosher slaughtering of animals, and that PETA supports violence and terrorist activities.

Journal Articles through the Web

http://www.ajc.com/metro/content/printedition/2006/12/05/
meshcdcpetal1205a.html

The Atlanta Journal-Constitution. "PETA: Gerberding Should Go" by Alison Young, December 5, 2006. The animal rights group PETA called for the resignation of the CDC (Centers for Disease Control) director Julie Gerberding, because of animal care problems at CDC. One problem was that monkeys were dying from dehydration. This evidently took place in 2002, when Gerberding just began her tenure as director; however, she was unaware of this problem until 2005 and then addressed this issue. The CDC claims it has a world-class animal care and use program.

http://www.theithacajournal.com/apps/pbcs.dll/article?AID=20061121/
OPINION02/611210307

The Ithaca Journal.Com. "The Struggle to Save a Sanctuary and a Movement" by Lee Hall, November 21, 2006. This article is about a primate sanctuary in San Antonio, Texas. The sanctuary, Primarily Primates, Inc., provided a home for chimpanzees that were used in cognition experiments at Ohio State University. PETA tried to have the sanctuary closed under a county ban on "dangerous wild animals." PETA wanted to send the animals to Louisiana's Chimp Haven. The issues were septic problems, sewage, and animals becoming ill due to bad hygienic atmosphere. The article is lengthy and presents both sides of this issue, including some litigation.

http://findarticles.com/p/articles/mi_mOFDE/is_1_21/ai_82552555

Vegetarian Journal. "Vegetarian Starter Kit Available from PETA—Veggie Bits," January–February 2002. This article is about a free offering from PETA. It is a booklet that includes data for new vegetarians and vegans. Included in this booklet are simple recipes, all "cruelty free," such as mushroom sandwiches and spinach lasagna. A phone number and website are also included to obtain a copy of this Vegetarian Starter Kit.

Books

The Fast Food Craze: Wreaking Havoc On Our Bodies and Our Animals by Tina Volpe (Canyon Publishing, LLC, 2005). 0976134306.

This is a guidebook for beginner vegetarians or people who consider their own health and the well-being of animals. There is a chapter on junk food, and other chapters on animals most often found on people's plates. There is much written about the treatment animals undergo on their way to becoming food. The author assails the fast food industry and the mistreatment of farm animals and is an advocate for vegetarianism.

The Animal Ethics Reader edited by S. Armstrong (Routledge, 2003). 041527589X.

180 *Encouraging and Supporting Student Inquiry*

This is an anthology of readings under the following headings: Theories of Animal Ethics, Animal Capacities, Animals for Food, Animal Experimentation, Genetic Engineering of Animals, Ethics and Wildlife, Zoos, Aquaria, Animals in Entertainment, Companion Animals, and Legal Rights for Animals. There is a balanced representation of these subjects.

Animal Rights: Current Debates and New Directions edited by Cass R. Sunstein and Martha C. Nussbaum (Oxford University Press, 2005). 0195305108.

The editors have included a number of contributors who explore the legal and political issues that involve animal rights and the opposition to it. The issues addressed are ethical questions about ownership and protection against unjustified suffering. The selections offer different perspectives on animal rights and animal welfare.

Public vs. Private School Education

The issues surrounding this controversy are many. One is the concept of vouchers that would enable parents to send their children to private schools which they assume would provide a better education. However, many private schools attract better students and may cater to parents who are more interested in their students' academic achievement. There are a number of private schools that have a religious orientation which raises the concern of vouchers to those schools and the issue of church–state separation. There is apprehension that funds for private schools might be diverted from public schools and diminish the effectiveness of the educational environment in the latter. Regarding public school education, suggestions have been made to have national standardized testing, academic standards for grade promotion, encouragement of parental interest in students' education, encouragement of more innovative technology use in school with interactive computer-based learning, and initiation of curriculum reform and teaching students how to think rather than what to think.

http://www.browardschools.com/info/education.htm
"Public vs. Private Education," Broward County, Florida Public Schools. This site offers a comparison of public vs. private education parameters. Public schools operate on 180 days; there is no such stipulation for private schools. There are no fees for public school attendance, yet there is tuition for attending private school. Public school educators must hold college degrees; private school teachers may not have the same requirement. Public schools may not be selective as are private schools in accepting students. Public school students need to meet state credit requirements; private schools do not have such criteria. Content and performance standards in public schools are required by the state; private schools may establish their own curriculum. Public schools must deal with collective bargaining with employees; private schools need not do so. Public schools must comply with federally qualified lunch programs; private schools do not have to do so.

http://www.greatschools.net/cgi-bin/showarticlefeature/ca/197
"Private vs. Public Schools: What's the Difference?" Public schools cannot charge tuition; private schools do charge tuition because they do not receive tax revenues. Public schools admit all children; private schools are selective. Public schools must follow federal, state, and local laws; private schools are not subject to such regulations. Public schools offer a general education program; private schools have the flexibility to create programs. Public school teachers are state-certified; private school teachers may not be required to have this stipulation. In public schools, students reflect the

neighboring community; private school students participate in a selection process and live in different communities. Public schools must educate all students and provide a special education curriculum for those in need; private schools do not have to accept those with special needs. Class size differs in both situations, with public schools having larger classes.

http://parentcenter.babycenter.com/refcap/bigkid/gpreschool/67271.html

"Public vs. Private: Which is Right for Your Child?" by Maureen Boland. The author indicates that parents must educate themselves about school quality, accountability, curriculum, and teacher training. Parents must investigate their local public schools, which may be better than private institutions. In public schools teachers are required to have more qualifications, students study core subjects, more activities are sponsored, and the student population is diverse. In private schools classes tend to have fewer students, there is less bureaucracy, and parent involvement is strong.

Journal Articles through the Web

http://www.nytimes.com/2006/07/19/opinion/19wed2.html?ex=
   1310961600&en=98f291b02d6b2fc38ei=5090&partner=
   rssuserland&enc=rss

New York Times editorial. "Public vs. Private Schools," July 19, 2006. Studies have shown that educational quality differs within all school categories: public, private, charter, and religious. The U.S. Education Department released a report on student achievement in federal math and reading tests known as the National Assessment of Educational Progress. When researchers looked at race, gender, parents' education, and income, there was no appreciable difference in scores. Private school students' raw scores were higher when considered alone, but not when the variables mentioned above were taken into consideration. However, public, private, charter, and religious schools all suffered from wide fluctuations in quality and effectiveness. The article concluded with the concept that *on average*, school children are not performing well in reading, math, and science, whatever type of school they attended.

http://www.associatedcontent.com/article/8063/education_private_versus_
   public.html

AC Associated Content. "Education: Private Versus Public; Which is a Better Choice?" by Valencia Higuera (The People Media Company, September 15, 2005). The author has discussed advantages and disadvantages of both types of education. Some private schools work at an accelerated pace because of smaller classrooms and a larger curriculum. Public schools generally have more than twenty-five students per class with students who learn at different speeds. Curriculum in public schools meets the needs of a majority of its students. Parents have misconceptions of these two educational opportunities and think that private schools are safer, have fewer crimes, and drugs are not as easy to obtain. The author does mention the difference in credentials required of teachers. She advises parents to consider a private education, if that is what is desired, and which type of private school, should it be coed or same sex.

http://www.onlineopinion.com.au/view.asp?article=2734

Online Opinion, Australia e-journal of social and political debate, November 11, 2004. "Private Boarding School vs. Public School Education for Indigenous Students" by Stephen Hagan. Some people react to private school education as an elitist education. A prominent indigenous leader, Noel Pearson, advocates sending students to schools away from their communities to overcome chronic academic underachievement. He was referring to aboriginal youth. He was concerned with these youth being competitive in the labor market. He offers statistics of the poor percentage of aboriginals who complete their education in their own neighboring schools.

Books

Public School Choice vs. Private School Vouchers edited by Richard D.
    Kahlenberg (Century Foundation Press, 2003). 0870784846.

This text is a compilation of articles, papers, and discussions on public school choice and private school vouchers. Contributors include law professors, newspaper education editors, Department of Education personnel, a representation from People for the American Way, and a representative from the American Federation of Teachers. The contributors discuss whether choice should occur within public schools, or extend to private schools, and the advantages and disadvantages of each approach. The federal No Child Left Behind Act has placed new emphasis on choice within the public school system.

School Choice: The Moral Debate edited by Alan Wolfe (Princeton University Press, 2003). 0691096619.

This is an essay collection, organized as a debate. Choice is seen as a way of improving educational opportunities for the underserved, those in low-income racial minorities, and to target vouchers to them. There are still a couple of perspectives. However, there is agreement that students' performance on reading and math is stagnant and that the U.S. system of schooling is inefficient and ineffective.

*Privatizing Education: Can the School Marketplace Deliver Freedom,
    Choice, Efficiency, Equity, and Social Cohesion?* edited by Henry M.
    Levin (Westview Press, 2001). 0813366402.

This book consists of a collection of essays about groups and lobbyists who wish to move education from the public to the private sector. This is occurring through tuition tax credits, vouchers, and some charter school initiatives. This text emanated from a conference held at Columbia University's Teachers College called "Setting the Agenda." The editor, a professor at Columbia, is initiating a center on school choice, the National Center for the Study of Privatization in Education.

USA Patriot Act (H.R. 3162)

(Full Title:
Uniting and Strengthening America by Providing Appropriate Tools Required to Intercept and Obstruct Terrorism Act of 2001)

This controversial act was devised to deter and punish terrorist acts in the United States and world-wide. The act also seeks to enhance law enforcement tools for investigative purposes. The several parts to this act were passed to enhance domestic security against terrorism, enhance surveillance procedures, deal with international money laundering, utilize bank secrecy provisions and activities of U.S. intelligence agencies, deal with currency crimes and protection, protect geographical borders and enhance immigration provisions, provide aid to victims of terrorism, and improve intelligence.

http://en.wikipedia.org/wiki/USA_PATRIOT_Act
This act was signed into law by President George W. Bush on October 26, 2001. The act was developed after the September 11, 2001, attacks on the United States. The *Wikipedia* site provides the entire scope of the act: Provisions, for example, Government access to library records; enforcement and sections which were considered unconstitutional by the courts; resistance by state and local governments to comply; and public opinion.

http://www.aclu.org/safefree/resources/17343res20031114.html
ACLU (American Civil Liberties Union) site. "Stop the Abuse of Power; Restore the Rule of Law." The ACLU discusses what they feel are significant flaws in the Patriot Act. These flaws would threaten fundamental freedoms because the act gives the U.S. government power—without probable cause—to access medical records, tax records, information about books one borrows from the library, and the power to break into one's home and conduct secret searches without revealing this to the owner. The site offers summaries and analyses of various aspects of the act.

http://www.ala.org/ala/oif/ifissues/usapatriotact.htm
This is the American Library Association/Office for Intellectual Freedom site, specifically dealing with the USA Patriot Act and Intellectual

Freedom. The site offers a number of PDF files on the Patriot Act: *Doe vs. Gonzalez*, Brochure for Patrons, Law Enforcement Inquiries, Legal Assistance with the Act, Reauthorization Analysis by the ALA Washington Office, plus links to frequently requested resources related to the act and guidelines for libraries and their staffs.

Journal Articles though the Web

http://www.boston.com/news/nation/articles/2006/03/24/bush_shuns_patriot_act_requirement/

Boston Globe. "Bush Shuns Patriot Act Requirement" by Charlie Savage, Globe staff, March 24, 2006. President George W. Bush signed the reauthorization of the USA Patriot Act and added an addendum that stipulated he did not feel obliged to obey any requirement that he needed to inform Congress about how the FBI (Federal Bureau of Investigation) was using the act's expanded police powers. However, the act did contain oversight provisions to be sure the FBI did not abuse special terrorism-related powers. The powers that President Bush have claimed have caused much consternation among members of both the Republican and Democratic representatives in Congress.

http://www.washingtonpost.com/wp-dyn/articles/A13970–2004Feb4.html

Washington Post. "N.Y. City Council Passes Anti-Patriot Act Measure" by Michelle Garcia, February 4, 2004. New York City, among many other cities, formally opposed the expanded powers that were granted to law enforcement agencies under the USA Patriot Act. The NYC Council actually condemned the law considering it unpatriotic and that it does away with civil liberties. The act infringes on privacy rights, basically the issue of viewing library patron records, and the easing of requirements for search warrants. New York City joined 246 other cities and counties and three states that passed legislation in opposition to the act.

http://www.fepproject.org/commentaries/patriotact.html

The Free Expression Policy Project, Brennan Center for Justice at New York University School of Law. "The Impact of the USA Patriot Act on Free Expression" by Nancy Kranich, Senior Research Fellow, May 5, 2003. The author, also a former President of the American Library Association, comments on the U.S. government threatening civil liberties in the name of national security. This article was in response to the fact that people were going to libraries for information on the Taliban, Islam, Afghanistan, and terrorism after the September 11, 2001 attacks on the United States. Ms. Kranich has stated the provisions of the USA Patriot Act which she feels deals a blow to freedom for information and expression. She is particularly concerned with roving wiretaps by monitoring electronic communications, extending telephone monitoring, and giving the FBI authority to obtain search warrants for business, medical, educational, library and bookstore records. There is an additional provision which prohibits people or institutions served with a search warrant from disclosing that this has taken place.

Books

How Patriotic Is the Patriot Act? by Amitai Etzioni (Routledge, 2004). 0415950473.

The author deals with how American society can protect its citizens against terrorist threats without infringing on individual rights. He also discusses the challenges that modern technology poses to individual freedoms. He suggests assessing various threats, for example, bioterrorism, and considers the benefits and threats of national ID cards. The author finds parts of the USA Patriot Act necessary—Student and Exchange Visitor Information System, and is disturbed by other parts—military tribunals.

America's Unpatriotic Acts: The Federal Government's Violation of Constitutional and Civil Rights by Walter M. Brasch (Peter Lang Publishing, 2005). 0820476080.

This act was drafted in secret within six weeks after the September 11, 2001 attacks on the United States. Congress did not have an opportunity to fully read the 342-page document. Congress was only given a few hours to peruse it, and there was virtually no debate on its contents. The author looks at the efforts of the USA Patriot Act on the nation and at the many civil rights violations conducted within the United States, as well as by the United States in foreign countries since the act was passed.

Opposing Viewpoints Series The Patriot Act edited by Louise I. Gerdes (Greenhaven Press, 2005). 0737730986.

This anthology presents differing views on whether the USA Patriot Act protects national security, violates civil liberties, and whether the act should be expanded. Most students reading the selections offered can easily determine the tone and subjectivity of the authors. The essays are short and get right to the core of the arguments.

Religion

Anti-Semitism

Atheism

Fundamentalism

New Age Spirituality

Opus Dei

Scientology

Sharia

Anti-Semitism

Anti-Semitism refers to prejudice against or hatred of the Jews. This issue has been in effect for at least 2000 years. Probably the most extreme example of anti-Semitism was the Holocaust, the persecution and murder of six million European Jews by Nazi Germany and its collaborators from 1933–1945, the end of World War II. There is a continuing threat of anti-Semitism today in America, in Europe, and in the Islamic world, with hate speech, violence particularly against Jews and Jewish institutions, and with the denial of the Holocaust.

http://en.wikipedia.org/wiki/Anti-Semitism

The *Wikipedia* site considers three forms of anti-Semitism: Religious (if Jews converted, attacks would stop); Racial (Jews are considered inferior); New anti-Semitism (focused opposition to the emergence of a Jewish homeland in the State of Israel). This site discusses the etymology and usage of the term; anti-Semitism and the Christian world in Europe and the Middle Ages with expulsions from England, France, Germany, and Spain; anti-Semitism in the nineteenth, twentieth, and twenty-first centuries; racial and new anti-Semitism; bans on kosher slaughter, and anti-Semitism in specific countries, and traces the history of anti-Semitism.

http://www.state.gov/g/drl/rls/40258.htm

United States Department of State. "Report on Global Anti-Semitism," January 5, 2005. There has been increased frequency of anti-Semitic incidents since 2000, particularly in Europe. This article is focusing on a definition of anti-Semitism as hatred toward Jews individually, and as a group. Israel has been demonized, sometimes compared with Nazi leaders. There are four main sources of global anti-Semitism: Traditional anti-Jewish prejudice that has pervaded Europe—includes ultra-nationalists and others who insist that the Jewish community controls governments, the media, international media, and the financial world; anti-Israeli sentiment; anti-Semitism within Muslim populations, and, criticisms of the United States and its relationship to Israel.

http://www.antisemitism.org.il/

Coordination Forum for Countering Anti-Semitism. This site provides a summary of anti-Semitic incidents in 2006. Jews were killed just for being Jewish, with crimes perpetrated in France, and the United States. Anti-Semitism is also a part of Russia's official policy. Iran has taken a lead, followed by Syria. The Forum lists ten most prominent incidents that took place in 2006:

1. United States (six shot and killed at Seattle Jewish Federation);
2. France (murder of a Jew in Paris);

3. Russia (eleven stabbed at Moscow Synagogue rampage);
4. Norway (shots fired at synagogue in Oslo);
5. Iran (Holocaust cartoon exhibition);
6. Iran (host of Holocaust Deniers at Tehran Conference);
7. Britain (Jewish girl beaten on London bus);
8. Belgium (attack on Jewish family on train to Antwerp);
9. France (attack on Jewish youth in Annecy);
10. Austria (release of Holocaust denier David Irving from prison).

Journal Articles through the Web

http://www.questia.com/PM.qst?a=o&d=5000833234&er=deny

Commentary. "On Ignoring Anti-Semitism" by Ruth R. Wisse, Vol. 114, October 2002. The author refers to an article in the *New Republic* magazine which indicated that the magazine's literary editor, Leon Wieseltier, said that American Jews were bringing up unwarranted fears by comparing the Arab war against Israel with Hitler's war against the Jews. The article provoked a number of rebuttals and defenses.

http://www.honestreporting.com/articles/45884734/reports/Anti-Semitism_at_Le_Monde_and_Beyond.asp

Honest Reporting. Media Critiques; "Anti-Semitism at '*Le Monde*' and Beyond" by Tom Gross, *Wall Street Journal* (Europe), June 2, 2005. A landmark ruling by a French court found its leading newspaper guilty of slandering Israel and the Jewish people. Three writers and the publisher of *Le Monde* were found guilty. Their article was published in 2002, "Israel-Palestine: The Cancer." *Le Monde* did not publish a condemnation of the article. The article referred to the Jews as "a contemptuous people taking satisfaction in humiliating others" and "imposing their unmerciful rule." The article refers to newspapers in other countries which also have articles misrepresenting the Jews.

http://www.engageonline.org.uk/journal/index.php?journal_id=5&article_id=15

Engage. "The Rise of a New Anti-Semitism in the UK" by Shalom Lappin, January 2006. The author writes of Israel pursuing increased repressive occupation of the Palestinians in the West Bank, East Jerusalem, and until July 2005, Gaza. The author feels that the actions of the Israeli government should be under scrutiny and criticism. Israel has been looked upon as the aggressor in racism, and oppression to dispossess the Palestinians. There are almost six million Muslims in Britain and these people have been influential in rejecting Israel's right to exist with strong support from Palestinian suicide bombings. The article continues with historical roots of the New Anti-Semitism in England and the dismay surrounding lack of support for organized Jewish life.

Books

Anti-Semitism: Myth and Hate from Antiquity to the Present by Marvin Perry and Frederick M. Schweitzer (Palgrave Macmillan, 2005). 1403968934.

The authors discuss the history of anti-Semitism, beginning in the first century AD, and analyze origins of anti-Semitic myths. There are chapters on Holocaust denial, anti-Semitism in the Muslim world, the writings and speeches of the Nation of Islam.

Why the Jews? The Reason for Anti-Semitism by Dennis Prager and Joseph Telushkin (Touchstone, 2003). 0743246209.

The authors discuss the replicating of Nazi anti-Semitism in the Arab world, the pervasive anti-Zionism/anti-Semitism on university campuses, the rise of anti-Semitism in Europe, why the United States and Israel are linked in the minds of anti-Semites.

The Changing Face of Anti-Semitism: From Ancient Times to the Present Day by Walter Laqueur (Oxford University Press, 2006). 0195304292.

The author traces the history of anti-Semitism and the evolution of this hatred from distrust in the pre-Christian era to a rage against "Christ killers" in the Medieval Christian world. In the nineteenth century, anti-Semitism and the racial hatred formed the basis of the Holocaust. The author feels that racial anti-Semitism is confined to the extreme right-wingers. There is also intense hostility toward the State of Israel.

Atheism

Atheism refers to the denial and//or disbelief in the existence of any deities. Many consider atheists to be non-spiritual or not religious. However, there are some religious beliefs that do not have any specific deities. This is the situation in some forms of Buddhism. The main organization which labors for the civil liberties of atheists is American Atheists.

http://en.wikipedia.org/wiki/Atheism

The *Wikipedia* site offers an etymology of this belief, types of atheism, the history of this belief system, lists atheist organizations, the reasons for atheism—scientific, historical, philosophical, logical, personal, social, and ethical, plus the site provides a section on criticism of atheism.

http://www.atheists.org/

This is the site of the organization, American Atheists. The organization was founded in 1963 as an outcome of a Supreme Court case which resulted in ending prayer and bible reading in public schools. There are a number of sections on this site to download that provide an overview of this belief. These sections raise provocative questions: Do religious accounts of creation make sense? Does religious doctrine and ceremony belong in government? Should seasonal religious displays be erected on public property? The site also provides articles about atheists.

http://atheism.about.com/

About: Agnosticism/Atheism. There are a number of sections on this site which reflect on atheism and its relationship to religion, the paranormal, tolerance vs. disagreement, and issues of church and state. Some of the sections are titled: How Moderate Should Atheists Be? or How Less Extreme? Religion vs. the Paranormal; Functional Definitions of Religion, and Secularism as Philosophy.

Journal Articles through the Web

http://www.americanatheist.org/

American Atheists, a journal of atheist news and thought. "A Dispute Over a College Course to Examine Creationism in the Context of 'Religious Mythology' Escalates in Kansas" by Conrad F. Goeringer, December 12, 2005. This article is about the religious studies professor, Dr. Paul Mirecki from the University of Kansas, who wanted to teach a course on evolution and creationism. The professor originally preferred his course title to have the words "religious mythologies." Kansas state education officials wanted "intelligent design" taught. They wanted this taught in science courses instead of classes teaching history, ancient philosophy, and religion. The professor was assaulted by two unidentified people after which Dr. Mirecki resigned as head of the University of Kansas Department of Religious Studies.

http://www.timesonline.co.uk/article/0,,2-1798944,00.html
Times Online, Britain. "Societies Worse Off 'When They Have God on Their Side'" by Ruth Gledhill, religion correspondent, September 27, 2005. The author feels that religious belief can be harmful for society. This belief could contribute to high murder rates, abortion, sexual promiscuity, and suicide. The author alluded to a study which indicated belief in and worship of God contribute to social problems. She also mentions that many conservative evangelicals in the United States consider Darwinism to be a social evil because it inspires atheism. Gregory Paul, a social scientist, authored the study and used data from the Gallup organization and other research bodies.

http://www.atheists.org/Atheism/
American Atheists, 2006. This article provides a definition of atheism which declares: "There are no forces, phenomena, or entities which exist outside of or apart from physical nature or which transcend nature, and that humankind is on its own." This definition and additional thoughts on atheists were communicated to the Supreme Court when atheists petitioned to have school prayer dropped from the public schools. Other comments about atheists were that they believe in their fellow man, not in God. They believe that no help can come to them through prayer, but instead find an inner conviction. An atheist strives to become involved in life, not to escape into death, and he wants man to understand and love man and to have an ethical way of life.

Books

The God Delusion by Richard Dawkins (Bantam Press, 2006).
0593055489.
The author is an atheist and asserts the irrationality of belief in God and the harm religion has caused on society from the Crusades to September 11, 2001. He examines God in all forms and comes to the conclusion that there is no supreme being. He discusses how religion fuels war and encourages bigotry. He considers himself to be a deeply religious nonbeliever.

The End of Faith: Religion, Terror, and the Future of Reason by Sam Harris (W.W. Norton & Company, 2005). 0393035158.
The author provides an analysis of the clash between reason and religion in the modern world. He warns against the infusion of organized religion into world politics. Harris has developed this theme from insights from neuroscience, philosophy, and Eastern mysticism. He believes in ethics and spirituality that is secular and humanistic.

Atheist Manifesto: The Case Against Christianity, Judaism, and Islam by Michel Onfray (Arcade Publishing, 2007). 1559708204.

The author discusses how the world's three major monotheistic religions have attempted to suppress knowledge, science, pleasure, and desire. Onfray mentions that God is very much alive, but controlled by fundamentalists who are a danger to the human race. He speaks of religious intolerance over the many millennia and believes that the three religions demand faith, belief, obedience, and submission, and praise the afterlife at the expense of life now.

Fundamentalism

This is a fairly new segment of Protestantism having had its roots in the late 1800s. The first phase lasted until 1925 with the Scopes trial. The movement developed and grew as a religious movement as a reaction to liberalizing trends in American Protestantism. The movement became strong around 1970 and has gained many adherents since then. In many Fundamentalist congregations, one-third to one-half of its members had belonged to the Catholic Church. Today, one out of six Hispanics in the United States are now Fundamentalists. The issues that drew new recruits to Fundamentalism were a liberalizing and secularizing trend within Protestantism that was purported to weaken the Christian message, the belief in Darwinism which questioned Scripture, and higher criticism of the Bible which originated in Germany. The Bible is basic to the faith of Fundamentalists. (The information in this paragraph is from http://www.catholic.com/library/Fundamentalism.asp.)

Even though the term Fundamentalism was coined in the United States, this movement has emerged in faiths worldwide: in Judaism, Islam, Sikhism, Confucianism, and Hinduism. Fundamentalism is a rebellion against secularism in the modern world. Fundamentalists wish to see religion, or God, reflected in public life. They want to see faith play an important part in the lives of people on a daily basis.

http://en.wikipedia.org/wiki/Fundamentalism

The *Wikipedia* site provides a definition of this religious movement; the historical background and development of the term Fundamentalism; controversy over use of the term; basic beliefs of religious fundamentalists from the perspective of Christians, Jews, Mormons, and Muslims; arguments in favor of their positions; and Fundamentalism and politics.

http://religiousmovements.lib.virginia.edu/nrms/fund.html

This site deals with new religious movements. It offers a profile of Fundamentalism including the origin of the concept (time and location) and its sacred text which is the Bible. Fundamentalists believe that the Bible is to be understood as literally true. The conservative estimate of the size of the membership would be at least thirty million in the United States alone. The site also deals with problems in analyzing Fundamentalism and how to define it. In addition, there are links to a number of Fundamentalist sites.

http://www.global-vision.org/sacred/fundamentalism.html

Science and the Sacred site. This site considers Fundamentalism to be a religious phenomenon, a political movement, and a state of consciousness. Members of this movement are dissatisfied with society; they are preoccupied with religious beliefs; they assume there is a battle between forces of good and evil; they also claim divine authority to justify violence against those they perceive as enemies. Fundamentalism appears in many forms, including Hindu, Jewish, Christian, and Islamic, and has led to genocides, crusades, jihads, witch hunts, inquisitions, deportations, pogroms, holocausts, terrorist attacks, revolutions, and human rights violations. There is much information on this site for study and debate.

Journal Articles through the Web

http://compass.bw.semcs.net/subject/history/article_view?article_id= hico_articles_bpl125

History Compass, peer-reviewed journal, College of William & Mary. "Islamic Fundamentalism and Political Islam" by Tamara Sonn, October 2005. This article is about political Islam, a movement which began in the late 1920s as a result of secular governments not securing economic independence, prosperity, and good governance in the Muslim world. The movement wanted a return to the sovereignty of Islamic law. Yet, within this movement are those who also advocate a peaceful approach to Islam through teaching which contrasts with those who are jihadists who believe only in violent revolution to achieve their goals.

http://www.findarticles.com/p/articles/mi_qa3821/is_200304/ai_n9174278

Journal of Third World Studies. "Religious Fundamentalism in Developing Countries" by Cecil B. Currey, Spring 2003. This review is based on a book of the same title published by Greenwood Press in 2001. The book consists of chapters contributed by different people on various subjects, but Islam is the focus in four of the eight chapters. One of those chapters concentrates on evangelical Christianity and black Pentecostals in London. The author indicated that black churches are highly critical of white ones and compromise on biblical teachings on marriage and divorce. Black ministers are distressed that the Church of England makes allowances for gays, lesbians, single mothers, and promiscuous sexuality. The author of the article reveals that the chapter author speaks of black theologians as pastoral and that they enjoy telling stories about God's love. The black theologians use the Bible to motivate action and to substantiate points made in stories by citing Scripture.

http://jci.sagepub.com/cgi/content/abstract/27/4/389

Journal of Communication Inquiry. "Communicating Islamic Fundamentalism as Global Citizenship" by Lina Khatib, Vol. 27, No. 4, pp. 389–409, 2003. This article examines Islamic Fundamentalism as being an imagined community, communicating both a local and global identity. The author reveals how Islamic Fundamentalists use the Internet. The latter becomes a "portable homeland." Internet use helps them to strengthen global ties. This shows that Islamic Fundamentalism is not at all an inward-looking force, but uses the Internet as a tool to carry out political conflicts.

Books

Fundamentalism and American Culture by George M. Marsden (Oxford University Press, 2006). 0195300475.

This text has been considered a classic in religious history. The author feels that Fundamentalists are not only religious conservatives, but conservatives who are willing to take a stand and fight for what they think is right. The author traces the origin of and direction of this influential religious movement. In this updated edition, the author compares Fundamentalism since the 1970s to that of the 1920s and the growth in political emphasis and power.

Fundamentalism: The Search for Meaning by Malise Ruthven (Oxford University Press, 2005). 0192806068.

The author discusses what Fundamentalism means. It was originally coined by American Protestant evangelicals in the 1920s, and now it includes radical conservatives—Islamic radicals in the Muslim world, the militant Israeli settlers who oppose them, and even the Sikh, Hindu, and Buddhist nationalists who justify their political agendas by divine edicts or religious tradition.

Strong Religion: The Rise of Fundamentalisms Around the World by Gabriel A. Almond et al. (University of Chicago Press, 2003). 0226014983.

The authors studied the research done from the Fundamentalism Project, a ten-year study of the militant movements on five continents and within seven world religions. The authors analyze social structures and political environments from Islamic Hamas and Hizbullah to the Catholic and Protestant paramilitaries of Northern Ireland and from the Moral Majority and Christian Coalition of the United States to the Sikh radicals and Hindu nationalists of India. The authors also provide details of the various cultures that nourish such militant movements.

New Age Spirituality

This religious movement, though it is not a formal one, has no sacred text, or central organization, membership, clergy, dogma or creed. Those who follow this spiritual movement believe in astrology to foretell the future, that crystals are a source of healing, Tarot Cards are a base for life decisions, that God is a state of higher consciousness, and that each person is God, which is the personification of human potential. New Agers represent about 20 percent of the population. (Information from http://www.religioustolerance.org/newage.htm).

http://en.wikipedia.org/wiki/New_Age
The New Age movement appeared in the late twentieth century and combines elements of spiritual traditions from both the East and West. These traditions borrowed ideas from modern science (psychology and ecology), and from major religions (spiritualism, Buddhism, Hinduism, Shamanism, Sufism, Taoism, and Neo-Paganism). The *Wikipedia* site also offers links to sites that deal with both criticism and skepticism about New Age practices.

http://www.godandscience.org/apologetics/newageintro.htm
"New Age Spirituality—An Examination of Beliefs." This site offers a discussion of New Age ideas: a) The New Age Paradigm with the possibility of reincarnation, aspects of humanistic psychology, Western criticism, and the possibility that astrology and use of crystals have a scientific basis; b) Does the Bible and science support reincarnation; c) what Does the Bible say about astrology? This site provides many links to various aspects of New Age Spirituality.

http://www.sideroad.com/New_Age_Spirituality/new_age_spirituality.html
"New Age Spirituality" by Elaine Murray. The author speaks of getting one's power back. New Age refers to the Age of Aquarius, an age of evolutionary change of consciousness in humanity for the good of everyone. New Age Spirituality requires that each person must take responsibility for everything that happens in life and to learn to love oneself. In order to create inner peace one should meditate, which is the practice of listening to God while in an altered state of consciousness. There is no need for a priest or minister to intercede.

Journal Articles through the Web

http://www.csicop.org/si/2004–05/new-age.html
Skeptical Inquirer Magazine. "Bridging the Chasm Between Two Cultures" by Karla McLaren, May 2004. The author discusses the conflict between the skeptical community and the metaphysical/new age community.

She believes there is a full clash of cultures between fact-based and faith-based viewpoints and between rationality and credulity. The author explains what encouraged her to become an adherent of new age culture and to develop an understanding of those who are critical thinkers and their expectations of life, peace, love, and humanity.

http://www.americanspiritnews.com/
American Spirit Psychic Newspaper. "Editorial Hello and Welcome" by Kathy Bibeau, October–November 2006. The author reflects on the holiday time and the fact that this is a good time for people to contemplate on what is holy or spiritual. This newspaper is dedicated to assisting people in understanding that their spirits are within their bodies and they have psychic talents and spiritual rights. The author comments on various articles in this issue of the newspaper. One article deals with the fact that holiday time is a time of energy to prepare oneself for the coming New Year. Another article deals with the here-after and a "doorway to beyond."

http://www.consciouscreation.com/journal/index.html
Conscious Creation Journal. "Do You Attract What You Want In Your Life" by Michael Roads, February 2004. The author looks at life through human energy. All of us generate and express physical, mental, and emotional energy. This energy could be under our control which the author believes is rare, or energy that one gathers as a reaction to situations one encounters. The author also feels that the energy one generates toward another person is a field of energy that attracts reciprocal energy. If you have negative energy toward someone or to a situation, you will be impacted negatively.

http://www.religioustolerance.org/newage.htm
ReligiousTolerance.org. "New Age Spirituality" by B.A. Robinson, October 1, 2006. This article provides the historical development of New Age Spirituality, and a description of each of the fundamental beliefs: Monism, Pantheism, Reincarnation, Karma, Aura, Personal Transformation, Ecological Responsibility, Universal Religion, and the New World Order. The article further deals with New Age practices: channeling, use of crystals, meditating, New Age music, divination, astrology, holistic health, and the Human Potential Movement.

Books

Another Gospel: Cults, Alternative Religions, and the New Age Movement
by Ruth A. Tucker (Zondervan, 2004). 0310259371.
The author surveys major alternative religions in the United States. She also investigates why crystals, shamans, guided imagery, and healing meditation, which are all New Age practices, have been so widely accepted. The author also highlights controversies with each movement.

In Search of New Age Spiritualities by Adam Possamai (Ashgate Publishing, 2005). 0754652130.

The author interviewed thirty-five people about how they followed their spiritual journey and what techniques or meditation they used.

The New Age Movement in American Culture by Richard Kyle (University Press of America, 1995). 0761800115.

The author offers a comprehensive cultural history of this movement. He found several prominent themes: New Age and the Occult Tradition, Science and Education in the New Age, Politics and Economics, Salvation through Psychology, and Health and Healing.

New Age and Neopagan Religions in America by Sarah M. Pike (Columbia University Press, 2004). 0231124023.

The author discusses the daily lives of adherents to these new religions, and what healing rituals they practice aside from self-awareness meditation and channeling. Within all the new religious groups there is an emphasis on nature, women's spiritual leadership, seasonal ritual, and personal transformation.

Opus Dei

This is a Catholic institution, founded in 1928 in Spain, whose mission is to spread the message that work and circumstances of everyday life are occasions that help one get closer to God, to serve others and to improve society. Opus Dei also complements the work of local churches by offering classes, talks, retreats, and pastoral care that help people develop their personal spiritual life. Diocesan priests may join the Priestly Society of the Holy Cross, which is a society united to the Opus Dei Prelature. This institution is governed by a Prelate in accord with canon law and its own statutes and is currently situated in sixty-one countries.

http://en.wikipedia.org/wiki/Opus_Dei
Opus Dei is Latin for "the Work of God." The organization is often referred to as "the Work." Opus Dei is part of the Catholic Church and it emphasizes the Catholic belief that "everyone is called to be a saint." The membership, which is approximately 85,000, is known as "Supernumeraries." These people lead traditional lives and have traditional careers. The *Wikipedia* site provides a historical account of this institution, its doctrine, structure and activities, different types of membership, papal support, controversy, corporal mortification (where pain and/or discomfort is inflicted on oneself), and Opus Dei within popular culture.

http://www.odan.org
ODAN Pus Dei Awareness Network. Three groups joined to create an awareness of harmful experiences they underwent with Opus Dei worldwide. They felt that the membership in Opus Dei no longer have personal freedoms, that they have been indoctrinated through aggressive recruiting techniques and the withholding of information so they cannot make informed choices. This website has posted new testimonies from people who were members and/or experienced the pressure to join. These testimonies are: Opus Dei Recruits Minors and Deceives Church Officials, Opus Dei Superiors Lied to Church Officials, and Government, Direction, and Control in Opus Dei. There are many links to help understand the pros and cons of this movement.

http://www.opusdei.us/art.php?p=7017
Opus Dei. This site offers a response to *The DaVinci Code* from the Prelature of Opus Dei in the United States. "*The DaVinci Code*, the Catholic Church, and Opus Dei," November 16, 2006. The site is clear about referring to *The DaVinci Code* as a work of fiction. This text has also indicated the increased public interest in the origins of the Bible and central Christian doctrines such as the divinity of Jesus Christ. The writers of this article consider that the data in *The DaVinci Code* lacks support among reputable scholars. They feel that Opus Dei was not portrayed realistically

202   Encouraging and Supporting Student Inquiry

or truthfully. The site offers additional information to dispel the impression one receives while either reading *The DaVinci Code* or seeing the movie. This information is found in such sections as: Opus Dei and Monks, Opus Dei and Crime, Opus Dei and Corporal Mortification, Opus Dei and Cult Allegations, Opus Dei and Women, and Opus Dei and the Vatican Bank.

Journal Articles through the Web

http://www.americamagazine.org/articles/martin-opusdei.cfm

America, the National Catholic Weekly. "Opus Dei in the United States" by James Martin, S.J., Vol. 196, No. 2, January 15, 2007. The author of this article is an associate editor of *America*. He speaks of Opus Dei as a very conservative group in the Catholic Church. He indicated that it is difficult to find balanced reporting of this movement because of the different views on the group and its influence in Vatican circles. Its critics believe Opus Dei is a cult-like organization that uses secrecy and manipulation to advance its agenda. This article is based on material written by Opus Dei, plus its critics, as well as interviews with current and former Opus Dei members and with priests, religious and lay persons, campus ministers, scholars, and journalists who have encountered Opus Dei in the United States.

http://www.time.com/time/magazine/article/0,9171,1184078,00.html

Time, in Partnership with CNN. "The Ways of Opus Dei" by David Van Biema, April 24, 2006, The author provides an inside look into Opus Dei, a controversial group within the Catholic Church. This article tries to dispel the myths surrounding Opus Dei as a result of the images presented in both the book, *The DaVinci Code,* and in the movie. The article addresses both supportive and critical views of the organization. It is a lengthy, interesting, objective eight-page article for those who wish to understand the precepts of the "liturgy."

http://www.findarticles.com/p/articles/mi_qa3944/is_200605/ai_n16410176

Church & State. "Breaking the Opus Dei Code" by Rob Boston, May 2006. The author writes about a religious bookstore in Washington, D.C., called the Catholic Information Center. The author believes this bookstore is an American outpost for Opus Dei. The author names some U.S. senators who are conservative Catholics and Opus Dei boosters. Opus Dei's Bishop reports directly to the Pope. The author believes that Opus Dei is dedicated to fending off liberalism in the Catholic Church and that it advances a hard-right political agenda.

Books

Opus Dei: An Objective Look Behind the Myths and Reality of the Most Controversial Force in the Catholic Church by John L. Allen (Doubleday Religion, 2005). 0385514492.

The author is a journalist who covers the Vatican. In this text he describes the organization, its clergy, and lay people. He visited Opus Dei outposts around the world, and conducted 300 hours of interviews with members and non-members. He also lived for five days in an Opus Dei residence. He objectively discusses Opus Dei's treatment of women, secrecy, financial holdings, wielding of Church and political influences and recruiting practices, and ways to improve the image of the organization.

Ordinary Work, Extraordinary Grace: My Spiritual Journey in Opus Dei by Scott Hahn (Doubleday Religion, 2006). 0385519249.

The author is a member of Opus Dei. He joined this group because he found in it a livelier faith than what he had known among fellow evangelical Protestants. He expounds on the group's tenets and offers some personal awareness as a member. As a teacher and biblical theologian he provides an insider's view of Opus Dei.

Their Kingdom Come: Inside the Secret World of Opus Dei by Robert Hutchison (St. Martin's Griffin, 2006). 0312357605.

The author exposes the inner workings of Opus Dei which is headquartered in Rome and whose members include the Pope's personal secretary, his spokesman, and several of his close ministers. The author portrays Opus Dei as an organization that has infiltrated the world's upper echelons of political, financial, and educational power. Opus Dei, both politically and theologically conservative, flourished during the papacy of John Paul II.

Scientology

The word Scientology means "the study of truth." It encompasses the study and handling of the spirit in relationship to itself, others, and all of life. Some of the fundamental truths are: man is an immortal, spiritual being; his capabilities are unlimited; he can solve his own problems, gain lasting happiness, and achieve higher states of awareness and ability. Man consists of three parts: spirit (the individual himself); mind (a communication and control system between himself and his environment); and body (but this is not really the person). There are also dynamics: infinity (God); spiritual; physical universe (matter, energy, space, and time); life forms (plant and animal life); mankind (species); group survival (friends, nation, race); family and children; self (information from: http://scientology.bridgeinc.us/scientology/fot.php).

http://www.scientology.org/
This is the Home Page for Scientology. It offers a brief description of this belief and has links to areas of one's life that a person might wish to explore: unhappiness, stress, anxiety, personal well-being, marriage, children, helping others, integrity, education and learning, job productivity, financial success, or drug and alcohol problems. The site also has sections on materials and services, Scientology in the news, and a church locator.

http://www.xenu.net/
Operation Clambake. This site is critical of Scientology. It offers Frequently Asked Questions, and debates with Scientologists. There are also sections on what is happening now and people in the news; L. Ron Hubbard who was the founder of Dianetics and the Church of Scientology. There are several sites about Hubbard. In addition, there are links to techniques of Scientology, the fact that it is the cult of celebrities and why, an archive of critical research, its propaganda, and personal accounts of former members, and Scientology and the press.

http://en.wikipedia.org/wiki/Scientology
The *Wikipedia* site offers background into the beliefs and practices of Scientology, church ceremonies, its origins, membership (Church of Scientology, Independent Scientology Groups, Scientology and Celebrities), controversy and criticism—as a state-recognized religion, as a cult, as a commercial venture, and its relationship to psychiatry.

Journal Articles through the Web

http://www.factnet.org/Scientology/dianetics.html
F.A.C.T.net (Fight Against Coercive Tactics Network), Scientology and Dianetics. This site is in opposition to the tenets of Scientology. Within

the Table of Contents one would find: Scientology Litigations and Lawsuits, Scientology's Fraud and Criminality, Scientology's Celebrities, Human Rights Abuses, and Freedom of Speech. There is a section on governments in opposition to Scientology, listing articles which discuss and reflect on this theme. The site is continually updated as current news articles and data about Scientology surfaces.

http://www.cs.cmu.edu/~dst/JeremyPerkins/Articles/buffalo-news-
   2005-02-xx-letters.html
   Buffalo News. "Letters to the *Buffalo News* Regarding Scientology," February 6, 2005. One letter, "Scientology Does Help With Life's Problems," which indicated that for eighteen years a particular person was helped to handle her problems through Scientology, was very negative about the newspaper's reporting. Another article, "Scientology Helped Save a Brother from Dying" was also a derogatory commentary on the *Buffalo News*. The writer indicated that her brother was a drug addict and homeless vagrant, but was helped by the Church's drug detox program. A writer of a third article, "Scientology has Helped Countless World Citizens," mentioned that he had been a member of Scientology for ten years and felt younger and happier than previously. He used Scientology to help children read, and said that in Buffalo the Church of Scientology had drug free marshals to help get children off drugs, expanded Buffalo's business community, and cared for victims of the September 11, 2001 attacks. There was also an article in support of the *Buffalo News* which exposed the harm Scientology can do.

http://www.sptimes.com/2004/07/18/Tampabay/About_Scientology.shtml
   St. Petersburg Times. "About Scientology," *Times* staff writer, July 18, 2004. This article gives some background on Scientology and then provides information on Scientology and the position the church takes toward gay marriage (against it, since the only recognized marriage is between a man and woman); abortion (against it because it can traumatize the mother and unborn child); birth control (not too negative on this procedure; however, procreation and child rearing are important); afterlife (the spirit lives many lifetimes); supreme being (do not necessarily believe in the worship of such a one), and female and/or married ministers (the ministry is open to men and women).

Books

The Challenge of the Cults and New Religions by Ron Rhodes (Zondervan, 2001). 0310232171.
   This book focuses on twelve of the primary representative cults. Each cult receives a separate chapter. The author, an authority on cults, explains what they are and why they are a cause of concern in the twenty-first century. Scientology is one of the twelve cults discussed in this text.

The Church of Scientology by J. Gordon Melton (Signature Books, 2000). 1560851392.

This book is a cogent study by one of the foremost experts on new and unconventional religions. Dr. Melton explores Scientology's good works and its help with addiction treatment, literacy, and civil rights programs. He also discusses mysticism and some secrecy within Scientology. In addition, the author examines the hierarchical structure of the church and its theology.

What is Scientology by L. Ron Hubbard (Bridge Publications, updated, 1998). 1573181226.

This text takes the reader through an extensive overview of what Scientology has to offer and explains why it has become the fastest growing religion in the world. The text purports to reveal that Scientology can restore honesty and trust, create happiness, raise IQ, and improve one's personality.

Sharia

This system of law is inspired by the Koran, the Islamic holy text, the Sunna, older Arabic law systems, and the work of Muslim scholars over the two first centuries of Islam. It is the Muslim law, but Islamic inspired. Sharia extends beyond law, as well. It is the totality of religious, political, social, domestic, and private life. Muslims are not totally bound by the Sharia when they live or travel outside the Muslim world. Regulations of the Sharia can be divided into two groups: regulations on worship and ritual duties, and regulations of juridical and political nature. The Sharia is important in domestic judicial fields like family, marriage, and inheritance. (Information from http://lexicorient.com/e.o/sharia.htm)

http://en.wikipedia.org/wiki/Sharia

The term Sharia means "way" or "path." Sharia deals with many aspects of daily life: politics, economics, banking, business law, contract law, sexuality, and social issues. This *Wikipedia* site presents the etymology of Sharia, sections of Sharia law, divergent developments after the nineteenth century, contemporary practice of Sharia law which encompasses marriage laws, divorce laws, penalty for theft, penalty for adultery, role of women under Sharia, dress codes, domestic punishments, customs and behavioral laws, festivals, dietary laws, illegal sexual relations like adultery and homosexuality, freedom of speech, democracy, and human rights.

http://www.answering-islam.org/Sharia/

"Differing Issues Regarding the Sharia Law." There are a number of links to articles on Islamic Sharia law: divorce, fatawas regarding women, Islamic law on female circumcision, Islamic law in general, temporary marriage, jihad in Islam, American Islam, jihad, and terrorism. There are also links to the beard in Islam, medical ethics, euthanasia, and organ transplants.

http://www.cfr.org/publication/8034/

Council on Foreign Relations. "Islam: Governing Under Sharia," March 14, 2005. The Council on Foreign Relations site answers many questions regarding Sharia. Some of the questions posed are: How have various Muslim countries applied Sharia? Does Sharia apply only to religious matters? Is there only one interpretation of Sharia? Do traditional Sharia laws continue to apply in modern countries? How is Sharia applied to banking and finance laws? How does Sharia influence modern criminal law? What are the traditional Sharia laws governing personal status issues? And are non-Muslims bound by personal status Sharia courts?

Journal Articles through the Web

http://www.guardian.co.uk/theissues/article/0,6512,777972,00.html

Guardian Unlimited. "Sharia Law" by Susie Steiner, August 20, 2002. The author explains the Islamic legal system which sentenced a Nigerian woman to be stoned to death. The woman had been accused of adultery. The act of stoning was originally delayed until the woman finished breast-feeding her daughter which would not be before January 2004. The Nigerian Supreme Court, though, ruled the Sharia practice unconstitutional and has caused much unrest in the country among those who are for and against carrying out the strict laws. The author revealed other cases of Sharia law being exercised in Nigeria: a teenage single mother given 100 lashes for adultery, although she argued she was raped by three men, and a death sentence imposed on a man of fifty for raping a nine-year-old. The latter case was unusual because men are rarely treated that harshly.

http://news.bbc.co.uk/1/hi/world/africa/621126.stm

BBC News. "The Many Faces of Sharia" by Michael Gallagher, June 21, 2000. The author indicated that Sharia differs greatly in its several implementations throughout the Islamic world. Saudi Arabia has practiced a harsh form of this law where murderers and drug smugglers may be executed, thieves lose their hands, and adulterers are stoned. Malaysia interprets Sharia differently and not as strictly. The author also discusses the Sharia Code for Living, which goes beyond criminal justice—prayers, fasting, and donations to the poor, women cover themselves, the sexes are segregated, and basically, the Koran becomes a country's constitution. In Pakistan, Sharia was made the supreme law in 1998. Sharia was abandoned in Turkey.

http://www.americanthinker.com/2005/08/top_ten_reasons_why_sharia_is.html

American Thinker. "Top Ten Reasons Why Sharia is Bad for All Societies" by James Arlandson, August 13, 2005. The author relates each of his top ten reasons why Sharia is bad:

10. Islam commands that drinkers and gamblers be whipped. The author feels there is no help to rehabilitate these offenders.

9. Islam allows husbands to hit their wives even if the husbands merely fear highhandedness in their wives. Women are continually oppressed—need to wear veils, are not mobile, cannot drive cars, and their testimony counts half that of men.

8. Islam allows an injured plaintiff to exact legal revenge—physical eye for physical eye.

7. Islam commands that a male and female thief must have hands cut off—repentance is acceptable only after the mutilation.

6. Islam commands that highway robbers be crucified or mutilated.

5. Islam commands that homosexuals be executed—thrown off a mountain or stoned to death.

4. Islam orders unmarried fornicators (having illegal sex) to be whipped and adulterers stoned to death.

3. Islam orders death for Muslims and possible death for non-Muslim critics of Muhammad and the Koran and for Sharia, as well.

2. Islam orders apostates to be killed—they are those who criticize clerical rule and leave Islam.

1. Islam commands offensive, aggressive, and unjust jihad. The rules of jihad are women and children are enslaved, jihadists can have sex with slaves, old men and monks could be killed. In war, civilian homes may be destroyed.

The author insists that this process of "law" be ended and that Islam must reform.

Books

Radical Islam's Rules: The Worldwide Spread of Extreme Sharia Law by Paul Marshall (Rowman & Littlefield Publishers, Inc., 2005). 0742543625.
In this book, noted human rights activists and scholars trace the growth of Sharia in Saudi Arabia, Iran, Pakistan, Sudan, Nigeria, Malaysia, and Indonesia. They document Sharia's threat to the status of women, religious freedom, and democracy, and they suggest how the rest of the world should respond.

Islamic Law: Theory and Practice edited by Robert Gleave and Eugenia Kermeli (I.B. Tauris, 2001). 1860646522.
This text deals with Islamic law in both the classic and modern periods and over a range of societies. The text is divided into four sections: legal theory, fatwas and muftis in classical Islamic law, the position of religious minorities under Islamic law, and modern developments in Islamic law. The book also explores the concept of jihad, where a jurist apprehends God's law and turns it into a legal ruling, and how this has formed law in both Sunni and Shiite Islam.

The Origins and Evolution of Islamic Law by Wael B. Hallaq (Cambridge University Press, 2005). 0521005809.
This study covers more than three centuries of legal history and presents an account of how Islam developed its own law from ancient Near Eastern legal cultures, Arabian customary law, and Koranic reform. The text explores the interplay between law and politics, and shows how the jurists and ruling elite allow Islamic law to become independent of the "state."

Sexuality

Homosexuality

Polygamy

Pornography

Same-Sex Marriage

Homosexuality

Homosexuality refers to the sexual attraction between individuals of the same sex. The relationships between these individuals may be just intimate or sexual, or both. There are three major forms of homosexual relationships: egalitarian—two partners, either two lesbians or two gay men, with no relevance to age, and practice the same-gender sex roles as heterosexuals of their sex; gender-structured—where each partner plays a different gender role; age-structured—partners of different ages, one may be an adolescent, another an adult, as in classical times.

http://en.wikipedia.org/wiki/Homosexuality

The *Wikipedia* site provides a wealth of information on this topic. The data delves into etymology and usage; academic study via an anthropology discussion; biological identification through physiological differences in people and homosexuality in animals; psychological and behavioral studies, nature vs. nurture; homosexuality and society—sexual practices, modern law; political aspects and scapegoating; homosexuality in the military ancient world, Middle Ages, and modern times; youth groups; same-sex love in pre-modern times; and modern developments—marriage/civil unions, parenthood, political and religious developments.

http://www.religioustolerance.org/homosexu.htm

ReligiousTolerance.org site. "Homosexuality and Bisexuality: All Sides to the Issue." This site offers differing viewpoints and beliefs about homosexuality. Trends—acceptance by older teens and young adults. Geographical Scope—references about homosexuality in the United States, Canada, the Netherlands, and Belgium. Specific topics covered are same-sex parenting and adoption; bisexuality; impact of religion; discrimination against homosexuality, its causes, and incidents; challenges facing gays and bisexuals—state laws, and the military; essays, sermons, testimonials; and a section on resources.

http://www.narth.com/menus/born.html

National Association for Research & Therapy of Homosexuality (NARTH). This site offers the following: *Psychological Issues*—"Born That Way" theory and social factors in same-sex attraction; sexual orientation and reorientation therapy; homosexuality and genes; biological basis. *Medical Issues*—clinical studies, gay-to-straight research; sexual orientation change (in some studies the latter is possible, others differ with this theory). *Social, Ethical, Political Issues*—gay activism in schools; use of social networks on the Internet, movie themes, for example, "Brokeback Mountain;" endorsements of same-sex marriage; tolerance education; ethical treatment; and opposing reparative therapy.

Journal Articles through the Web

http://www.narth.com/docs/risks.html

The American Journal of Public Health. "The American Journal of Public Health Highlights Risks of Homosexual Practices" by A. Dean Byrd, Vol. 93, No. 6, June 2003. Much of this article deals with quotes and information from other articles on homosexuals and risky behavior, especially contracting HIV/AIDS. The medical issues surrounding contracting HIV/AIDS concern lack of condom use, slow development of biomedical interventions, and separation of prevention and treatment. The author of this article believes that homosexuality is not innate, not an orientation, but a choice, which does differ with the medical community definitions.

http://www.leaderu.com/orgs/narth/journalarticle.html

Leadership U. journal at Regent University of Counseling & Services, Virginia Beach, Virginia. This site reports on two journal articles in *Psychotherapy*, Vol. 35, Summer 1998: "When Clients Seek Treatment for Same-Sex Attraction: Ethical issues on the 'Right to Choose' Debate" by Dr. Mark Yarhouse. This article encourages reparative-type therapies as a treatment option. The author feels it is ethically correct to offer conversion therapy. Dr. Yarhouse's second article, "When Families Present with Concerns about An Adolescent's Same-Sex Attraction" stresses the importance of respecting the client's cultural and religious values. This article also urges the client to either confirm or deny his homosexuality through therapy.

http://www.nsba.org/site/doc_cosa.asp?TRACKID=&VID=50&CID=488&DID=36123

School Law, National School Boards Association. "Court Refuses to Overturn Principal's Ban on Student Newspaper Articles about Homosexuality," June 2005. The California Supreme Court refused to overturn this ban, but it allowed a student lawsuit to proceed. The students at East Bakersfield High School were represented by the ACLU (American Civil Liberties Union). California law permits censorship of a student publication that may incite students to create a danger or disruption. The principal was concerned about violence. The article includes, with permission, photographs and interviews with gay students. The student Editor-in-Chief indicated that the featured students were already open about their sexual orientation and they would not be threatened. The principal said he was concerned about safety. Appended to the article are links to the full story in *Whittier Daily News* and *Mercury News*.

Books

Social Issues Firsthand—Homosexuality edited by David M. Haugen and
  Matthew J. Box (Greenhaven Press, 2005). 0737728914.
  Contributors to this anthology discuss gays and lesbians coming to

terms with their own identity as homosexuals in a primarily heterosexual world. Gays and lesbians feel oppressed by American society since homophobia and violence remain threats to their living an openly gay lifestyle.

Coming Out Straight: Understanding and Healing Homosexuality by Richard A. Cohen and Laura Schlessinger (Oakhill Press, 2001). 1886939470.

This text was written by Cohen, an ex-gay therapist and contains a foreword by Schlessinger. Cohen writes for gays and lesbians who want to transition to heterosexuality. Cohen believes his homosexuality was a symptom of disrupted affiliation with the same-sex parent and incomplete feelings of maleness/femaleness. Cohen's approach is sympathetic and leans on psychological factors. He feels that homophobia must be healed and those who do not wish to change should not be coerced to do so.

Homosexuality and Civilization by Louis Crompton (Belknap Press, 2006). 0674022335.

The author chronicles the history of homosexuality in Europe and parts of Asia from Homer to the eighteenth century. He relates stories of men and women who have been immortalized, celebrated, shunned, or executed for their homosexuality. The focus of the text is the account of persecution of homosexuals under Christian regimes throughout the centuries. During the time of Alexander the Great, in the high ranks of the Han Dynasty in China, in the bisexual poetry of Arab Spain, and among the samurai of Japan, same-sex male love flourished. The author indicated it was more difficult to find information on lesbianism.

Polygamy

Polygamy is a form of marriage where a person has more than one spouse. The word comes from Greek, meaning "many marriages." There are other types of arrangements related to this term. *Polygyny* refers to one man having more than one wife and *polyandry* where one woman has more than one husband. There is also a group marriage arrangement which is a combination of *polygyny* and *polyandry*. Other terms which recognize other types of marriage arrangements are *bigamy*, being married to two people at the same time; *trigamy*, having three spouses at the same time; *polyamory*, a romantic or sexual relationship involving multiple partners at once, and not necessarily involving marriage. There is also *serial monogamy*, people who have married a number of times and divorced many times.

http://en.wikipedia.org/wiki/Polygamy

The *Wikipedia* offers an extensive accounting of forms of polygamy. It also provides information on polygamy around the world, with patterns of occurrence. There are sections on polygamy and religion, legal aspects of this marriage arrangement, data from both proponents and opponents, and polygamy today with Mormon fundamentalism, with Muslims, and traditionalist cultures. In addition, there was a listing of polygamy in fiction.

http://news.google.com/news?q=Polygamy&hl=en&um=l&sa=x&oi=news_group&resnum=4&ct=title

This is a Google News site that provides links to a number of sites related to polygamy:

1. Fundamental Mormons seek recognition for polygamy
2. Polygamy, polyamory and same-sex marriage to be opposed at rally
3. Polygamy case heats up, June 7, 2007
4. Best bets on TV tonight on HOB's Big Love polygamy drama
5. Inheritance: What place for wives?

http://www.absalom.com/mormon/polygamy/faq.htm

Polygamy—Frequently Asked Questions. This site answers many questions related to this form of marriage: What is the difference among polygamy, polyandry, and polygyny? How much of Utah is Mormon? How many polygamists are there in Utah? Why aren't all those polygamists in jail? Is bigamy accepted within the Mormon religion? Is the Law of Polygamy forced within Mormonism? What are Mormon Fundamentalists? Are there different types of polygamists? Are polygamist marriages valid? Why is polygamy banned in the Utah constitution?

Journal Articles through the Web

http://www.brusselsjournal.com/node/301

The Brussels Journal. "First Trio Married in the Netherlands" by Paul Belien, September 26, 2005. The author has indicated that in the Netherlands polygamy had been legalized in all but name. He referred to a civil union of three partners, a man with two women. This was a civil union, not an official marriage. The male partner mentioned that this threesome relationship worked because the two women were bisexual.

http://www.reason.com/news/show/117323.html

Reason Online. "One Man, Many Wives, Big Problems; the Social Consequences of Polygamy are Bigger Than You Think" by Jonathan Rauch, April 3, 2006. The author indicated that polygamy had been out of the news until an HBO television series "Big Love" was aired. This series portrayed one husband with three wives in Utah. After this airing a federal lawsuit (now on appeal) was issued, but organizations such as the ACLU (American Civil Liberties Union) and its stand for polygamist rights and pro-polygamy groups like TruthBearer.org (an evangelical Christian group) and Principal Voices (a Utah-based group run by wives of polygamous marriages) are against the federal law suit. The author's concern is that he feels no polygamous society is a true liberal democracy; there is no equal opportunity. In his research, the author has found crime rates to be higher in polygamous societies. He further states that polygamy destabilizes individuals, couples, communities, and society by withdrawing marriage from many who have it.

http://www.questia.com/PM.qst?a=o&d=5000780713&er=deny

Ethnology. "Best of Friends and Worst of Enemies: Competition and Collaboration in Polygamy" by Sangeetha Madhavan, Vol. 41, 2002. The author discusses the fact that much research seems to portray polygamy as harmful to women, pitting co-wives against each other and that they feel subjugated. Yet, other research shows these relationships to be collaborative. Regarding the latter, the author indicates these can only be fully understood within particular socio-cultural and personal contexts. The author studied two ethnic groups in Mali, West Africa to show how co-wives negotiate their status through both competitive and collaborative strategies.

Books

The Secret Story of Polygamy by Kathleen Tracy (Sourcebooks, 2001). 1570717230.

The author, a journalist, discusses examples of polygamous abuse. Her analysis was developed through a 1999 case study of two brothers who were involved in unlawful sexual contact, physical abuse, and incest. The author further stated that many women of polygamous marriages are treated as breeders of children. They are often young girls who are forced to become servants to their husbands.

His Favorite Wife: Trapped in Polygamy by Susan Ray Schmidt (Kassidy Lane Publishing LLC, 2006). 097797300X.

This is an autobiography of a fifteen-year-old girl who became the sixth wife in a polygamous marriage. She indicated that many girls embrace this relationship to pursue the highest degree of glory. She describes the life situation as one of obedience, unquestioning acceptance of this marriage arrangement, and giving birth to large families to assure them pure life in heaven. The book reviews describe the text as providing both heartbreak and triumph.

Modern Polygamy and Mormon Fundamentalism: The Generations After the Manifesto by Brian C. Hales (Greg Kofford Books, 2006). 1589580354.

The author is an active member of the Church of Jesus Christ of Latter-Day Saints (Mormon Church), and a former missionary. He provides background for understanding the practice of polygamy within the Mormon Church and the discontinuance of that practice in 1904. However, he discusses those groups and individuals who dissented the end of this practice and the Mormon fundamentalist organizations that are perpetuating the practice.

Pornography

According to the *Oxford American Desk Dictionary and Thesaurus*, 2nd edition, 2002, pornography is the "explicit description or exhibition of sexual activity in literature, films, etc." The Media Awareness Network extends the above definition and adds "photography" to literature and films and suggests that the depiction of sexuality activity is intended to stimulate erotic, rather than aesthetic or emotional feelings. The definitions of pornography on the Web from the Google site add that the depictions are intended to arouse sexual desire.

http://en.wikipedia.org/wiki/Internet_pornography

Internet pornography on the *Wikipedia* site refers to pornography distributed via the Internet. Pornography can be found on websites, peer-to-peer file sharing, and through Usenet news groups. When viewed through the Internet, people are able to view pornography in private. This site offers a review of the history and methods of distribution, whether the material is free or commercial. The *Wikipedia* site also provides information on formats: image files, video files, and streaming videos. There is data on legal issues where each country deals with Internet pornography differently since there are no international laws regulating pornography.

http://www.asacp.org/

Association of Sites Advocating Child Protection. This association, founded in 1996, is nonprofit and dedicated to eliminating child pornography from the Internet. The association urges adults to report on pornography they view through a hotline. The association then forwards these reports to government agencies and associations, like the FBI (Federal Bureau of Investigation) and the National Center for Missing and Exploited Children. The offending sites are then flagged and labeled.

http://internet-filter-review.toptenreviews.com/internet-pornography-statistics.html

This site lists all sorts of Internet pornography statistics. Some are revenue statistics. Pornography is a $57 billion worldwide industry, with $12 billion being spent in the United States. Adult videos are the most successful revenue producers. Pornography revenue is larger than the combined revenues of all professional football, baseball, and basketball franchises. Child pornography generates $3 billion annually. There are 4.2 million pornography websites with 68 million daily pornography search engine requests. The average age of first Internet exposure to pornography is eleven years old. The twelve–seventeen age group are the largest consumers of Internet pornography. Forty million adults regularly visit pornographic sites.

Journal Articles through the Web

http://mensstudies.metapress.com/content/6721r77044761463

International Journal of Men's Health. "Use of Internet Pornography and Men's Well-Being" by Andreas G. Philaretou et al., Summer 2005. The cybersex pornographic industry is very profitable. The authors found that a sizable male minority are cybersex compulsives and at-risk users. They spend much time, money, and energy to view cybersex but the results are often accompanied by bouts of depression, anxiety, and problems with intimacy with their life partners. College and university authorities report academic failure and breaking of student rules as a result of cybersex. Divorce attorneys find that compulsive cybersex viewing tends to be a leading factor in divorce. The 100,000 or so websites feature all kinds of sexual content—erotic photos, videos, live sex acts, and web-cam strip sessions.

http://www.jsonline.com/story/index.aspx?id=498915

Milwaukee Journal Sentinel Online. "Child Porn Sting Snares Children—Four Juveniles Charged This Year After Police Track Down Downloads" by Mary Zahn, September 18, 2006. Milwaukee police had a search warrant to investigate home computers of high school honor roll students. The students were charged with felony possession of child pornography. The investigation was part of a national effort funded by the federal office of Juvenile Justice and Delinquency Prevention. A psychologist was interviewed and felt these children were *not* sex offenders and that each case must be viewed separately before there is any prosecution. The psychologist indicated that years ago *Playboy* magazine and others like it would have been read, but now students are using computers which are monitored by police.

http://jama.ama-assn.org/cgi/content/abstract/288/22/2887

JAMA; The Journal of the American Medical Association. "Does Pornography-Blocking Software Block Access to Health Information on the Internet?" by Caroline R. Richardson, M.D. et al., Vol. 288, No. 22, December 11, 2002. The authors contend that the Internet has become an important source to search for health information, especially among adolescents. Yet, some computers block out sites which may not be pornographic in nature. The authors investigated twenty-four health searches and six pornography searches and they compiled a list of top teen health information sites. About 10 percent of health sites found using search terms related to sexuality (safe sex, condoms) and homosexuality were blocked. The authors were concerned, therefore, that adolescents were not always able to search for legitimate sexuality related information because sites were blocked.

Books

Pornography and Sexual Representation: A Reference Guide (in three volumes) by Joseph W. Slade (Greenwood Press, 2001). 0313315213.

This text discusses the history of pornography in the United States and in the media. It offers a chronology of important dates and a discussion of child pornography. The author also shows how this topic has had a major impact on research and policy in the medical and social sciences, the law in the United States, and the economics/marketing of pornography.

Obscenity and Pornography Decisions of the United States Supreme Court edited by Maureen Harrison and Steve Gilbert (Excellent Books, 2000). 1880780232.

This text offers major obscenity and pornography decisions of the U.S. Supreme Court edited into non-legal English for the general adult and young adult reader. The twentieth century had many challenges to materials in this area: in books, theatrical performances, radio shows, and on the Internet. The editors investigated data to show how laws enacted by Congress have come into conflict with social change, community values, and the growth of technology.

Defending Pornography: Free Speech, Sex, and the Fight for Women's Rights by Nadine Strossen (New York University Press, 2000). 0814781497.

Ms. Strossen, President of the American Civil Liberties Union (ACLU) and Professor of Law at New York Law School, sees censoring pornography as advocating for the right wing's agenda to control the media and an attack on the First Amendment. She traces the recent history of censorship in relation to sexual speech.

America's War on Sex: The Attack on Law, Lust and Liberty by Marty Klein, Ph.D. (Praeger, 2006). 027598785X.

The author discusses issues of government censorship of many sexuality issues, plus the limiting of access to contraception, and to the encouragement of abstinence-only sexuality programs in schools. He reports on the continuing struggle to receive medically accurate information about sexual issues, to making personal choices regarding contraception, abortion, and about sexual partners. He documents right-wing assaults in the area of sexuality.

Same-Sex Marriage

This issue has caused much consternation and debate for a number of years. The institution of marriage, whether same-sex, inter-racial, inter-ethnic, has been addressed by many different groups in many different eras. After the American Civil War, African-Americans were permitted to marry in the United States. A Supreme Court decision in 1967 stipulated that mixed race couples could marry in the United States. However, only recently have there been states and countries that have permitted same-sex couples to marry.

In 2001 the Netherlands considered a new definition of marriage, which included opposite sex and same-sex. In 2003 Belgium followed with this definition as well. In 2004 most Canadian provinces approved of this arrangement. Spain passed such a law in 2005. The Scandinavian nations, England, and the United States (Vermont, California, and Hawaii) all recognized committed relationships with some benefits. Presently, thirty-seven states ban same-sex marriage. Five states (Connecticut, New Jersey, New York, New Mexico, and Rhode Island), and the District of Columbia have no explicit prohibition against same-sex marriage. Massachusetts allows same-sex marriage but there are residency requirements.

http://www.religioustolerance.org/hom_marr.htm

ReligiousTolerance.org. "Same-Sex Marriages (SSM) and Civil Unions." Aside from discussing same-sex marriages this site also discusses civil unions and domestic partnerships. These types of committed relationships recognize that couples would be permitted certain state benefits that were previously granted only to married heterosexual couples. The site offers PDF files for Statewide Marriage Laws, Relationship Recognition in the United States, Statewide Anti-Discrimination Laws and Policies, Statewide Hate Crimes Laws, Second-Parent/Stepparent Adoption Laws in the U.S., and laws and policies affecting state employees.

http://en.wikipedia.org/wiki/Same-sex_marriage

The *Wikipedia* site includes information on the status of same-sex marriage in the United States and in other countries, including those where this institution is still being considered. The site also discusses debates over specific terminology, the history of same-sex unions, controversies involving religious and social arguments, arguments about tradition, concerning children and equality, and parallels to interracial marriages.

http://www.samesexmarriage.ca/

"Equal Marriage for Same-Sex Couples." This site contains many articles on this topic that appeared in Canadian news outlets in November/December 2006. The articles reflect both support for this institution and divisive comments about this arrangement. Same-sex marriage is legal in Canada, but there are fundamentalists trying to change the legality.

Journal Articles through the Web

http://www.timescommunity.com/site/tab5.cfm?newsid=17611977&BRD= 2553&PAG=461&dept_id=565197&rfi=6

The Fairfax (VA) County Times. "Same-Sex Marriage Letter 'Unfair'" by Bob Sihler, December 19, 2006. A woman complained the *Times* did not print articles or letters supporting the same-sex marriage ban. The person who responded to this woman's concern indicated that he voted against the ban, but also defended the newspaper which is published in Northern Virginia, an open, liberal, progressive part of the state. The author of this article does not want same-sex marriage or adoptions by gay couples to be legalized in Virginia, but he wants Virginia's elected leaders to make those decisions, rather than have a constitutional amendment to that effect.

http://www.sfgate.com/cgi-bin/article.cgi?file=/c/a/2006/12/10/ EDGRML]]8Q1.DTL

San Francisco Chronicle. "From Civil Unions to Marriage Lite" by Debra J. Saunders, December 10, 2006. The author discusses a new bill being sponsored that would expand civil unions to heterosexual couples—calling this arrangement a non-marriage marriage. Senator Migden introduced this bill to allow same-sex couples to register as domestic partners. A state bill cannot offer all the protections given to heterosexual couples like Social Security survivor benefits, so this senator's bill reflected the idea that heterosexual couples with one partner older than sixty-two years of age could register as domestic partners to allow seniors to protect their pensions while enjoying some benefits of marriage. Migden's rationale was that more than 50 percent of couples in the United States are living together without getting married and she wants these arrangements to be protected as much as same-sex couples.

http://www.hometownannapolis.com/cgi-bin/read/2006/12_03-54/TOP

The Capital Online. "Annapolis Becomes Gay Marriage Battleground: State's Highest Court Hears Case Tomorrow" by Eric Hartley, staff writer, December 3, 2006. An attorney for the American Civil Liberties Union (ACLU) will be arguing the case that will challenge the state's definition of marriage. That definition says that only a marriage between a man and woman is valid. A judge had ruled that the law violates the state constitution's provision against discrimination on account of gender. The article mentions situations where same-sex partners have been in that situation for many years and adopted children and were living responsibly, but had no legal protections like medical decision-making for the children.

Books

America's Struggle for Same-Sex Marriage by Daniel R. Pinello (Cambridge University Press, 2006). 0521848563.

This book examines the political controversies of this social movement. The text focuses on the Massachusetts law passed in 2003 that stipulated that marriage conferred only on heterosexual couples violated constitutional principles of respect for individual autonomy and equality under law. The author relied on interviews to offer insider accounts of how courts, politicians, and activities dealt with this social policy.

Same-Sex Marriage?: A Christian Ethical Analysis by Marvin Mahan Ellison (Pilgrim Press, 2004). 0829816594.

This book discusses the modern debate of whether same-sex couples should have the right to marry. The author conducted dialogues with legal scholars and theologians to better understand how advocates and critics of this social movement shape their arguments. This text presents relevant ethics from both a Christian and human point of view.

Same-Sex Marriage and the Constitution by Evan Gerstmann (Cambridge University Press, 2003). 0521811007.

This text relates constitutional law and theory of equal protection, plus the right to privacy to the politics of whether the Supreme Court should decide on the right to same-sex marriage. The author exposes weaknesses on both sides of the debate and offers a convincing case on behalf of same-sex marriage rights—applicable to all regardless of their sexual orientation.

Index

AASL/AECT Information Literacy Standards for Student Learning, xli
abortion, 3–5
Abortion Law Homepage, 3
The Abortion Rights Controversy in American History (Hull and Hoffer), 5
accessing: controversial materials, xiii; library media center, xviii–xxii
Access to Resources and Services in the School Library Media Program (ALA), xlviii
accommodating students with special needs, xxxi
Achenbach, Joel, 127
acid rain, 77–79
active euthanasia, 24
Activist Cash website, 178
administrative staff, relationship with, xxviii, xxix
administrative support, xxiii–xvii
administrator commitment to library media program, xxi–xxii
Adoption History Project website, 57
Adoptive Families website, 57
advocacy for library media program, xxiv–xxvi. *See also* public relations
Ahmadinejad, Mahmoud, 120
AIDS, 6–9
AIDS: Science and Society (Fan, Conner, and Villarreal), 9
AIDS: Virus Or Drug Induced? (Duesberg), 7
AIDS in the Twenty-First Century (Barnett and Whiteside), 9
AIDS Vaccine Clearinghouse, 8
Alarcon, Walter A., 90
Alcor Life Extension Foundation, 20
Allen, D., 87
Allen, John L., 202–3

Allende, Isabel, 134–35
Allende, Salvador, 133–35
Alm, Leslie R., 79
Almond, Gabriel A., 197
Alterman, Eric, 66
Alternative Health News Online, 10
alternative medicine, 10–11
Alternative Medicine Homepage, 10
America, Russia, and the Cold War, 1945–2002 (LaFeber), 164–65
American Anthropological Association website, 45
American Association of School Librarians, @ Your Library Campaign, xxiii–xxiv
American Atheists website, 192
American Civil Liberties Union, 184, 221
American Library Association: *Access to Resources and Services in the School Library Media Program*, xlviii; Office for Intellectual Freedom website, 184–85
American Life League, 12
American Society for Reproductive Medicine website, 29
American Veterans Committee for Puerto Rico Self-Determination website, 101
America's Colony (Malavet), 103
America's Struggle for Same-Sex Marriage (Pinello), 223–24
America's Unpatriotic Acts (Brasch), 186
America's War on Sex (Klein), 221
Aminmansour, Morteza, 99
Amnesty International USA website, 48
Anabolic Steroid Abuse website, 39
anarchism, 157–59
Anarchism (Ward), 158
The Anatomy of Fascism (Paxton), 168

225

Index

Anderson, Brian C., 66–67, 69
And the Band Played On (Shilts and Greider), 9
Angels of Death (Magnusson), 25
The Animal Ethics Reader (Armstrong), 179–80
Animal Rights (Sunstein and Nussbaum), 180
Annas, George J., 27
annotated bibliography/webliography, xxi
annual report, xxxiii
Another Gospel (Tucker), 199
Answers.com website, 95, 123, 160
Anti-Defamation League website, 104, 121, 145
Anti-Immigration Movement, 104
anti-Semitism, 189–91
Anti-Semitism (Perry and Schweitzer), 191
apartheid in South Africa, 111–13
Arafat, Yasser, 136–38
Arafat (Walker and Gowers), 137
Arafat's War (Karsh), 137–38
Area 51, 126
Arlandson, James, 208–9
Armstrong, S., 179
Artigas, Mariano, 149
Association of Sites Advocating Child Protection website, 219
As They See It (Downing), 7
atheism, 192–94
Atheist Manifesto (Ontray), 194
At Issues Series—Performance-Enhancing Drugs (Haley), 51
Atkinson, Rick, 100
Authentically Black (McWhorter), 162
authentic learning, xxxvi–xxxvii
The Autobiography of Malcolm X, 151
The Autobiography of Martin Luther King, Jr., 154
Avery, Dennis T., 91

Back Rooms (Messer and May), 4
Bader, Eleanor, 4
Baird, Robert M., 69
Baird-Windle, Patricia, 4

Bakalar, James B., 33
Baker, N., 87
Barchfield, Jenny, 105
Bard, Mitchell Geoffrey, 97
Barnett, Tony, 9
Bateman, Geoffrey, 173
Baumgardner, Jennifer, 171
Beam, Ted, 33
Bearing Right (Saletan), 4
Becker, Michael W., 51
Belien, Paul, 217
Belkin, Aaron, 173
The Bell Curve (Hernnstein and Murray), 46–47
Berliner, Don, 128
Bernstein, Matthew, 72
Bersa, Misha, 68
Bibeau, Kathy, 199
BIG6 Skills model, xxxix
birth control, 12–14
The Birth Control Book (Cadoff and Pasquale), 14
black separatism, 160–62
Blackwell Complementary and Alternative Medicine (Herring), 11
Blumenthal, Max, 146
Bock, Alan W., 33–34
The Body website, 8
Bonilla-Silva, Eduardo, 130
Borowiec, Andrew, 115
Boston, Rob, 202
Box, Matthew J., 214
Boyd, Billy Ray, 17
Bradner, Tim, 84
Brasch, Walter M., 186
Breitman, George, 151
Briggs, Laura, 57
Britt, Lawrence, 166
Bryant, Rebecca, 116
Bryza, Matthew, 114
Burlein, Ann, 130
Byrd, A. Dean, 214

Cadoff, Jennifer, 14
Caldicott, Helen, 85
Campbell, Keith, 19
Card, Orson Scott, 66

Carroll, Robert Todd, 45
Carroll, Will, 51
Carson, Clayborne, 151, 154
Carson, Rachel, 91
A Case for Nuclear-Generated Electricity (Heaberlin), 85
The Case for Peace (Dershowitz), 97
Centers for Disease Control and Prevention, 54, 179
A Century of Genocide (Weitz), 119
Cesar Chavez Foundation website, 139
The Challenge of the Cults and New Religions (Rhodes), 205
The Changing Face of Anti-Semitism (Laqueur), 191
Chavez, Cesar, 139–41
Chavez, Hugo, 142–44
Chavez (Chavez, Deutschmann and Salado), 144
Chemical Pesticides (Stenersen), 91
Chesterton, G.K., 23
Chomsky, Noam, 158–59
Chomsky On Anarchism (Chomsky and Pateman), 158–59
Christian, Mark, 130
Christian, Shirley, 134
The Church of Scientology (Melton), 206
Chyka, Peter A., 50
circumcision, 15–17
Circumcision (Boyd), 17
Circumcision (Gollaher), 17
Circumcision Information and Resource Pages, 15–16
Clarks, Michael F., 51
classroom teachers: assisting research of, xxvi; cultivating interest of, xxxiii–xxxiv; professional development opportunities for, xvii; relationship with, xxviii, xxix; role of, xiii–xiv; surveying, xxi–xxii; working with library media specialist, xviii–xix
Climate Change, Ozone Depletion and Air Pollution (Gillespie), 88
Climate Change (Victor), 82
Climate of Fear (Moore), 82

Clinton, Bill, 172–73
Clinton, Hillary Rodham, 173
cloning, 18–19
Cloning Information Website, 18
CNN.com website, 4
Cockcroft, James D., 134
Cohen, Richard A., 215
Cole, Tim, 122
Collins, Ray, 116
Colonial Subjects (Grosfoguel), 102–3
Coloring the News (McGowan), 67
The Color of Guilt & Innocence (Holbert and Rose), 49
Columbia Encyclopedia website, 175
Coming Out Straight (Cohen and Schlessinger), 215
Commercial Nuclear Power (Ramsey), 85
communism, 163–65
community, relationship with, xxxi
complementary and alternative medicine, 10–11
Complementary and Alternative Medicine (Kelner and Wellman), 11
Complementary and Alternative Medicine in the United States (Institute of Medicine), 11
Conner, Ross F., 9
content descriptors for computer and video games, 63
Contraception (Guillebaud), 13
Controlling Hollywood (Bernstein), 72
controversial issues: definition of, xv, xliii; ground rules for discussion of, xliii–xliv; policy regarding, xliv–xlv; presentation of, xlix; researching, xlvii–xlviii
controversial materials, accessing, xiii
Coordination Forum for Countering Anti-Semitism website, 189–90
Copernican System, 147
Costello, Edward, 115
Council on Foreign Relations website, 207
The Covenant with Black America (Smiley), 162
creationism, 26–28

Crompton, Louis, 215
Crossing Borders, Crossing Boundaries (Alm), 79
Crozier, Brian, 112
cryonics, 20–21
Currey, Cecil B., 196
curriculum development, xxxv
Cyprus (Borowiec), 115
Cyprus dispute, 114–16

Dale, Brian, 30
The DaVinci Code (Brown), 201–2
Davis, Nathaniel, 135
Dawkins, Richard, 193
Day, Kristen, 5
Dean, Howard, 161
Deats, Richard, 154
debates, xliii–xliv
Deen, Thalif, 96
Defending Pornography (Strossen), 221
deKlerk, F.W., 111
Deloria, Vine, Jr., 27, 160
de Marneff, Peter, 44
Democrats for Life (Day), 5
Denying History (Shermer and Grobman), 122
department meetings, xxxiv
Department of State website, 189
Derbez, Luis Ernesto, 104
Dershowitz, Alan, 97
Deutschmann, David, 144
Dialogue Concerning the Two Chief World Systems (Galileo, Einstein and Drake), 148
Dictionary of Labor Law Talk website, 71
Disarmed (Goss), 177
discussion, ground rules for, xliii–xliv
displaying student work, xxi–xxii
district school board meetings, xxvi–xxvii
Don't Ask, Don't Tell (Belkin and Bateman), 173
doping, 39–41
Dougherty, Jon E., 106

Dowbiggin, Ian, 25
Downer, Alexander, 114
Downing, Raymond, 7
Drake, Stillman, 148
Driving While Black (Meeks), 49–50
drugs: medical marijuana, 32–34; performance-enhancing, 39–41; psychoactive, 42–44
Drugs in Sport (Mottram), 51
Drugs 101 (Hyde), 44
Drug War Facts website, 32
Du Bois, Denis, 84
Duesberg, Peter H., 7
Duke, David, 145–46
Dyson, Michael Eric, 151

Earleywine, Mitch, 33
Ecology and the Crisis of Overpopulation (Shah), 38
Educational Testing Service, xvii
Effects of Acid Rain on Forest Processes (Godbold and Huttermann), 79
Ehrenfeld, Rachel, 137
Ehrlich, Anne H., 38
Ehrlich, Paul R., 38
Einstein, Albert, 148
Elder, Kay, 30
Ellison, Marvin Mahan, 224
Ellner, Steve, 144
Embracing Cyprus (Green and Collins), 116
eMedicine Health website, 29
employers, needs of, xvii
Encyclopedia of Astrobiology Astronomy and Spaceflight website, 126
The End of Faith (Harris), 193
English department, collaborative effort with, xxxii–xxxiii
Environmental Canada website, 77
Environmental Protection Agency website, 77, 80, 89
Environmental Tobacco Smoke (Watson and Witten), 55
Epstein, Barbara, 157

Eralp, Doga Ulas, 115
Essential Skills for Information Literacy, xl
ethical use of information, xxi
Ethics of Abortion (Hurley), 4–5
The Ethics of Transracial Adoption (Fogg-Davis), 58
Etzioni, Amitai, 186
eugenics, 22–23
Eugenics and Other Evils (Chesterton), 23
euthanasia, 24–25
evolution, 26–28
Evolution, Creationism and Other Modern Myths (Deloria), 27
Evolution vs. Creationism (Scott), 27
exhibition of student work, xxi–xxii
extending services of media center, xxxiii–xxxiv
Extension Toxicology Network website, 89

F.A.C.T.net website, 204–5
Fan, Hung, 9
fascism, 166–68
Fascism (Passmore), 168
Fascists (Mann), 168
The Fast Food Craze (Volpe), 179
female circumcision, 15
Female Genital Mutilation (Skaine), 17
feminism, 169–71
Feminism Is for Everybody (hooks), 170
Feminist Majority Foundation Online, 169
Ferriss, Susan, 140–41
The Fight in the Fields (Ferriss), 140–41
filtering software, xlvii–xlviii
Findlen, Barbara, 170
Fish, Jefferson M., 46
Fitz-Gibbon, Jorge, 176
Fleiss, Paul M., 16
Foer, Franklin, 160
Fogg-Davis, Hawley, 58
Fong, Mei, 69

Food and Drug Administration, 13
Forever for All (Perry), 21
Fowler, Geoffrey A., 69
Franklin, Benjamin, 20
Franzini, L.R., 170
From Genesis to Genetics (Moore), 27
Fundamentalism, 195–97
Fundamentalism (Ruthven), 197
Fundamentalism and American Culture (Marsden), 197

Gaddis, John Lewis, 164
Galileo Galilei, 147–49
Galileo in Rome (Shea and Artigas), 148–49
Galileo, Science, and the Church (Langford), 148
Gallagher, Michael, 208
Game Coding Complete (McShaffry), 64
Garcia, Michelle, 185
Gardner, Christine J., 13
Gardner, Howard, xxxviii
Gardner, Richard L., 52
gays in military, 172–74
Gellately, Robert, 118
genocide, 117–19
Genocide in International Law (Schabas), 118
Genocide Watch website, 117
Gentile, Douglas A., 64
Gerberding, Julie, 179
Gerdes, Louise I., 186
Gerstmann, Evan, 224
Gilbert, Craig, 167
Gilbert, Steve, 221
Gillespie, Alexander, 88
Givel, Michael, 54–55
Gleave, Robert, 209
Gledhill, Ruth, 193
global warming, 80–82
Global Warming (Houghton), 82
Godbold, Douglas L., 79
The God Delusion (Dawkins), 193
Goeringer, Conrad F., 192
Gollaher, David L., 16, 17

Gore, Al, 80, 82, 173
Goss, Kristin A., 177
Gott, Richard, 144
Gottlieb, David, 52
Gowers, Andrew, 137
Green, Pauline, 116
Greider, William, 9
Grinspoon, Lester, 32, 33
Griswold, Daniel T., 106
Griswold v. Connecticut, 62
Grobman, Alex, 122
Groseclose, Tim, 66
Grosfoguel, Ramon, 102
Guerin, Daniel, 158
Guillebaud, John, 13
Gulf/2000 Project website, 99
gun politics, 175–77
Guttenplan, D.D., 121, 122

Hagan, Stephen, 183
Hagen, Bruce, 120
Hahn, Scott, 202–3
Haith, Douglas A., 90
Hales, Brian C., 218
Haley, James, 51
Hallaq, Wael B., 209
Halutz, Dan, 95
Harris, David, 49
Harris, Deborah, 118
Harris, Robie H., 14
Harris, Sam, 193
Harrison, Maureen, 221
Hartley, Eric, 223
Hartzell, Gary, xxiv–xxv
Haudricourt, Tom, 50
Haugen, David M., 214
Haustein, Knut-Olaf, 55
Haynes, John Earl, 165
Hayworth, J.D., 106–7
Heaberlin, Scott W., 85
Hellinger, Daniel, 144
Herring, Mary A., 11
Herrnstein, Richard J., 46
Hezbollah, 95
Higuera, Valencia, 182
Hillstrom, Laurie Collier, 100
Hirst, David, 136

His Favorite Wife (Schmidt), 218
Hodgkinson, Neville, 6–7
Hoffer, Peter Charles, 5
Holbert, Steve, 49
Hollingsworth, Leslie D., 58
Holly, Stephen, 49
Hollywood v. Hardcore (Lewis), 72–73
Holocaust Denial (Zimmerman), 122
Holocaust revisionism, 120–22
The Holocaust on Trial (Guttenplan), 122
homosexuality, 172–74, 213–15, 222–24
Homosexuality and Civilization (Crompton), 215
Homsher, Deborah, 177
hooks, bell, 170
Horowitz, Sara R., 118
"hot topics," xv, xlvii
Houghton, John, 82
Howell, Susan E., 146
How Patriotic Is the Patriot Act? (Etzioni), 186
Hubbard, L. Ron, 204, 206
Huber, Peter W., 84
Hugo Chavez (Gott), 144
Hull, N.E.H., 5
Human Genome Project Information, 18
Human Rights Watch website, 96
Hunter, Melanie, 96
Hurd, Dale, 142
Hurley, Jennifer, 4
Husak, Doug, 44
Hutchison, Robert, 202–3
Huttermann, Aloys, 79
Hyde, Margaret O., 44
Hymowitz, Kay S., 169
Hynek, J. Allen, 128

Illegals (Dougherty), 106
Imagining the Modern (Bryant), 116
Immigration's Unarmed Invasion (Wooldridge), 106
An Inconvenient Truth (Gore), 82
INFOhio DIALOGUE Model, xl

information literacy skills models, xxxix–xli
information literacy standards, xxxviii
Information Power; Building Partnerships for Learning (ALA/AECT), xxvi, xxxv, xxxviii
inquiry process, steps of, xxxviii–xxxix
In Search of New Age Spiritualities (Possamai), 200
intelligence and race, 45–47
Intelligence Resource Program website, 133
intelligent design, 26
International Coalition for Genital Integrity, 15
International Law and the Administration of Occupied Territories (Playfair), 97
Internet sites: evaluation of, xli–xlii; filtering of, xlvii–xlviii; safety and "netiquette" issues, xlviii. *See also specific websites*
In the Company of Soldiers (Atkinson), 100
In Their Own Voices (Simon and Roorda), 59
In the Name of Eugenics (Kevles), 23
"The Invisible School Librarian" (Hartzell), xxiv–xxv
in vitro fertilization, 29–31
In Vitro Fertilization (Elder and Dale), 30
In Vitro Fertilization (Sher et al.), 30
involuntary euthanasia, 24
Irving, Dianne N., 52
Islamic law, 207–9
Islamic Law (Gleave and Kermeli), 209
Israeli-occupied territories, 95–97
Is the Temperature Rising? (Philander), 81–82
It's Not the Media (Sternheimer), 69
It's Perfectly Normal (Harris), 14

Jarhead (Swofford), 100
Jensen, Richard, 140
Jewish Supremacism (Duke), 146
Johnson, Carole A., 55–56
Johnson, David L., 55–56
Joskow, Paul L., 79
Journal for MultiMedia History website, 22
The Juice (Carroll et al.), 51
Julien, Robert M., 44

Kaffir Boy (Mathabane), 113
Kahlenberg, Richard D., 183
Karsh, Efraim, 137
Kass-Annese, Barbara, 14
Kelner, Merrijoy, 11
Kermeli, Eugenia, 209
Kevles, Daniel, 23
Khatib, Lina, 196
Kiernan, Bon, 118
King, Martin Luther, Jr., 153–54
Kirton, Derek, 58
Kitei, Lynn D., 128
Kitzmiller v. Dover Area School District, 26
Klehr, Harvey, 165
Klein, Marty, 221
Kopel, David B., 175, 176
Koppel, Ted, 142
Korff, Kal K., 124
Kowalok, Michael E., 87
Kranich, Nancy, 185
Kunich, John Charles, 19
Kushner, David, 64
Kuypers, Jim A., 67
Kwok, Chi T. Steve, 29
Kyle, Richard, 200

LaFeber, Walter, 164
Lake, Eli, 145
Lambright, W. Henry, 88
Lang, Joann, 58
Langford, Jerome J., 148
Lappin, Shalom, 190
Laqueur, Walter, 191
The Last Two Years of Salvador Allende (Davis), 135
learning: authentic, xxxvi–xxxvii; constructs of, xxxv; styles of, xxxviii

Learning and Libraries in an Information Age; Principles and Practice (Stripling), xxxviii, xxxix
Lee, Janet, 170
The Legalization of Drugs (Husak and de Marneff), 44
Lehring, Gary L., 173
Leinbach, Glenn, 164
Lendman, Stephen, 143
Levin, Henry M., 183
Levine, Harry G., 43
Levy, Anne, 146
Lewis, Jon, 72
library media center: accessing for assignments and class discussions, xviii–xxii; extending services of, xxxiii–xxxiv
library media specialists: characteristics of, xxiii; as consultants, xvi; curriculum development and, xxxv; one-on-one meetings with administrator/principal and, xxvi; partnership between administrator and, xxiv–xxv; role of, xiii–xiv; working with classroom teachers, xviii–xix
Lift High the Cross (Burlein), 130
Limb, Peter, 112
Lindorff, Dave, 99
Listen Up (Findlen), 170–71
locating materials, xxi
Loges, William E., 69
Long, Anthony, 121
Long Walk to Freedom (Mandela), 113
Losing the Race (McWhorter), 162
Love, Aaron Michael, 130
Lynn, Richard, 46

MacDonald, Heather, 48
Madhavan, Sangeetha, 217
Mae-Won, Ho, 7
Magnusson, Roger S., 25
Making Malcolm (Dyson), 151
The Making of Modern South Africa (Worden), 112–13
Malavet, Pedro A., 103
Malcolm X, 150–52
Malcolm X (Myers), 152
Malcolm X Speaks (Breitman), 151–52
male circumcision, 15
Mandela, Nelson, 111, 113
Manifesta (Baumgardner and Richards), 171
Mann, Michael, 168
Marable, Manning, 151
Marching to an Angry Drum (Mitchell), 174
Marijuana (Grinspoon and Bakalar), 33
Marijuana Medical Handbook (Rosenthal et al.), 33
Markets for Clean Air (Joskow et al.), 79
Marsden, George M., 197
Marshall, Paul, 209
Martin, James, 202
Martin, Thomas, 157
Martin Luther King, Jr. (Deats), 154
Marx, Karl, 163
Masters of Doom (Kushner), 64
material selection policy, xlvii
Mathabane, Mark, 113
Matshak, Daniel R., 52
Matthews, Graham, 90
Matthews, Mike, 27
Maxwell, Carol J.C., 5
May, Kathryn E., 4
Mayo Clinic website, 50
McCarthy, John, 83
McConnell, Edwina A., 29
McCuen, Richard H., 78
McDaniel, George, 146
McGowan, William, 67
McGregor, Ann, 140
McGregor, Joy H., xxxviii
McLaren, Karla, 198
McMullen, Emerson Thomas, 148
McShaffry, Mike, 64
McWhorter, John, 161, 162
media bias, 65–67
media center. *See* library media center
media coordinators. *See* library media specialists
media literacy, xli–xlii

The Media & Morality (Baird, Loges and Rosenbaum), 69–70
Media Ratings for Movies, Music, Video Games and TV (Gentile et al.), 64
media restrictions, 68–70
medical marijuana, 32–34
Medical Marijuana Pro Con website, 32
Meeks, Kenneth, 49
Meinert, Rolf, 90
Meltdown (Michaels), 82
Melton, J. Gordon, 206
Meltzer, Albert, 157
A Merciful End (Dowbiggin), 25
Messer, Ellen, 4
Mexico–United States border dispute, 104–7
Michaels, Patrick J., 82
Miele, Frank, 162
Miller, J.L., 64
Mills, Mark P., 84
Milyo, Jeff, 66
mind control, 35–36
Mirecki, Paul, 192
Mises Institute, 158
Mitchell, Carl G., 174
Model Information Literacy Guidelines (Colorado), xl–xli
Modern Mummies (Quigley), 21
Modern Polygamy and Mormon Fundamentalism (Hales), 218
monthly report, xxxiii
Moore, John, 27
Moore, Thomas Gale, 82
Mottram, D.R., 51
MPAA film rating system, 71–73
multiple intelligences, xxxviii
Murray, Charles, 45–46
Murray, Elaine, 198
Museum of Communism website, 163
Myers, Walter Dean, 152
My Invented Country (I. Allende), 134–35
The Mystery of Arafat (Rubinstein), 138
Myths and Facts: A Guide to the Arab-Israeli Conflict (Bard), 97

The Naked Clone (Kunich), 19
NASA and the Environment (Lambright), 88
National Academy of Sciences website, 86
National Assessment of Educational Progress, xvi–xvii
National Association for Research & Therapy of Homosexuality website, 213
National Association of Theater Owners, 71
National Center for Complementary and Alternative Medicine, 10, 11
National Center for Science Education website, 27
National Institute on Drug Abuse website, 43
National Institutes of Health website, 51
National Organization for the Reform of Marijuana Laws website, 43
National Right To Life website, 24
National Youth Violence Prevention Resource Center website, 43
Natural Birth Control Made Simple (Kass-Annese), 14
Negotiating a Good Death (Pool), 25
Neuhaus, Richard, 46
Nevins, Joseph, 106
New Age and Neopagan Religions in America (Pike), 200
The New Age Movement in American Culture (Kyle), 200
New Age spirituality, 198–200
Newman, Alex, 140
NewsTarget.com website, 8
Night Siege (Hynek), 128
Nizkor Project website, 120–21
No Child Left Behind Act, xvi
No Future Without Forgiveness (Tutu), 113
No Gods No Masters (Guerin), 158
Nogues, S., 87
Nordenberg, Tama, 13
note taking, xx–xxi
nuclear power, 83–85

Nuclear Power Is Not the Answer (Caldicott), 85
Nussbaum, Martha C., 180

Obscenity and Pornography Decisions of the United States Supreme Court (Harrison and Gilbert), 221
ODAN Pus Dei Awareness Network website, 201
Officially Gay (Lehring), 173–74
Oguzlu, H. Tarik, 115
Olick, Diane, 30–31
On Denial (Haynes and Klehr), 165
one-on-one meetings with administrator/principal, xxvi
Onfray, Michel, 194
Operation Clambake website, 204
Operation Gatekeeper (Nevins), 106
Opposing Viewpoints Series The Patriot Act, 186
Opus Dei, 201–3
Opus Dei (Allen), 202–3
oral presentation, xxxviii
Ordinary Work, Extraordinary Grace (Hahn), 202–3
The Origins and Evolution of Islamic Law (Hallaq), 209
overpopulation, 37–38
Overpopulation (Zeaman), 38
ozone depletion, 86–88

Pachman, Tracey S., 29
Pacula, Rosalie Liccard, 33
parents, relationship with, xxx
Parson, Edward A., 87
Pasquale, Samuel, 14
passive euthanasia, 24
Passmore, Kevin, 168
Pateman, Barry, 158
Pathways to Knowledge Model, xl
Patrick, Ian, 16
Paxton, Robert O., 168
Pay to the Order of Puerto Rico (Odishelidze and Laffer), 103
PBS Teacher Source website, 22
Pence, Gregory E., 19
People for the Ethical Treatment of Animals (PETA), 178–80
Peres, Shimon, 136
performance-enhancing drugs in sports, 38–41
Perry, Marvin, 191
Perry, Paul, 128
Perry, R. Michael, 21
Persian Gulf, 98–100
pesticides, 89–91
Pesticides (Matthews), 90–91
Pesticides Safety Directorate Home Page, 89
PETA (People for the Ethical Treatment of Animals), 178–80
Pew Research Center for People and the Press website, 68
Pflock, Karl T., 125
Philander, S. George, 81
Philaretou, Andreas G., 220
Philpott, Paul, 6
The Phoenix Lights (Kitei and Perry), 128
Pike, Sarah M., 200
Pinello, Daniel R., 223
plagiarism, xx–xxi
Planet Out website, 172
Playfair, Emma, 97
policy: material selection, xlvii; regarding controversial issues, xliv–xlv
The Politics of Gun Control (Spitzer), 176
polygamy, 216–18
Ponnuru, Ramesh, 102
Pool, Robert, 25
The Population Explosion (Ehrlich and Ehrlich), 38
pornography, 219–21
Pornography and Sexual Representation (Slade), 220–21
Possamai, Adam, 200
Pournelle, Jerry, 125
Powell, Lawrence N., 146
Prager, Dennis, 191
Preaching Eugenics (Rosen), 22–23

Press Bias and Politics (Kuypers), 67
A Primer of Drug Action (Julien), 44
Privatizing Education (Levin), 183
problem-solving processes, xix
"Professional Library" collection, xxvi
Profiles in Injustice (Harris), 49
Pro-Life Activists in America (Maxwell), 5
promoting new materials, xxxii
Propaganda, The Press and Conflict (Willcox), 69
Protecting the Ozone Layer (Parson), 87–88
psychoactive drugs, 42–44
Public Eye Organization website, 129
public relations: with community, xxxi; cultivating interest of teachers, xxxiii–xxxiv; with English department, xxxii–xxxiii; meetings in media center, xxxiv; monthly reports, xxxiii; with parents, xxx; promoting new materials, xxxii; purposes of, xxviii–xxix; special events in, xxxii, xxxiii; with students, xxix–xxx; surveying staff and students, xxxi–xxxii; with teachers and administrators, xxix
Public School Choice vs. Private School Vouchers (Kahlenberg), 183
public school environment, xv
public vs. private school education, 181–83
Puerto Rico self-determination, 101–3
Pynes, Christopher A., 53

quality-based learning, xxxvi
Quigley, Christine, 21

Rabaka, Reiland, 150
Rabin, Yitzhak, 136
A Race Against Time (Taylor and McDaniel), 146
Race (Sarich and Miele), 162
race and intelligence, 45–47
Race Differences in Intelligence (Lynn), 46

Race and Intelligence (Fish), 46
racial profiling, 48–50
Racial Profiling Data Collection Resource Center website, 48
Radical Islam's Rules (Marshall), 209
Ramsey, Charles B., 85
Randle, Kevin D., 124–25
ratings symbol for computer and video games, 63
rating systems: film, 71–73; software, 63–64
Rauch, Jonathan, 217
Rausch, Andrew, 73
Rauscher, Megan, 44
Ray, Dixy Lee, 79
"reading across the curriculum," xvi
Reagan, Leslie J., 4
Reeves, Eric, 118
Refuting Evolution 2 (Sarfati and Matthews), 27
Reinarman, Craig, 43
relationship with faculty and administrative staff, xxviii, xxix
Religious Movements website, 195
ReligiousTolerance.org website: abortion, 3; euthanasia, 24; gays in military, 172; homosexuality, 213; New Age spirituality, 199; same-sex marriage, 222
Remembering Cesar (McGregor), 140
researching: controversial issues, xlvii–xlviii; for topic, xxi
resource-based instruction, xviii
Rhodes, Ron, 205
Richards, Amy, 171
Richardson, Caroline R., 220
Richman, Sheldon, 166
Risen, James, 4
Roads, Michael, 199
Roberts, Adam, 95
Robertson, Pat, 143
Robinson, B.A., 199
Roe v. Wade, 4, 62
Romero-Barcelo, Carlos, 102
Roorda, Rhonda, 59
Rose, Lisa, 49

Rosen, Christine, 22
Rosenbaum, Stuart E., 69
Rosenthal, Ed, 33
Ross, Loretta, 129
Roswell (Pflock and Pournelle), 125
The Roswell UFO Crash (Korff), 124
Roswell UFO Crash Update (Randle), 124–25
Roswell UFO incident, 123–25
Roth, Chris, 72
Rowland, F. Sherwood, 86
Rubin, Barry, 137
Rubin, Judith Colp, 137
Rubinstein, Danny, 138
The Rural Face of White Supremacy (Schultz), 130
Ruse, Michael, 53
Rush, Erik, 143
Ruthven, Malise, 197

Sachs, Jeffrey, 81
safety online, xlviii
Salado, Javier, 144
Saletan, William, 4
Salvador Allende Reader (Cockcroft), 134
same-sex marriage, 222–24
Same-Sex Marriage and the Constitution (Gerstmann), 224
Same-Sex Marriage? (Ellison), 224
Sanders, Stafford, 55
Sarfati, Jonathan, 27
Sarich, Vincent, 162
SAT exam, xvii
Saunders, Debra J., 223
Savage, Charlie, 185
Saving the Planet with Pesticides and Plastic (Avery), 91
Schabas, William A., 118
Schlessinger, Laura, 215
Schmidt, Susan Ray, 218
School Choice (Wolfe), 183
The School Library Media Manager (Woolls), xlii
Schultz, Mark, 130
Schulz, Nick, 81
Schweitzer, Frederick M., 191

Science and the Sacred website, 195–96
The Scientific Conquest of Death (Immortality Institute), 21
Scientology, 204–6
Scott, Eugenie, 27
The Second Creation (Wilmut, Campbell, and Tudge), 19
The Secret Story of Polygamy (Tracy), 217–18
Selig, Bud, 50
Sell, Stewart, 52
Selling the Holocaust (Cole), 122
Semmens, Kristin, 167
Shah, Anup, 38
Sharia, 207–9
Shaw, Susan M., 170
Shea, William R., 148–49
Sher, Geoffrey, 30
Shermer, Michael, 122
Shilts, Randy, 9
Shweder, Richard A., 16
Sihler, Bob, 223
Silent Spring (Carson), 91
Simon, Rita James, 59
Skaine, Rosemarie, 17
Slade, Joseph W., 220
Smiley, Tavis, 162
Social Issues Firsthand—Homosexuality (Haugen and Box), 214–15
Software Rating Board, 63–64
Sonn, Tamara, 196
Sorokin, Ellen, 140
Soulos, Greg, 55
South Africa, apartheid in, 111–13
Southern Poverty Law Center website, 22, 104
South Park Conservatives (Anderson), 66–67
The Specter of Genocide (Gellately and Kiernan), 118–19
Spitzer, Robert J., 176
Stanford Encyclopedia of Philosophy website, 24
Steele, Shelby, 161
Steiner, Susie, 207
Stem Cell Biology (Matshak, Gottlieb and Gardner), 52

The Stem Cell Controversy (Ruse and Pynes), 53
Stem Cell Handbook (Sell), 52
Stem Cell Research (Viegas), 52
stem cells, 51–53
Stenersen, Jorgen, 91
Stephens, Bret, 137
Sternheimer, Karen, 69
steroids, 39–41
Stop Smoking and Chewing Tobacco for Life Changes (Johnson and Johnson), 55–56
Streiber, Whitley, 128
Stringham, Edward, 158
Stripling, Barbara, xxxviii–xxxix
Strong Religion (Almond et al.), 197
Strossen, Nadine, 221
student advisory group, xxiv
student inquiry, fostering and encouraging, xiii–xiv
students: relationship with, xxix–xxx; with special needs, accommodating, xxxi; surveying, xxi–xxii
Sullivan, Meg, 65
Sullivan, Scott, 143
Sunnucks, Mike, 130
Sunstein, Cass R., 180
surveying staff and students, xxi–xxii
Swofford, Anthony, 100

Talk.Origins archive site, 26
Taranto, James, 66
Targets of Hatred (Baird-Windle and Bader), 4
Taylor, Jared, 146
Tedeschi, Sara K., 133
Telushkin, Joseph, 191
Their Kingdom Come (Hutchison), 202–3
thinking critically, xliii
Thomas, David E., 124
Thomas, Judy, 4
Thompson, Kimberly M., 63, 72
Tobacco or Health?: Physiological and Social Damages Caused by Tobacco Smoking (Haustein), 55
tobacco smoking, 54–56

topic suggestion, xxxvii
Toufexis, Anastasia, 38
Tracy, Kathleen, 217–18
transracial adoption, 57–59
Transracial Adoptions (Lang), 58
Trashing the Planet (Ray), 79
Troubled Memory (Powell), 146
troubleshooting possible misinterpretation of assignments, xix
Tucker, Ruth A., 199
Tudge, Colin, 19
Turning Points in Film History (Rausch), 73
Tutu, Desmond, 113
2006 Report on the Global AIDS Epidemic, 8

UFO Briefing Document (Berliner and Streiber), 128
UFO Museum and Research Center website, 123
Understanding Marijuana (Earleywine), 33
unidentified flying objects (UFOs), 126–28
United Farm Workers, 139
United States–Mexican border dispute, 104–7
Unraveling AIDS (Mae-Won), 7
USA Patriot Act, 184–86

Van Biema, David, 202
VAX bulletin, 8
Venezuelan Politics in the Chavez Era (Hellinger and Ellner), 144
Victor, David G., 82
Viegas, Jennifer, 52
Villarreal, Luis P., 9
Vince, Gaia, 87
visual presentation, xxxviii
Volpe, Tina, 179
vouchers, for education, 181–83

Waiting to Inhale (Bock), 33–34
Walker, Theodore, Jr., 160
Walker, Tony, 137
Ward, Colin, 158

War in the Persian Gulf (Hillstrom), 100
Watson, Ronald R., 55
Waxman, Sharon, 72
webbing process for topic: abortion, 3; example of, xx; overview of, xix
Web Genocide Documentation Center website, 117
Web of Addictions website, 43
Weiss, Philip, 96
Weitz, Eric D., 119
Wellman, Beverly, 11
We Now Know (Gaddis), 164
Wetzstein, Cheryl, 140
Whatever It Takes (Hayworth), 106–7
What is Scientology (Hubbard), 206
What Liberal Media? (Alterman), 66
When Abortion Was a Crime (Reagan), 4
When Nature's Not Enough (Olick), 30–31
Whiteside, Alan, 9
white supremacy, 129–30
White Supremacy and Racism in the Post-Civil Rights Era (Bonilla-Silva), 130
Who's Afraid of Human Cloning (Pence), 19
Why the Jews? (Prager and Telushkin), 191
Why We Can't Wait (King), 154
Wikipedia website: abortion, 3; Allende, 133; anarchism, 157; anti-Semitism, 189; Arafat, 136; atheism, 192; birth control, 12–13; black separatism, 160; categories of, xlix; C. Chavez, 139; H. Chavez, 142; communism, 163; cryonics, 20; Cyprus dispute, 114; Duke, 145; euthanasia, 24; fascism, 166; Fundamentalism, 195; Galileo, 147; gays in military, 172; genocide, 117; gun politics, 175; Holocaust deniers, 120; homosexuality, 213; King, 153; Malcolm X, 150; media restrictions, 68; MPAA film rating system, 71; New Age spirituality, 198; nuclear power, 83; Opus Dei, 201; Persian Gulf, 98; pesticides, 89; PETA, 178; polygamy, 216; pornography, 219; Puerto Rico, 101; race and intelligence, 45; racial profiling, 48; same-sex marriage, 222; Scientology, 204; Sharia, 207; stem cells, 51; tobacco smoking, 54; UFOs, 126; USA Patriot Act, 184; in vitro fertilization, 29; white supremacy, 129
Willcox, David R., 69
Williams, Linda S., 29
Williams, Ted, 20
Wilmut, Ian, 19
Winograd Commission, 95
Wisse, Ruth R., 190
Witten, Mark L., 55
Wolfe, Alan, 183
Women & Guns (Homsher), 177
Women's Health.gov website, 12
Women's Voices, Feminist Visions (Shaw and Lee), 170
Wooldridge, Frosty, 106
Woolls, Blanche, *The School Library Media Manager,* xlii
Worden, Nigel, 112
The Words of Cesar Chavez (Chavez and Jensen), 140
Wrath of Angels (Risen and Thomas), 4
"writing across the curriculum," xvi
writing skills, xvi–xvii
written presentation, xxxviii

Yamey, Gavin, 55
Yarhouse, Mark, 214
Yasir Arafat (Rubin and Rubin), 137
Yokota, Fumie, 72
Young, Alison, 179

Zeaman, John, 38
Zimmerman, John C., 122

About the Author

HARRIET S. SELVERSTONE is a retired high school library media specialist and department chair of the Library Media Department at Norwalk High School, Norwalk, CT. She is a former president of the American Association of School Librarians and two-term president of the Connecticut Educational Media Association. She served two terms on the American Library Association's Intellectual Freedom Committee, and was Chair for several years of the Connecticut Educational Media Association's Intellectual Freedom Committee. She has authored chapters on censorship issues in two texts, *Children and Books* (1996) and *Collection Management for School Library Media Centers* (1985–1986). She is Series Adviser to Libraries Unlimited Professional Guides in School Librarianship Series. She received a masters degree in Library Science, an advanced certificate in Information Management and an honorary doctorate degree from Pratt Institute.

Recent Titles in Libraries Unlimited's Professional Guides in School Librarianship Series

100 More Research Topic Guides for Students
Dana McDougald

Curriculum Partner: Redefining the Role of the Library Media Specialist
Carol A. Kearney

Using Internet Primary Sources to Teach Critical Thinking Skills in Geography
Martha B. Sharma and Gary S. Elbow

Using Internet Primary Sources to Teach Critical Thinking Skills in World Languages
Grete Pasch and Kent Norsworthy

Leadership for Today's School Library: A Handbook for the Library Media Specialist and the School Principal
Patricia Potter Wilson and Josette Anne Lyders

Using Internet Primary Sources to Teach Critical Thinking Skills in Mathematics
Evan Glazer

Using Internet Primary Sources to Teach Critical Thinking Skills in Government, Economics, and Contemporary World Issues
James M. Shiveley and Phillip J. VanFossen

Creating Cyber Libraries: An Instructional Guide for School Library Media Specialists
Kathleen W. Craver

Collection Development for a New Century in the School Library Media Center
W. Bernard Lukenbill

Using Internet Primary Sources to Teach Critical Thinking Skills in the Sciences
Carolyn M. Johnson

Using Internet Primary Sources to Teach Critical Thinking Skills in World Literature
Roxanne M. Kent-Drury, PhD

Information Literacy and the School Library Media Center
Joie Taylor